Warfare and Culture
in World History

WARFARE AND CULTURE SERIES
General Editor: Wayne E. Lee

*A Rabble in Arms: Massachusetts Towns
and Militiamen during King Philip's War*
Kyle F. Zelner

*Empires and Indigenes: Intercultural Alliance, Imperial
Expansion, and Warfare in the Early Modern World*
Edited by Wayne E. Lee

Warfare and Culture in World History
Edited by Wayne E. Lee

Warfare and Culture in World History

EDITED BY

Wayne E. Lee

NEW YORK UNIVERSITY PRESS

New York and London

NEW YORK UNIVERSITY PRESS
New York and London
www.nyupress.org

References to Internet websites (URLs) were accurate at the time of writing.
Neither the author nor New York University Press is responsible for URLs
that may have expired or changed since the manuscript was prepared.

Library of Congress Cataloging-in-Publication Data
Warfare and culture in world history / [edited by] Wayne Lee.
p. cm.
Includes bibliographical references and index.
ISBN 978-0-8147-5277-7 (hardback) — ISBN 978-0-8147-5278-4 (pb)
1. Military art and science—History. 2. War and society—History.
3. Political culture—History. 4. Military history. I. Lee, Wayne E., 1965–
U27.W345   2011
355.0209—dc23   2011020455

New York University Press books are printed on acid-free paper,
and their binding materials are chosen for strength and durability.
We strive to use environmentally responsible suppliers and materials
to the greatest extent possible in publishing our books.

Manufactured in the United States of America

c   10 9 8 7 6 5 4 3 2 1
p   10 9 8 7 6 5 4 3 2 1

Contents

List of Maps

Warfare and Culture

WAYNE E. LEE

Ideas matter in warfare. Machine guns may kill, but ideas decide where to place them, how to man them, and when the most effective moment is to begin firing them. The answers to those questions might seem obvious now, but in fact the answers varied for different times and places, reflecting an evolving process of ideas interacting with technological capability.[1] Military historians have been adept at explaining where machine guns, or other weapons, came from, but they have been less attentive to the origins of the ideas that brought them to bear on the battlefield. Traditionally, when historians examined such ideas, they often explained them simply as rational calculations of advantage: Soldiers put machine guns in what they deemed were the best places, where they would do the most damage. Over the last few decades, however, this perspective has been changing. A real paradigm shift has emerged in military history, in which historians are closely examining how societies conceptualized war, weapons, violence, military service, and a host of other ideas that produced specific battlefield effects. "Rational" now is understood to be a highly idiosyncratic and contextual adjective. Rather than a single objective solution to a given problem, specific ideas or "solutions" emerge from a web of overlapping influences, mental and material, rooted in past ideas, modified by changing conditions, and perhaps best summed up by the word *culture*.

This book, and indeed the series to which this book belongs, arises from the ongoing work of military historians to contextualize war and military institutions more deeply within the culture that produced them. This book further seeks to address those questions within the broad context of world history. American universities are increasingly attuned to the needs of the "globalizing" world. Economics, immigration patterns, security concerns, and other such issues all suggest the need for citizens educated in the history and condition of the world, not just the United States. *Warfare and Culture in World History* contributes to that effort by providing case studies from both inside and outside the Western experience of warfare. It is our sense that for too long, military history has been taught from an exclusively "Western" perspective. Doing so has limited our ability to see the wide array of possible military responses to technology, to material circumstance, to social organization, and so on. Comparing France with Britain has real value, and indeed doing so often exposes surprising variables, but it can be even more enlightening to compare, for example, Britain with Japan. Comparing two societies with vastly different assumptions or, better, different cultural conceptions of war brings those assumptions to the surface, as they become clearer by contrast. Or in some cases, we might detect the overriding influence of material factors that seem to generate similar results *despite* different cultural conceptions.[2] Taking a world history perspective is not, though, to discard the significance of the Western experience. It not only is the heritage of the country in which this book is published, but it also is the military system that dominates the world. Explaining war's origins, nature, and, yes, its "culture" in the Western experience therefore matters. A quick glance at the table of contents shows that Western warfare dominates in this book, but we hope nevertheless to provide a broad comparative perspective, both chronologically and geographically.

Although using a world history approach helps provide a framework for contrasts, the real unit of analysis in this book is "culture," especially its impact on the operational behavior of armies. Culture, however, is a vast, amorphous, and potentially troublesome word, so some explanation is required. In one sense, claiming culture as a tool of analysis is simply about striving for a more holistic examination of the relationship between a society and the wars it fights. According to this definition, a cultural approach merely seeks to avoid technological determinism, or the study of battles otherwise divorced from their social context. But such a simplistic, essentially negative, definition does not get us very far, nor does it do justice even to so-called traditional military history, which has long been sensitive to social and political context. We need, therefore, to be more specific about what is meant by "culture" and what we want to find from using culture as a category of analysis.

Culture

As will quickly become clear to the reader of this book, there is more than one way to define culture or, even better, more than one level at which to seek it. The problem of defining it, especially in its sense as a source of specific ideas or choices, occupies virtually every humanistic discipline and has gained considerable input from anthropology and evolutionary psychology as well.[3] Without recapitulating the long evolution of the use and meaning of the term, I suggest that in essence, any group of humans living or working together over time develops "habitual practices, default programs, hidden assumptions and unreflected cognitive frames" that inform their choices, or indeed they will have created "a repertoire or 'tool kit' of habits, skills, and styles from which people construct 'strategies of action.'"[4] Crucially, if the community persists, it will then transmit that repertoire to the next generation "through teaching, imitation, and other forms of social transmission." Finally, such transmission occurs not merely through words but also through symbols and actions.[5]

I suggest this cobbled-together definition because it immediately offers several things to us. First, it insists that culture provides a repertoire of choices; it does not limit individual possibility, but it shapes individual vision. Second, this definition reminds us that the evidence for culture can be found in action as well as words. Discernible repeated patterns of behavior reveal the underlying cultural assumptions behind these choices. Third, this definition indicates a program of research: cultural values must be transmitted to survive, and especially in an institutional context like a modern military, the process of "teaching, imitation, and other forms of social transmission" can be found in doctrine, training, theoretical literature, and stated policy. Fourth, this definition cautions against assuming too much in that visible recorded form of transmission: the "hidden assumptions" also must also be teased out because they may in fact contradict stated policy. Fifth, this definition works at multiple levels of human community formation: societal, organizational, or even incidental. Finally, and crucially to this book, it demands that we investigate the role of all these aspects of culture in shaping choices, and for the military historian, that includes operational or battlefield choices.

This definition of culture suggests as well that there are multiple "levels" at which one can investigate the interaction of warfare and culture, and the contributors to this book have made different, sometimes overlapping, choices about level. Military history has at least five, also sometimes overlapping, levels or types of culture: societal, strategic, organizational, military, and "soldiers."[6] Military organizations, or even just groups of people coalescing to embark on a violent mission, are in some sense a subset of their parent society. They therefore bring with them to the military environment all their "societal" culture's values and assumptions, some of which may directly relate to warfare. Indeed, those societal cultural values likely played a very large role in determining who was fighting and who was not. But analyzing linkages between societal culture and battlefield behavior can be extraordinarily difficult. Sometimes the fundamental assumptions that organize and (more or less) regulate an entire society seem to be a long way from the specific ways in which this society then makes choices in wartime. Contributors Kenneth M. Swope, David Silbey, and Adrian R. Lewis all try to tease out the long tangled threads that connect a society's values to its wartime choices.

Swope confronts a long-held assumption that Chinese society strongly preferred to cultivate civilian values (*wen*) over more martial ones (*wu*), and therefore China has struggled to field truly effective militaries. In his case study from the late Ming dynasty, Swope finds it "too easy to characterize imperial Chinese officials as 'Confucian' or pacifistic." Instead, he provides a detailed narrative of how one set of imperial commanders, who technically were "civilians," negotiated the competing tugs of Confucian values, which favored mercy for peasant rebels, against the recommendations of other equally civilian factions, who favored strategies of extermination. Indeed, the "culture" in play here was not "Confucian" or "a rational military establishment" so much as a culture of competition within the imperial court that fostered the production of competing solutions solely or primarily for the purpose of gaining and keeping the emperor's favor. Swope's narrative has many twists and turns, but considered as a whole, it is emblematic of the constant interaction of what I have elsewhere called "mind and matter": logistical, topographic, and demographic limits profoundly shaped conscious choices about how to solve the peasant rebellion.[7] Equally powerful were notions of the appropriate relationship between the emperor and his subjects, between civilian officials and the emperor, and between civilian officials and their military subordinates. These relationships depended on more than mere institutional structure; they turned around a contested imagination of the role of power in an ordered polity.

In his chapter, Silbey discusses the cultural "needs" of the Dominions, especially Australia, New Zealand, and Canada, and how they were slotted into the operational plans for "British" offensives in 1918 in France. There are complexities here: British officers, with their own cultural predilections, dominated the planning process, but they felt compelled to acknowledge the explicitly articulated demands of their Dominion subordinates. In turn, those subordinates were moved by their nations' emergent nationalist feelings about their own unique qualities to demand special roles in the order of battle. In cyclical fashion, demanding and being given a special role as "shock troops" for the offensive further contributed to a culture of nationalism in Australia, New Zealand, and Canada. Here Silbey treats nationalism as a specific aspect of societal culture, in some ways one of the oldest components of any self-defined society:

the desire to stand apart, to reinforce distinctiveness. In the context of imperial war planning, that desire had specific operational consequences.

Lewis also situates his analysis at the societal level. He finds a dramatic transformation in the American public's understanding of war in the years after World War II, a transformation that has contributed to, if not demanded, a particular set of operational tendencies within the U.S. military establishment. American disenchantment with limited war, and a simultaneous willingness to substitute technological cost for personal sacrifice, has led to a tendency to rely on airpower, to avoid the commitment of ground forces, to count on the surgical application of force, and to ignore both the long-term budgetary costs and the short-term human costs of those choices.

In one way, Lewis's argument is about the influence of societal culture on American "strategic culture." Strategic culture is a more specific category (or level), focusing specifically on how members of a military or political elite approach the problem of winning. Leaders' decisions and choices tend to be conscious and reflective, perhaps based on careful calculations of available resources and their knowledge of the situation.[8] But even such conscious weighing of moral and material factors is conditioned by past experience, beliefs, and expectations about the nature of war and what actions would not only define victory but also produce it.

Like Lewis, Sarah C. Melville's chapter on the surprisingly sudden end of the Assyrian Empire similarly combines societal and strategic culture in her analysis, and she further emphasizes the potential consequences of an emerging competitor that does not share the assumptions of that culture. Melville sees the Assyrians as having been participants in a shared urban Mesopotamian set of values about war, in which its function and its limits were clear even to competing or successive empires. The Assyrians did, however, have one key idiosyncrasy. They had come to strongly prefer offensive operations, even when on the strategic defensive. After all, she argues,

> The Assyrians had perfected an extremely effective system of conquest and control that brought peace to their heartland and much of the empire as well. Even though peace profoundly shaped their concept of how war should and would be waged, it also inevitably seduced them into taking the heartland's invulnerability for granted.

Those assumptions evaporated under the destructive and consuming style of attack waged by the invading nomadic Medians, and Assyrian strategic culture proved unable to adapt quickly enough to prevent the empire's collapse.

Likewise, Isabel V. Hull's chapter describes imperial German strategic culture, particularly the wider impact of German societal and political culture, but focuses on how Germany's peculiar strategic culture became so fixed in the army's institutional fabric—indeed, in its "organizational" culture—that it continued to pursue certain operational/battlefield habits even when they had clearly become dysfunctional.[9] As she notes, organizations develop "habits, basic assumptions, default programs, and scripts that seem so obviously correct and natural that those inside the organizational culture have trouble thinking beyond or against them." For a military, some of those basic assumptions are about victory and its pursuit, and thus "strategic culture" is a kind of subset of organizational culture. Faced in some ways with a challenge not unlike that facing Swope's Ming commanders—pursuing elusive "rebels"—the German military simply shifted into its accustomed operational practice. What followed was a "logical unfolding of the German military's standard operating procedures on the levels of both doctrine and of practice (that is, on both the conscious and the habitual and un-self-reflexive levels)," which in this case meant pursuing the destruction of the enemy through a single battle of annihilation followed by ruthless pursuit. Enacted against the Herero in desert Southwest Africa and adding other basic assumptions of the German military's organizational culture, the result could only be called genocide, a result neither sought nor desired by the German colonial or imperial government. Accordingly, the Germans' strategic culture and their specific operational choices emerged from their larger organizational culture. That organizational culture, however, also had other effects. The Germans' disregard for logistics and their assumptions about appropriate rations for non-German detainees combined to create horrifying conditions and wholesale death for the interned Herero people.

Mark Grimsley also looks specifically at organizational culture, here with an eye to how organizations resist or accept change. Using a model partly derived from the modern business world's concern with such issues, he refines it to examine not only the culture of leadership at the high command level but also the more "clannish" organizational culture of a U.S. Civil War regiment. His analysis distinguishes among an organization's levels and identifies the idiosyncrasies within that war's different field armies. Although societal culture mattered, especially in the clannish regiments, the individual personalities and styles of high commanders in a hierarchical organization like an army imprinted distinctive values and assumptions on it that proved hard to change later. Even more important to this book's goal, Grimsley is able to tie specific operational consequences to all these descriptions of command and regimental culture.

These organizational and strategic culture paradigms may be most useful in analyzing those long-established military institutions about whose internal workings we have detailed sources. The strategic culture of premodern, prestaff, pre-"doctrinal" armies may be reconstructed to a certain degree through their patterns of behavior, but historians more often turn to the somewhat broader category of "military culture." One scholar defined this term as "the ethos and professional attributes, both in terms of experience and intellectual study, that contribute to a common core understanding of war within military organizations."[10] We might fairly ask how this differs from organizational or strategic culture. In essence, I have defined those terms as dealing with specific aspects of military activity (institutional processes and operational predilection, respectively), whereas military culture refers to a broader, somewhat more nebulous set of assumptions and values associated with being a part of a separate military subculture. A group of individuals long associated with military activity may, and usually do, develop a host of values that they believe are distinct from those of their parent society. Examples might be a particular construction of honor, masculinity, uniformity, and/or obedience. In hierarchical societies, this military culture is determined primarily by those men who lead it, most often a social elite. I have argued elsewhere that in addition to this military culture, soldiers often form a contradictory subset of this military culture.[11] This "soldiers' culture" arose from the shared experience of a non-elite soldiery, which often is in defiance of their elite masters but which they saw as essential to their survival and which they passed on to new recruits.

John A. Lynn II's and Lee L. Brice's chapters provide examples of both military and soldiers' culture. Lynn's chapter is a fine example of the interactive and overlapping qualities of several levels of cultural analysis. He agrees that technology surely set some parameters around the eighteenth-century European infantry battle but that the real key to the "battle culture of forbearance" was aristocratic self-perception, as well as the aristocratic attitude toward the common soldier. Indeed, the elite needed a battle system that emphasized their role as controllers of an unruly lower class. The soldiers' social reality, however, differed from their masters' perceptions of them, and when those perceptions were altered by the political changes of the French Revolution, the soldiers' capacity to flourish under a different tactical regime was unleashed.

Brice's chapter describes even more explicitly the difference between a Roman military culture designed to impose control over its soldiers, and the contrarian soldiers' culture that developed during the late Republic's civil wars. Brice undermines the popular stereotype of the intensely corporally disciplined Roman legionary by instead emphasizing a deeply embedded "matrix of discipline" that relied on remuneration and religion as well as physical coercion. Rome's was an evolved military culture that had been created by a hierarchical society through a long fractious negotiation between the upper and lower social strata. During the civil wars, however, factional leaders, including Octavian, found themselves leaning heavily on the promises of material rewards. As the civil wars dragged on, a soldiers' culture emerged that demanded more and more such bonuses, without which they threatened to change sides. Brice contends that Octavian gradually realized the flaw in this perversion of the traditional disciplinary system. In essence he and the other factional leaders had encouraged the emergence of a soldiers' culture opposed to hierarchical control, one that now threatened the stability of the state. That flaw could arguably be said to have returned in later centuries to help bring down the empire. But when Octavian became Augustus, he restored the *disciplina militaris* and its full matrix of discipline "from oath to whip."

Change and Agency?

The distinction among these five "levels" of cultural analysis (societal, strategic, organizational, military, and soldiers'), and indeed even the definition of culture itself, clearly remains vague, and these levels may overlap in any number of ways. But this is all right; we do not need to straitjacket the historical imagination with overly rigid categories and definitions. In part, I define these levels as suggestions for research and analysis. For example, historians can look for those occasions when a military culture has emerged that diverges from societal culture or when a soldiers' culture has arisen in opposition to the supposedly dominant military culture. In fact, readers will find that the contributors have not necessarily adhered to the definitions described in this introduction.

The final analytical issue that I want to consider here is the theoretical problem to which students of culture repeatedly return: the problem of change. That is, if cultural values and assumptions are so deeply embedded and so influential in shaping individual behavior, then how do those values and assumptions change—something they demonstrably do—especially in the context of military behavior? Furthermore, some military historians worry that an emphasis on culture undermines the role of contingency and agency in history, that is, the choices and actions of specific individuals at key moments that seem to create decisive military consequences for both the short and the long term.

These are not trivial concerns. Defeat, for example, is often cited as critical motivator of a military system's or institution's innovation (although it does not have to be!). Furthermore, individuals do seem to make decisions at odds with cultural norms, and sometimes those decisions can have outsized effects in a fast-moving wartime context. To acknowledge change and agency, however, is not to undermine the value of cultural analysis. Indeed, the definitions of culture just explored already suggest some of the means by which change occurs. Intergenerational "transmission," for example, can become garbled, and cultural habit provides a tool kit, not a single solution. In addition, some theorists of culture have suggested mechanisms for change that account for the contingency of individual decisions. Peter Richerson and Robert Boyd, for example, argue that "culture consists of an interrelation between norms and actual behavior (practices) tested through time, both affecting each other. It is not simply an idea template that stamps out approved behavior."[12] In the 1970s, Pierre Bourdieu emphasized that "practices" derived from cultural predilection are always subject to individual "improvisation." Each individual act serves as a precedent that both reinforces and ever so slightly modifies the cultural "norm." Furthermore, Bourdieu pointed out, when material conditions change substantially, more and more individuals may modify their actions in a similar direction in order to account for the changes, and by doing so, they rewrite the norm; that is, they establish new precedent.[13] Although military institutions can be notoriously conservative, they also are environments in which the "material conditions" can change rapidly, and thus "culture" can do so as well. Soldiers recruited into an army away from their civilian life find dramatically different conditions and thus quickly create new cultural norms that shape their actions, as both individuals and groups. Armies as institutions, especially in the modern era, are constantly confronting material (usually technological) changes, and they do so in peculiarly conscious ways as they evaluate the probable future efficacy (or not) of a given weapons system. In doing so, they may try to rewrite their strategic culture, although they often find themselves struggling against established norms in their societal culture, or even the norms in their own military culture.

We hope that this book will expand military historians' understanding of culture, military institutions, and behaviors. It presents the work of both distin-

guished and more recent scholars in the field, and it represents the sophistica-
tion and complexity that characterizes the best work in military history. Military
history written in the 1970s or 1980s (and certainly in the 1990s) often predicted
that war had a limited future on this planet. But *Warfare and Culture in World
History* offers no such hopes. In this era of warfare in which ideas about violence
and its use have very often proved far more threatening than any new weapons
do, it behooves us to consider ever more carefully where ideas come from, how
they change, and how our own culture of warfare might need adjusting.

NOTES

1. Consider, for example, debates in the British army about the machine gun's usefulness even after World War I had begun. See John Ellis, *The Social History of the Machine
Gun* (New York: Pantheon Books, 1975), 111–45.

2. For examples of this sort of comparative work, see Stephen Morillo, "Guns and Government: A Comparative Study of Europe and Japan," *Journal of World History* 6 (1995):
75–106; and Kenneth Warren Chase, *Firearms: A Global History to 1700* (Cambridge:
Cambridge University Press, 2003).

3. Useful reviews of the meaning and role of culture in various disciplines can be found
in Lynn Hunt, "Introduction: History, Culture, and Text," in *The New Cultural History*,
ed. Lynn Hunt (Berkeley: University of California Press, 1989), 1–22; Victoria E. Bonnell and Lynn Hunt, introduction to *Beyond the Cultural Turn*, and William H. Sewell Jr.,
"The Concept(s) of Culture," both in *Beyond the Cultural Turn*, ed. Victoria E. Bonnell
and Lynn Hunt (Berkeley: University of California Press, 1999), 1–34 and 35–61. Explora-
tions of the role of cultural analysis in military history also can be found in Wayne E.
Lee, "Mind and Matter—Cultural Analysis in American Military History: A Look at the
State of the Field," *Journal of American History* 93, no. 4 (2007): 1116–42; John Shy, "The
Cultural Approach to the History of War," *Journal of Military History* 57 (1993): 13–26; John
A. Lynn, "The Embattled Future of Academic Military History," *Journal of Military History*
61 (1997): 777–89; and Jeremy Black, "Determinisms and Other Issues," *Journal of Military
History* 68 (2004): 1217–32.

4. Isabel V. Hull, *Absolute Destruction: Military Culture and the Practices of War in Imperial Germany* (Ithaca, NY: Cornell University Press, 2004), 2; Ann Swidler, "Culture in
Action: Symbols and Strategies," *American Sociological Review* 51 (1986): 273–86.

5. Peter J. Richerson and Robert Boyd, *Not by Genes Alone: How Culture Transformed
Human Evolution* (Chicago: University of Chicago Press, 2005), 5. Also critical here is
Clifford Geertz, "Religion as a Cultural System," in *The Interpretation of Cultures*, by Clif-
ford Geertz (New York: Basic Books, 1973), esp. 89.

6. In his *Battle: A History of Combat and Culture* (Boulder, CO.: Westview Press, 2003),
xx, John A. Lynn defines three categories of culture in the study of military history: societal, military, and strategic. Here I expand on and modify his definitions.

7. Lee, "Mind and Matter."

8. Alastair Ian Johnson, "Thinking about Strategic Culture," *International Security*
19 (summer 1995): 34.

9. As an indicator of how fluid these labels are, Hull uses the term *military culture* rather than *strategic culture*. As I observed, the definitions substantially overlap, but her chapter's focus on operational planning places it more closely in my definition of strategic culture. Similarly, Peter Wilson conflates military culture with organizational culture, primarily because of his focus on modern institutional militaries. His analytical subcategories for analyzing the institutional/organizational culture of a military, however, are very useful. They include the military's mission, its relationship to the state and other institutions, its social basis and relationship to society, its internal structure embodying its norms and assumptions, and its resource requirements. See Peter H. Wilson, "Defining Military Culture," *Journal of Military History* 72 (2008): 11–42, esp. 17.

10. Williamson Murray, "Does Military Culture Matter?" *Orbis* 43 (winter 1999): 27–42, esp. 27.

11. Wayne E. Lee, *Barbarians and Brothers: Anglo-American Warfare, 1500–1865* (New York: Oxford University Press, 2011), chap. 4. See also Wilson, "Defining Military Culture," 18.

12. Richerson and Boyd, *Not by Genes Alone*, 5.

13. Pierre Bourdieu, *Outline of a Theory of Practice,* trans. Richard Nice (Cambridge: Cambridge University Press, 1977), 72, 79, 81, 8. Compare the discussion in Sewell, "The Concept(s) of Culture," 44–45. Guy Halsall makes fine use of this theory of change in his *Warfare and Society on the Barbarian West, 450–900* (New York: Routledge, 2003), 8.

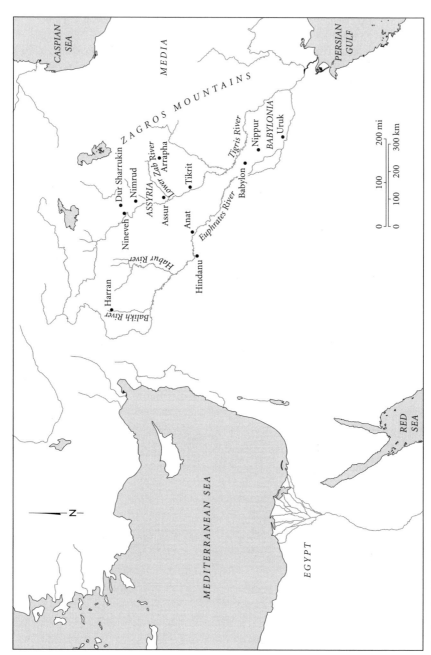

The Assyrian Heartland, ca. 640 BCE

The Last Campaign

The Assyrian Way of War and
the Collapse of the Empire

SARAH C. MELVILLE

At its height in the mid-seventh century BCE, the Assyrian Empire held sway over the entire Near East; it was the largest, best organized empire the ancient Western world had yet seen.[1] With sophisticated central and provincial administrations and a standing army second to none, the Assyrians appeared to be invincible. Yet, just fifty years after reaching its zenith, the empire faced annihilation at the hands of a Babylonian-Median coalition. Modern studies have struggled to explain how the power that had dominated the Near East for more than four hundred years could succumb so quickly to invasion. Citing causes such as resource depletion, internal and external dissention, economic decline, and dwindling provincial populations, most explanations have ignored warfare altogether except to assume a fundamental military weakness that the sources do not confirm.[2] In fact, the Assyrians were a militaristic society whose long-held and deeply ingrained assumptions about warfare played a crucial role in rendering their heartland vulnerable to the type of attack that destroyed it.[3]

One consequence of Assyria's violent downfall is that comparatively little written or material evidence has survived from the period in question (ca. 630–610). When the Babylonians and Medes destroyed all the palaces and administrative centers in the Assyrian heartland, they also obliterated decades of economic records, royal inscriptions, and other state documents, thus leaving large gaps in our knowledge of Assyria's internal situation and foreign relations during the period leading up to the war. For example, despite ample evidence for Median-Assyrian contact up to about 656 BCE, sources after that date are completely silent about the Medes until their sudden invasion of Assyria in 614. As a result, much of the attack's political context has been lost. In Assyria, the archaeological record is all that is left to bear witness to the empire's fate.[4]

Indeed, the only near-contemporary account of Assyria's collapse presents the victor's point of view. The Nabopolassar Chronicle (NC) and the Fall of Nineveh Chronicle (FNC) are part of the group of cuneiform tablets, known collectively as the Babylonian Chronicle, that documents important events in Babylonian history.[5] Written in a terse, seemingly objective style, these reports contain only selected facts with little elaboration. In addition to the chronicles, scattered economic texts, royal inscriptions, and other miscellaneous tablets help establish the chronology and provide additional details.[6] Later, external sources such as the Bible, Berossus, and the classical authors Herodotus, Xenophon, and Ctesias generally corroborate the earlier evidence but otherwise contribute little that is new or reliable.[7] Though fragmentary and difficult to interpret, the surviving evidence nevertheless reveals valuable information about how the Assyrian Empire met its end.

The Armies

None of the extant sources includes information on such basic military matters as the size or composition of armies, troop deployments, tactics, or strategies. However, by extrapolating from slightly earlier material, it is possible to get a general idea of the armies involved.[8] In the mid-seventh century BCE, the Assyrian armed forces consisted of a standing core, deportee units, and men performing *ilku*-service (corvée duty / national service). In addition, allies and clients were required to send men to serve alongside the Assyrians, and from the mid-eighth century on, specialized contingents (usually chariots or cavalry) captured from defeated armies were incorporated into the standing Assyrian army. The Assyrians employed a regular chain of command, which ran from the king, his generals, and division commanders all the way down to officers in charge of small units of varying size.

Infantrymen—light armed auxiliaries and Assyrian levies (archers and spearmen) and heavy armed regulars (archers, spearmen, and slingers)—were variously outfitted with bows, spears, swords, daggers, slings, and, less commonly, maces or battle-axes. Soldiers' armor differed according to their unit type, and some units, such as Assyrian light archers, wore only head protection.[9] Fully armed soldiers carried a heavy shield and wore a conical helmet made of bronze or iron, as well as a metal breastplate or scale armor. The army employed a number of shield types, including heavy round shields (akin to the later Greek *hoplon*), small bucklers, and tower shields made out of wicker.

Chariots were manned by teams of three or four, a driver, fighter (archer/ spearman), and one or two shield bearers. In the late seventh century, chariots were large and heavy—their wheels almost as tall as a man—and were probably used on parade and at sieges rather than in battle.[10] Cavalry were armed with bows or lances, daggers, and short swords. Although at this time, horsemen had neither proper saddles with girth straps nor stirrups, well-designed bridles and bits helped riders control their mounts. Because horses were expensive and difficult to train, they were accoutered with thick leather armor, which proved a disadvantage in action against the lighter, faster horses of opponents such as the Medes. The Assyrians were the first sedentary power of the Near East to develop cavalry (in the ninth century BCE), but since the heartland was not ideal for raising horses, the acquisition of suitable mounts was a perennial problem. The Assyrians went to great lengths to procure heavy breeds from Nubia for chariot teams, and smaller breeds from the western Zagros polities and Media for cavalry use.[11] The Medes' success against the Assyrians has sometimes been attributed to a severe shortage of horses in the Assyrian army, and while such a hypothesis is plausible, it remains unproven.

The arid environment of the Near East restricted armies and caravans to routes with good access to water and food; hence control of roads and navigable waterways was strategically essential. On the march through friendly territory, the army lived off food collected by the local authorities (client rulers or provincial governors) at forward supply depots. In enemy territory the Assyrians foraged for food, although soldiers also received rations of barley and oil.[12] Campaign season typically began after the spring rains and lasted until the onset of winter, which soldiers passed in camp or at home. Battle tactics included standard maneuvers such as flanking and envelopment, but because of the many untrained levies in their ranks, only the elite heavy infantry units, chariotry, and cavalry could perform complex movements.[13] Excellent engineers, the Assyrians were particularly adept at siege warfare; they built siege ramps; employed siege towers, battering rams, ladders, and grappling hooks; and mined under walls. Artillery such as catapults had not yet been invented.

We assume that the Babylonian army was similar in character to the Assyrian army, but since it consisted mainly of urban Babylonians and tribal Arameans and Chaldeans, it was probably a more homogeneous force. Lacking the Assyrians' sophisticated imperial administrative system to facilitate levying troops, the Babylonians mustered soldiers from the rich estates of major temples, from specially designated bow fiefs, and from among the citizenry.[14] Having fought the Assyrians regularly for centuries, the Babylonians were well acquainted with all aspects of Assyrian military operations and probably organized their forces according to the Assyrian model. The Medes, too, were familiar with the Assyrians, whose kings they had both fought and served in the past.[15] In the late seventh century, the Median army consisted of a large elite cavalry and massed infantry, at least some of whom would have been armed similarly to the Assyrian heavy infantry.[16] Each of the Assyrian, Babylonian, and Median armies that fought this war probably numbered in the tens of thousands.

The War

The war that brought down the Assyrian Empire and destroyed its heartland began unremarkably as the latest phase in the protracted struggle for control of Babylonia. During the eighth and seventh centuries BCE (the heyday of the empire), the Assyrians employed a number of strategies to pacify their southern neighbors: direct rule by the Assyrian king or his designated representative (e.g., the king's son or brother), indirect rule via a Babylonian puppet king, or, as a last resort, subjugation by brute force. Babylonia's ethnic and political diversity made Assyria's task even more difficult. Although Assyria had some success gaining the support of Babylonia's urban populations, tribal factions—particularly the Chaldeans and Arameans in the south and east—would not submit to the *Pax Assyriaca* and rebelled at the slightest opportunity. In spite of the prolonged military effort and the tremendous cost of subduing Babylonia, the Assyrians considered the area too important strategically and too lucrative economically to relinquish. Rare peaceful interludes only masked underlying problems and gave the would-be rebels time to regroup. No matter what steps the Assyrians took to pacify Babylonia, the political situation invariably devolved into a state of volatility and violence. Between 745 and 648 the Assyrians fought several major wars there, although each victory achieved only temporary peace. Eventually, Assyria's failure to solve its "Babylonian problem" proved catastrophic.

The endgame began around 627 BCE after both the long-lived Assyrian king, Ashurbanipal, and the last Assyrian-appointed ruler of Babylonia, Kandalanu, had died, thereby ending an unusually long interlude (around twenty years) of relative peace and prosperity.[17] There ensued a period of upheaval and civil war in both countries as rival claimants to the respective thrones struggled for supremacy. By 626 Sin-shar-ishkun, one of Ashurbanipal's sons, had established himself as king of Assyria, and Nabopolassar, a Babylonian official of nonroyal descent, had declared himself king in that country.[18] For the next ten years or so, these two men vied for control of Babylonia. During the initial phase of the war, which took place entirely on Babylonian soil, the advantage oscillated dramatically between the two opponents. The Nabopol-assar Chronicle describes a typical episode of this type of maneuver warfare:

> The first year of Nabopolassar (626 BC): . . . On the twenty-first day of the month Iyyar (April/May) the army of Assyria entered Raq[mat] and carried off its property. . . . On the ninth day of the month Ab (July/August) Nabopolassar and his army [marched] to Raqm[at]. He did battle against Raqmat but did not seize the city. The Assyrian army arrived so he retreated before them and withdrew.[19]

After suffering early reverses, Nabopolassar gradually gained the upper hand by attrition, and by 617 he had pushed the Assyrian army out of Babylonia. Pro-Assyrian factions remained in cities such as Nippur and Ur, whose continued support of Assyrian rule hindered Nabopolassar's consolidation of power for some time.[20]

The end of the Assyrian occupation of Babylonia marked the beginning of a new phase in the war, though this would not have been recognized as particularly significant at the time. Up until this point, the conflict had been characteristic of previous Assyro-Babylonian wars: all the fighting took place in Babylonia, with no decisive outcome. Since the Assyrians were accustomed to occasional reverses against the Babylonians, historical precedents would have suggested that Sin-shar-ishkun's situation was a temporary inconvenience. This view could not have been more wrong.

In 616 BCE Nabopolassar took the war outside Babylonia for the first time when he campaigned up the Euphrates into Assyrian-held territory in Syria. He took possession of the city of Hindanu and then defeated an Assyrian army near Gablini on the Balikh River, after which he pushed even farther north to the Habur River, cutting a wide swath of destruction as he went. In response, the Assyrian army (including Egyptian allies) regrouped and pursued the Babylonians back to Gablini without engaging them in battle. Both sides then withdrew, although Nabopolassar retained control of Hindanu.[21] The Babylonians now held the middle Euphrates and thus the western portion of the main east-west travel corridor.[22] Taking control of the central Euphrates was probably the main objective in this campaign and the first step in a strategic plan to keep the Assyrians out of Babylonia. However, Nabopolassar's withdrawal before the oncoming Assyrian army indicates that he was not yet prepared to mount an all-out invasion of enemy territory. At this juncture, his plans did not include the conquest of Assyria but simply aimed to secure Babylonian independence and his own rule.

After achieving success on Assyria's western flank, Nabopolassar approached Assyria via its eastern side later in the same year. The two armies fought near Arraphka (modern Kirkuk) and "the Assyrian army retreated before the army of Akkad (Babylonia). They (the Babylonians) inflicted a major defeat on it and pushed it back as far as the Zab River. They seized their chariots and horses and robbed them greatly."[23] In so doing, the Babylonians effectively eliminated Assyria's grip on the sparsely populated middle-Tigris buffer zone between the two countries. For the first time in centuries the Babylonians controlled the area right up to the southern edge of the Assyrian heartland. Moreover, control of the entire Mesopotamian section of the east-west road afforded Nabopolassar new commercial and military advantages while impeding his enemy's mobility and access to important resources.[24] The Babylonian king had achieved his initial objectives with relative ease, and with his throne now fairly secure, there was nothing to prevent him from continuing offensive operations against Assyria. What had begun as another chapter in the struggle for hegemony over Babylonia soon became a fight for Assyria's very survival.

For the next two years, Nabopolassar kept up the pressure on Assyria. In 615 Babylonian forces entered the heartland and briefly assaulted Assur, the empire's principal cult center and its southernmost city. Moving swiftly to counterattack, Sin-shar-ishkun managed to lift the siege and push the Babylonians back to Takrita'in (modern Tikrit), where he besieged them in turn until he was forced to retreat.[25] Although the territorial scope of the conflict had changed now that Nabopolassar was the aggressor, the war was still being fought in the style of maneuver, attack, counterattack, and retreat that characterized its first phase. Neither side yet had the means or the confidence to seek a decisive confrontation. Even after repeated setbacks, the Assyrian army remained capable of rapid response and swift counteroffensive. The war thus far was entirely "normal," both sides having fought according to standard military practice. All that was about to change.

The war's turning point came in 614 when a new enemy, the Medes, launched a surprise attack against the Assyrian heartland from the east.[26] A seminomadic tribal people, the Medes had long controlled territory in the eastern Zagros range but, from the eighth century on, had become increasingly involved in the mountain states bordering Assyria and Babylonia. It is possible that internal political strife caused by the war's disruption of their economy, which was tied to those of Assyria and Babylonia, inspired the Medes' intervention.[27] Whatever motivated it, the Medes' entrance into the war delivered a shock from which the Assyrians could not recover, for their new enemies gave no quarter and destroyed all they could not carry off.

The Medes swept through the heartland, sacking Tarbisu and Assur and attacking Nineveh and Nimrud, both of which managed to hold out. Even so, at Nimrud the Medes ravaged the lower town and substantially damaged the fortification wall of its arsenal, Fort Shalmaneser.[28] The destruction of Assur, Assyria's holiest city, had a profound impact on people throughout the Near East. The Babylonian Chronicle's report of these events emphasizes the violence of the Medes, who "inflicted a terrible defeat on a great people, pillaged and looted them, and [robbed them]."[29] Nabopolassar, eager to gain valuable military support (and just as eager to avoid making the Medes his enemies), immediately made an alliance with the Median leader, Cyaxares. Winter brought the Assyrians a brief respite as uncertain weather and lack of supplies forced their enemies to return to their respective homelands.

Despite being badly outnumbered and facing invasion on two fronts, the Assyrians did not recognize the gravity of their situation; they did not fall back into defensive positions. On the contrary, rather than hastening to repair the damage to the fortifications that the Medes had inflicted, the people of Nimrud dismantled parts of the wall in preparation for renovating it at some later date.[30] The renovations would never be completed. In the meantime, Sin-shar-ishkun continued to press the attack. In a bold attempt to forestall joint enemy operations and move the war's center of gravity away from Assyria, he went on the attack in 613. His eastern flank protected by tribal (possibly Scythian) allies,[31] the Assyrian king was able to force Nabopolassar out of Anat (on the middle Euphrates), where he had been trying to suppress the Assyrian-backed rebellion of a local tribe, the Suhu.[32] Babylonia's subsequent withdrawal from the area did not significantly alter Assyria's fortunes, however, and it may have been at this point that Sin-shar-ishkun finally grasped the severity of the crisis.

Two cuneiform documents, a fragmentary letter from Sin-shar-ishkun and Nabopolassar's possible response, show that a diplomatic exchange between the two kings might have taken place around this time. If, as is likely, these tablets are genuine and belong together, their contents suggest that they date to the period just before the fall of Assyria.[33] In his letter, the Assyrian king attempts to appease Nabopolassar in order to "quiet his fiery heart" and prevent further bloodshed.[34] But it seems that Sin-shar-ishkun had waited too long to open negotiations; he had nothing to offer that Nabopolassar could not simply take now that the Medes were his allies. Nabopolassar rejected Sin-shar-ishkun in the harshest of terms, declaring that "the wall of Nineveh, which is made of strong stone [by the command of] the god Marduk, great lord, I shall pile up like a mound of sand. The city . . . its roots I shall pluck out and the foundations of the land I shall obliterate."[35] If the Babylonian king had started the war looking for a negotiated peace with Assyria, nothing less than total victory would now suffice. Nevertheless, he did not anticipate the extremes to which his Median allies would go.

Within a few months of the failed negotiations, the combined Babylonian and Median armies had penetrated deep into Assyria, forcing Sin-shar-ishkun and the remnants of his army to make a last stand at Nineveh.[36] An enormous city with fifteen gates, Nineveh stood little chance against a determined enemy. After a siege of only three months, the city fell in August 612 when two or more of its gates were breached. Excavations have uncovered grisly evidence of Nineveh's final hours, notably the skeletal remains of numerous men and boys (aged ten to forty-five) who died defending the Halzi gate.[37] The subsequent sack of Nineveh was calculated and thorough: the Babylonians and Medes looted the city, symbolically mutilated images of the Assyrian kings, and eventually burned the entire place to the ground. But the violence did not stop with the destruction of the capital city and the death of Sin-shar-ishkun. The survivors retreated to Harran (in southern Turkey), where under the leadership of a new king, Assur-uballit II, they held out until their final defeat in 609.

In the meantime, the Assyrian heartland was systematically devastated. At sites such as Assur, Nineveh, Nimrud, Dur-Sharrukin, Tarbisu, Imgur-Enlil, and Khirbet Khatuniyeh, excavations have uncovered evidence of intense fires and widespread destruction. Only two cities, Assur and Arbela, appear to have been used later by the Babylonians or Medes, whereas the other sites show (at best) only sparse occupation by poor squatters.[38] As one archaeologist observed, "It is difficult to exaggerate the intensity of this destruction and few if any sites and buildings seem to have escaped unscathed."[39] In fact, what happened to Assyria—particularly the destruction of its temples—shocked the Babylonians. In his inscriptions, Nabopolassar carefully ascribed his victory to divine intervention.[40] By contrast, Nabonidus (555–539), the last king of the dynasty founded by Nabopolassar, blamed Cyaxares for the destruction of Assyria, declaring that the Median leader "demolished the sanctuaries of all the gods of Subartu (Assyria). . . . None of the cult(-centers) he omitted, laying waste their (sacred) towns worse than a flood storm." Nabonidus then claimed a more respectful attitude by his conquering ancestor, Nabopolassar, "for whom the sacrilegious action of (the god) Marduk was horrible, did not raise his hand against the cult(-places) of any of the great gods, but left his hair unkempt, (and) slept on the floor (to express his pious desperation)."[41] Although the Babylonians had defeated Assyria, in the process they and their Median allies had violated normal codes of conduct. Indeed, they had inflicted so much damage that the heartland began to recover only a hundred years later under Persian occupation.

The Assyrian Way of War

From the account given here, it would be easy to conclude that the Medes and Babylonians had simply outfought a weakened Assyrian military led by an incompetent king. After all, if the Babylonian Chronicles are to be believed, the Assyrians did not win a single battle after 620 BCE. Nor did they do much to defend their territory. Even so, the Assyrians proved remarkably hard to beat: they managed to field an army after each devastating defeat, continued to carry out offensive operations, and maintained the loyalty of their allies to the bitter end. The oft-invoked image of the imperial core as shrunken, dysfunctional, and isolated also does not stand up to scrutiny, for even though the empire had lost control of some strategically and economically important areas such as Babylonia and parts of Palestine, its provinces in Syria and in the northern Tigris region continued to function for some time after the destruction of the heartland.

If fundamental military weakness does not account for Assyria's defeat, then what does? The sources, albeit limited, allow us to make three crucial observations: first, that the Assyrians never implemented an effective defensive strategy; second, that they repeatedly took the offensive against Nabopolassar; and third, that the Medes' intervention entirely changed the nature of the war. However, the significance of these points becomes clear only when they are examined in their wider cultural and historical context.

The polities of the ancient Near East—Assyria, Babylonia, Egypt, Hatti, Urartu, and the city-states of Syria-Palestine and southern Turkey—were urban-based monarchies subject to similar environmental constraints, and as such, they developed many of the same core social and political institutions, even as they differed in cultural specifics. Assyria and Babylonia had a particular cultural affinity: a common language (different dialects of Akkadian) as well as shared religious and intellectual traditions. As Near Eastern states fought one another repeatedly over the centuries, they developed common war-fighting styles, conventional behaviors, and an unwritten code of conduct.[42] This convergence created shared expectations of warfare and its consequences. The effect was to limit somewhat the material and human cost of war. Kings usually went to war for security reasons, to quell rebellion or to gain control of resources and territory. Achieving these objectives involved diplomacy, negotiation, selective violence, and calculated destruction rather than the type of wholesale ruin meted out to Assyria. Conventional warfare was unquestionably brutal, but defeat was not intended to be so absolute as to preclude recovery under a new regime. In the normal course of war, targeted cities might be sacked and villages destroyed, but the general infrastructure, temples, and the conquered peoples' way of life usually were left intact for the victor to rule. Over decades of war fought in Babylonia, for example, the Assyrians never inflicted the kind of indiscriminate and comprehensive devastation that they suffered at the hands of the Medes.[43]

Despite Assyria's modern reputation as a brutal oppressor that cowed the hapless peoples of the ancient Near East through torture and terrorism, Assyrian military methods were generally in line with those of other ancient states. The Assyrian practice of taking heads, for instance, can be traced back to third-millennium Syria and is considered by some to have transferred to Assyria through "cultural migration."[44] Furthermore, the ruthless treatment of defeated enemies and the punishment of rebels were prevalent throughout the ancient world.[45] In at least one important respect, however, the Assyrians seem to have exceeded contemporary practices, namely, by the pervasive and graphic representation of violence in royal inscriptions and on sculptured palace reliefs. Whether the celebration of bloodshed expressed some dark cultural trait or had a more overtly political purpose remains hotly contested. The huge corpus of royal correspondence dealing with the realities of imperial rule is singularly devoid of sadism, a fact that belies the popular perception of the Assyrians as barbaric despots. Whatever else may have been at play, the element of calculation in Assyrian cruelty has long been recognized.[46]

The most successful kings carefully weighed the ratio of cost to benefit of all official undertakings, military or otherwise. Warfare and punitive actions were subject to the same type of calculation that diplomatic, political, or economic endeavors received. Although the Assyrians recognized the effectiveness of clemency in dealing with subject peoples, they also believed, along with many other ancient powers, that when conquered territories or clients rebelled, the response had to be swift and merciless. If rebellions were not quelled decisively, they would spread; all the more reason to make examples of the ringleaders in horrific public executions. More important, the king who failed to avenge a broken treaty would incur the wrath of his own gods, whose honor the rebels had affronted. Under these circumstances, punishments such as flaying or impaling—far from being imposed at the ruler's whim for his personal enjoyment—were carried out according to the precepts of divine justice. The subjects of any Near Eastern state would have understood this concept implicitly even as they feared its application.

By contrast, the Medes, unlike the centralized, literate, urbanized societies of Assyria or Babylonia, were a loose confederation of tribes and small, fortress-based chiefdoms that had come together temporarily under the leadership of Cyaxares in order to plunder and destroy Assyria. Although Nabopolassar's vision of the Babylonians as the natural "heirs of Assyria" conformed to age-old Mesopotamian tradition, the Medes did not share that tradition, had no imperial ambitions, and lacked the level of state organization required to administer an empire even if they had wanted to do so.[47] Had events followed historical precedent, Assyria would not have been laid waste and abandoned but would have been reorganized into the provinces of a new Babylonian empire. That the Babylonians later minimized their own role while blaming the Medes for the extreme devastation reveals the disjunction between the Near Eastern and Median expectations of war.[48] Because the Medes did not "play by the rules," their entrance into the war constituted a "strategic shock," meaning an event that "suddenly discredits many or all preexisting assumptions about the environment and those conventions that govern effective navigation through it."[49] What happened to Assyria truly stunned contemporary Near Eastern societies, not just because it was sudden, but because destruction on that level did not follow accepted norms. For their part, the Assyrians could not adapt to the new situation but doggedly pursued their customary way of war.

Although it was part of the larger Mesopotamian cultural and military tradition, the Assyrian army developed its fundamental character as a result of the state's unique historical circumstance. During the Middle Assyrian period (ca. 1600–1100), surrounded by enemies and with no geographical barriers to aid defense, Assyria struggled to survive among the era's great powers (Egypt, Kassite Babylonia, Mitanni, and Hatti). The humiliation of Mitannian hegemony in the fifteenth century BCE, followed by Aramean incursions that drastically reduced Assyrian territory at the end of the period, transformed the Assyrians into an aggressive military power whose fundamental understanding of warfare was that it should be preemptive and offensive rather than defensive. In short, the Assyrians decided that the best defense was a good offense. By the ninth century BCE, the impulse to secure the heartland of Assyria had combined with the religious mandate for imperial expansion to reinforce Assyrian assumptions about warfare. As the empire acquired more territory, war naturally gravitated to the periphery, but this situation simply validated what had become the Assyrians' automatic military response to threat: take war to the enemy with overwhelming force.

This offensive principle is nowhere more apparent than in the royal annals in which Assyrian kings celebrated their military deeds. After the introduction of the genre in the eleventh century BCE, Assyrian campaign narratives invariably depicted the king and his army leaving their homeland and entering enemy territory to wage war. Each new military operation was introduced with statements such as "In the fourteenth year of my reign: I mustered the country; I crossed the Euphrates; twelve kings came against me; I fought with them; I accomplished their defeat"; or "In my next campaign, I moved swiftly against Babylon whose destruction I sought, and like the onset of a storm, I attacked"; or "In my eighth campaign, at the command of the gods Assur and Ishtar, I levied my troops and went straight against Ummanaldash, king of Elam."[50] The annals are essentially military travelogues. Not only do all campaigns take place outside the Assyrian heartland, but (with one or two notable exceptions) they all are prosecuted the same way and follow a predictable pattern. The always victorious king marches his army out of Assyria into enemy territory, which he proceeds to devastate until his opponents submit. Rarely, if ever, do the Assyrians admit to giving ground. Assyrian armies might muster in the heartland, but they do not fight there.[51] The purpose of royal inscriptions was to celebrate the king's fulfillment of divine imperatives, not to elucidate royal political goals and military strategy or to report mere facts. These texts represent a fundamental unification of ideology and practice: Assyrian kings did not passively await attack but met any threat aggressively, as their sacred duty required.

Because tradition mandated that every king expand the borders of the empire,[52] the army from its inception became an offensive force. Nevertheless, no king could field a large enough army to conquer, police, and pacify a huge empire. Maintaining a hold on territory thus depended on a shrewd balance of diplomacy and ruthlessly applied violence. As long as the threat of retaliation or the promise of reward prevented rebellion among client states and provinces, the army could operate anywhere outside the core without threat to national security. Although some soldiers garrisoned strategically placed forts and provincial cities throughout the empire, the Assyrian army was more often used to attack than to occupy or defend. To that end, the Assyrians developed appropriate organizational and operational capabilities: superior training, weapons, and logistical support; an aptitude for maneuver and rapid deployment; and a facility for combined arms operations involving chariots, cavalry, and variously armed infantry units. Imperial expansion and continuing military success constantly reinforced expectations of how wars should be waged, and the notion that wars were fought on the periphery far from the imperial core became ingrained.

Assyria's military achievements brought unprecedented security to its heartland. After Tiglath-pileser I (1114–1076) evicted the Babylonians from Ekallate (slightly northeast of Assur) at the end of the twelfth century, no heartland city was besieged and no organized foreign invasion force penetrated its borders until 615 when the Babylonians first attempted to take Assur. The Assyrian core was free of invasion for more than five hundred years—an astounding record that no other Near Eastern state could even approximate. The Assyrians had perfected an extremely effective system of conquest and control that brought peace to their heartland and much of the empire as well. Even though these prevailing conditions profoundly shaped the Assyrians' concept of how war should and would be waged, they also inevitably seduced people into taking the heartland's invulnerability for granted.

The main goal of imperial expansion was to supply and enrich the core. Assyria's primary mode of production was agriculture, and the country lacked many essential resources, including wood, metal, and stone. As the empire grew, its kings struggled to secure and manage the vital commodities that urban growth demanded and that the local rural population could not furnish.[53] Indeed, such goals might even be termed the very function of empire. By the seventh century, the large size of Assyria's cities—Nimrud, Nineveh, Assur, and Dur-Sharrukin—had a significant impact on local settlement patterns and the rural population. Even Assur, the smallest of these, was reasonably large, at about 70 hectares.[54] More than ten times larger, Nineveh covered about 780 hectares and had an estimated population of as many as 230,000.[55] The demand for supplies and the uncertainties of climate and agriculture meant that food had to be shipped into the cities from the provinces, and because the cities took in much more than they produced, they eventually became a burden on the economy.[56] In response, kings undertook substantial public projects to provide housing and fresh water, facilitate the transportation of goods, and enhance communication between the heartland and distant parts of the empire.

As centers of commerce and intellectual and religious activity and as symbols of royal power, cities not only had to be easily accessible to a variety of groups (e.g., tribute-bearing foreign delegations and merchants' caravans), but they also had to be appropriately impressive. The most successful kings spared no expense in making capitals fabulous, but in their desire to stimulate production and glorify Assyria, they occasionally sacrificed defensive utility.[57] Sargon II (720–705), who built a new capital, Dur-Sharrukin, on virgin soil, claimed in his inscriptions that his purpose was to "provide the wide land of Assyria with food to repletion."[58] Its martial designation *dûr* (Akkadian for fort or wall) notwithstanding, the city's location on an open plain devoid of protective topographical features indicates that the ideological message it conveyed took precedence over military considerations. The fortification wall, though augmented by towers and possibly topped by stone crenellations, was only about twelve meters high, and each of the city's seven double-gates had a straight-axis approach. In addition, the platform of the citadel projected beyond the city wall, an innovation that traded security for the visual effect of "riding on the walls."[59]

Sargon's son Sennacherib (704–681) was even more ambitious than his father. After more than doubling the size of Nineveh, Sennacherib initiated massive improvements, some of which involved elaborate fortifications: a huge wall, a moat, and an outer rampart. He made Nineveh's water supply system, rather than the city's defenses, his priority and built some 150 kilometers of canals, tunnels, aqueducts, and dams in order to supply water to the city, its surrounding fields, and his splendid gardens.[60] As a result, the full fortification program was never completed. Nineveh's twelve-kilometer perimeter wall exceeded fifteen meters in height and included numerous towers, but any defensive advantage it afforded was compromised by the city's fifteen gates, which opened directly onto wide roadways that linked Nineveh to Assyria's other main cities.[61] Here, as at Nimrud, Dur-Sharrukin, and Assur, convenient access in peacetime became a lethal vulnerability during a siege.

This is not to say that the Assyrians skimped on fortifications. Masters of siege warfare, they employed all the standard defensive measures: double walls, ramparts, moats, ditches, glacis, and deep gates with towers to provide enfilading fire. Yet, after Assyrian prosperity began to wane toward the end of Ashurbanipal's reign, economic and political constraints prevented subsequent kings from matching their predecessors' building achievements. Construction projects of all types declined in number and scope. Under these circumstances, extending defenses that had not been needed since time immemorial would have been unconscionable. Although the last kings of Assyria made necessary repairs to city defenses, they undertook no improvements and made no attempt to address the access problem posed by the gates. The fact that Assur, Nimrud, and Nineveh held out the first time they were attacked belies the notion that city defenses had seriously deteriorated.

On the contrary, what proved Assyria's undoing was the belief that fortifications, however elaborate, would be enough to stop a determined enemy. Centuries of peace had made the idea of invasion seem far-fetched.

Conclusion

The Assyrians had no defensive strategy for the heartland because experience confirmed that they did not need one and because they were entirely confident in the way they waged war. Consequently, when the unthinkable actually happened and foreign armies penetrated the Assyrian heartland for the first time in five hundred years, Assyria was not prepared to defend itself. Throughout the war, Sin-shar-ishkun's actions were characteristic; he did not stay to defend his territory, but faithful to the Assyrian way of war, he kept pressing the attack. It probably never occurred to him to do anything else. Sin-shar-ishkun applied proven military principles: protect the flank, foment rebellion in enemy territory, take the war to the enemy, and concentrate the attack on one point of the enemy's position. Under the circumstances, he seems to have been a capable general who mustered all the resources at his disposal and deployed them rationally (particularly with regard to mobility and the use of allies), but in the end he had neither the means nor the time to adapt to the new conditions. More important, he simply was not prepared to mount an effective defense against a numerically superior enemy whose goal was destruction rather than conquest.

The Assyrians developed expectations of warfare in accordance with their social and economic organization in order to meet their political objectives. Great success over a long period of time created the deep-seated conviction that the heartland was inviolate and that warfare was best executed offensively. Weakened by economic circumstances and the strategic complacency that often accompanies long success, Assyria could not withstand the "game-changing" strategic shock that the Medes delivered. In the case of Assyria, we clearly see the dangers inherent in a social and military conservatism that adhered too stubbornly to preconceived notions about how war should be waged and that could not adapt to new challenges.

This chapter has stressed the need to evaluate warfare in its cultural context. Viewed in isolation, the Assyrians' last war is an unenlightening concatenation of events: the significance of the Medes' participation is lost; Sin-shar-ishkun's offensive strategy remains merely "puzzling";[62] and the vulnerability of the heartland becomes just another example of the standard paradigm for imperial collapse. Studied in their proper context, however, these events reveal a great deal about the relationship between warfare and culture in the ancient Near East. The Assyrian way of war did more than meet the practical exigencies of war; it expressed the Assyrians' (or the Assyrian elites') view of themselves—their values, standards, and codes of behavior. Assyria's cultural beliefs, in keeping with those of the wider Near Eastern community, both guided and gave meaning to their actions on the battlefield. Perhaps more than any other factor, their assumptions about warfare condemned the Assyrians to defeat.

NOTES

1. An earlier version of this chapter, "A New Look at the End of the Assyrian Empire," appeared in *Homeland and Exile: Biblical and Ancient Near Eastern Studies in Honour of Bustenay Oded*, ed. G. Galil, M. Geller, and A. Millard, Vetus Testamentum Supplements 130 (Leiden: Brill, 2009), 179–202.

2. See, for example, Stefan Zawadzki, *The Fall of Assyria and Median-Babylonian Relations in Light of the Nabopolassar Chronicle* (Poznan: Eburon, 1988); Joan Oates, "The Fall of Assyria," in *The Cambridge Ancient History*, 2nd ed., vol. III/2 (Cambridge: Cambridge University Press, 1991), 162–93; Amelie Kuhrt, *The Ancient Near East c. 3000-330 BC*, 2 vols. (London: Routledge, 1994), 540–46 ; Peter Machinist, "The Fall of Assyria in Comparative Ancient Perspective," in *Assyria 1995*, ed. Simo Parpola and Robert M. Whiting (Helsinki: Neo-Assyrian Text Corpus Project, 1997), 179–96; and Mario Liverani, "The Fall of the Assyrian Empire: Ancient and Modern Interpretations," in *Empires: Perspectives from Archaeology and History*, ed. Susan E. Alcock et al. (Cambridge: Cambridge University Press, 2001), 374–91.

3. Mark Altaweel, "The Land of Ashur: A Study of Landscape and Settlement in the Assyrian Heartland," 2 vols. (PhD diss., University of Chicago, 2004), 4 . Altaweel demarcates the heartland as the 150 km x 79 km area having a north-south axis from the Lower Zab to Eski Mosul and an east-west axis from Wadi Tharthar and Jebel Sheikh Ibrahim to Wadi Fadha, Qara Chauq, and the Khazir River. This area formed the nucleus of the Assyrian Empire and included the capital cities. It was at the core of the Assyrian concept of "the land of Assur," although in practice (and over time) this notion proved quite elastic.

4. See especially David Stronach, "When Assyria Fell: New Light on the Last Days of Nineveh," *Mâr Šipri* 2 (1989): 2–3; David Stronach, "Notes on the Fall of Nineveh," in *Assyria 1995*, ed. Simo Parpola and Robert M. Whiting (Helsinki: Assyrian Text Corpus Project, 1997), 307–24; Peter Miglus, "Die letzten Tage von Assur und die Zeit danach," *ISIMU* 3 (2003): 85–99; Diana Pickworth, "Excavations at Nineveh: The Halzi Gate," in *Nineveh: Papers of the XLIXe Rencontre Assyriologique Internationale, London, 7–11 July 2003*, vol. 2, ed. D. Collon and A. George (London: British Museum, 2005), 295–316; John E. Curtis, "The Assyrian Heartland in the Period 612–539 BC," in *Continuity of Empire(?): Assyria, Media, Persia*, ed. G. Lanfranchi, M. Roaf, and R. Rollinger, History of the Ancient Near East Monographs 5 (Padova: S.A.R.G.O.N. Editrice, 2003), 157–167.

5. For editions of these chronicles, see Albert Kirk Grayson, *Assyrian and Babylonian Chronicles* (Winona Lake, IN: Eisenbrauns, 2000), 87–96; and Jean-Jacques Glassner,

Mesopotamian Chronicles (Atlanta: Society of Biblical Literature, 2004), 218–24. References to these chronicles are given here by abbreviation and line numbers, for example, FNC 10 refers to the Fall of Nineveh Chronicle, line 10.

6. For the highly problematical chronology of the period, see Zawadzki, *The Fall of Assyria*; Nadav Na'aman, "Chronology and History of the Late Assyrian Period (631–619 BC)," *Zeitschrift für Assyriologie* 81 (1991): 243–67; Stefan Zawadzki, "A Contribution to the Chronology of the Last Days of the Assyrian Empire," *Zeitschrift für Assyriologie* 85 (1995): 67–73; Paul-Alain Beaulieu, "The 4th Year of Hostilities in the Land," *Baghdader Mitteilungen* 28 (1997): 367–94; John A. Brinkman, "Nabopolasser," *Reallexikon der Assyriologie und Vorderasiatische Archaeologie* 9 (1998): 12–16; and Michael Liebig, "Aššur-etel-ilani, Sin-šum-lišir, and Sin-šar-iškun und die Babylonische Chronik," *Zeitschrift für Assyriologie* 90 (2000): 281–84.

7. Machinist, "The Fall of Assyria in Comparative Ancient Perspective"; Aaron Pinker, "Nineveh's Defensive Strategy and Nahum 2," *Zeitschrift für alttestamentliche Wissenschaft* 118 (2006): 618–25; Aaron Pinker, "Nahum and Greek Tradition on Nineveh's Fall," *Journal of Hebrew Scripture* 6 (2006): 2–16; Stanley M. Burstein, *The Babyloniaca of Berossus*, Sources from the Ancient Near East 1/5 (Malibu, CA: Undena 1978); Robert Drews, "The Babylonian Chronicles of Berossus," *Iraq* 37 (1975): 39–55; R. J. Van Der Spek, "Berossus as a Babylonian Chronicler and Greek Historian," in *Studies in Near Eastern World View and Society Presented to Marten Stol on the Occasion of his 65th Birthday*, ed. R. J. Van Der Spek (Bethesda, MD: CDL Press, 2008), 277–318.

8. Thomas Deszö, "The Reconstruction of the Neo-Assyrian Army as Depicted on the Assyrian Palace Reliefs, 745–612 BC," *Acta Archeologica Academiae Scientiarum Hungaricae* 57 (2006): 87–130 and its bibliography.

9. Ibid., 100.

10. Ibid., 125.

11. Stephanie Dalley, "Foreign Chariotry and Cavalry in the Armies of Tiglath-pileser III and Sargon II," *Iraq* 47 (1985): 31–48.

12. F. M. Fales, "Grain Reserves, Daily Rations, and the Size of the Assyrian Army," *State Archives of Assyria Bulletin* III (1989): 23–34.

13. Deszö, "The Reconstruction of the Neo-Assyrian Army," 108. See also JoAnn Scurlock, "Neo-Assyrian Battle Tactics," in *Crossing Boundaries and Linking Horizons: Studies in Honor of Michael C. Astour on His 80th Birthday*, ed. G. Young, M. Chavalas, and R. Averbeck (Bethesda, MD: CDL Press, 1997), 491–517; Davide Nadali, "Assyrian Open Field Battles: An Attempt at Reconstruction and Analysis," in *Studies on War in the Ancient Near East*, ed. J. Vidial, Alter Orient und Altes Testament 372 (Münster: Ugarit Verlag, 2010), 117–52.

14. John MacGinnis, "Mobilization and Militarization in the Neo-Babylonian Empire," in *Studies on War in the Ancient Near East*, ed. J. Vidial, Alter Orient und Altes Testament 372 (Münster: Ugarit Verlag, 2010), 153–63.

15. In the early seventh century, Median contingents served as palace guards and bodyguards of the Assyrian crown prince. See Mario Liverani, "The Medes at Esarhaddon's Court," *Journal of Cuneiform Studies* 47 (1995): 57–62. See also Julian E. Reade, "Why Did the Medes Invade Assyria?" in *Continuity of Empire(?): Assyria, Media, Persia*, ed. G. Lanfranchi, M. Roaf, and R. Rollinger, History of the Ancient Near East Monographs 5 (Padova: S.A.R.G.O.N. Editrice, 2003), 149–56.

16. Herodotus (1.103) attributes this development to Cyaxares.

17. The exact date of Ashurbanipal's death is unknown but certainly took place between 631 and 627 BCE. Kandalanu, whom Ashurbanipal appointed to rule Babylonia in 648, died in 627. For a discussion of the evidence, see Grant Frame, *Babylonia 689–627 B.C.: A Political History* (Istanbul: Nederlands Historisch-Archaeologisch Instituut, 1992), 300–306.

18. Beaulieu, "The 4th Year of Hostilities in the Land," 391–93; Michael Jursa, "Die Söhne Kudurrus und die Herkunft der neubabylonischen Dynastie," *Revue d'assyriologie et d'archéologie orientale* 101 (2007): 125–36. Beaulieu argues that Nabopolassar was a native of Uruk (in southern Babylonia), and more recently, Jursa suggested that Nabopolassar was the eldest son of a governor of Uruk who was killed by the Assyrians.

19. NC 18–24. The ancient site of Raqmat, or Sallat, as it is sometimes transliterated, has not yet been located. According to convention, in translations of cuneiform sources the information enclosed in parentheses is explanatory and not part of the original text. Material included in square brackets represents the translator's reconstruction of words or phrases that are missing from the original because of a break in the text.

20. Steven W. Cole, *Nippur in Neo-Assyrian Times: C. 755–612 B.C.* State Archives of Assyria Studies 4 (Helsinki: Helsinki University Press, 1996), 80; Brinkman, "Nabopolassar," 14.

21. FNC 1–12. The site of Gablini has not yet been identified.

22. For the key roads in Assyria, see Sabrina Favaro, *Voyages et voyageurs à l'époque néo-Assyrienne*, State Archives of Assyria Studies 18 (Helsinki: Helsinki University Press, 2007), plates 4 and 6.

23. FNC 11–13.

24. Kuhrt, *The Ancient Near East*, 545.

25. FNC 16–22.

26. The Medes had been active in the area around Arrapha some months earlier, but the chronicle is broken at that point, and it is not possible to determine what happened (FNC 23). For more information about the Medes and their relationship to the Assyrians and Babylonians, see especially G. Lanfranchi et al., *Continuity of Empire*.

27. Kuhrt, *The Ancient Near East*, 545. For more on the Medes' role in the east-west trade, see K. Radner, "An Assyrian View on the Medes," in *Continuity of Empire(?): Assyria, Media, Persia*, ed. G. Lanfranchi, M. Roaf, and R. Rollinger, History of the Ancient Near East Monographs 5 (Padova: S.A.R.G.O.N. Editrice, 2003), 51–52.

28. M. E. L. Mallowan, *Nimrud and Its Remains,* 2 vols. (London: British Museum, 1966), 82; Joan Oates and David Oates, *Nimrud: An Assyrian City Revealed* (London: British School of Archaeology in Iraq, 2001), 148.

29. FNC 27.

30. Mallowan, *Nimrud and Its Remains*, 82; and Oates and Oates, *Nimrud*, 148.

31. Herodotus 1.103 mentions the Scythians attacking the Medes. There is earlier evidence of an alliance between the Assyrian king Esarhaddon (680–669), the grandfather of Sin-shar-ishkun, and the Scythian leader Bartatua. Esarhaddon might have cemented the alliance with a diplomatic marriage. See Ivan Starr, *Queries to the Sungod: Divination and Politics in Sargonid Assyria*. State Archives of Assyria 4 (Helsinki: Helsinki University Press, 1990), 20.

32. FNC 31–37.

33. For the Sin-shar-ishkun letter and discussion of both texts, see Wilfred G. Lambert, "Letter of Sîn-šarra-iškun to Nabopolassar," in *Cuneiform Texts in the Metropolitan Museum of Art*, ed. I. Spar and W. G. Lambert, vol. 2, *Literary and Scholastic Texts* (New York: Metropolitan Museum of Art, 1995), 206. For the Nabopolassar text, see Pamela Gerardi, "Declaring War in Mesopotamia," *Archiv für Orientforschung* 33 (1986): 30–38. The colophon of the Sin-shar-ishkun letter identifies it as a Hellenistic copy of a purported Babylonian original, so although Lambert argues convincingly that it is genuine, the possibility remains that it is the product of scribal imagination. In the other text, Nabopolassar's name is not preserved, but the contents make the attribution virtually certain.

34. Lambert, "Letter of Sîn-šarra-iškun to Nabopolassar," 205.

35. Gerardi, "Declaring War in Mesopotamia," 36.

36. FNC 41–46.

37. Pickworth, "Excavations at Nineveh."

38. Stephanie Dalley, "Nineveh after 612 BC," *Altorientalische Forschungen* 20 (1993): 134–47; Curtis, "The Assyrian Heartland."

39. Curtis, "The Assyrian Heartland," 164.

40. Rocío Da Riva, *The Neo-Babylonian Royal Inscriptions: An Introduction* (Munster: Ugarit Verlag, 2008), 6.

41. A. Leo Oppenheim, "Nabonidus," in *Ancient Near Eastern Texts Related to the Old Testament*, ed. J. B. Pritchard (Princeton, NJ: Princeton University Press, 1955), 309.

42. Mario Liverani, *Prestige and Interest: International Relations in the Near East ca. 1600–1100 B.C.* (Padova: S.A.R.G.O.N. Editrice, 1990).

43. Marc Van Der Mieroop, "Revenge, Assyrian Style," *Past & Present* 179 (2003): 19–22. Van Der Mieroop argues that the thorough destruction of Nineveh was a deliberate act of vengeance for Assyria's earlier sacking of Babylon (689 BCE). However, revenge does not account for the harsh treatment of the rest of Assyria. Sennacherib besieged and sacked Babylon to avenge the death of his own son, whom the Babylonians had betrayed, captured, and delivered to the Elamites. Even though Sennacherib's vengeance was both thorough and brutal, it was localized, and he did not systematically devastate all of Babylonia. See John A. Brinkman, *Prelude to Empire: Babylonian Society and Politics, 747–626 B.C.*, Occasional Publications of the Babylonian Fund 7 (Philadelphia: University Museum, 1984), 67–68; Frame, *Babylonia*, 52–63.

44. Rita Dolce, "The 'Head of the Enemy' in the Sculptures from the Palaces of Nineveh: An Example of 'Cultural Migration'?" See also Dominik Bonatz, "Ashurbanipal's Headhunt: An Anthropological Perspective"; and Zainab Bahrani, "The King's Head"; all in *Nineveh: Papers of the XLIXe Rencontre Assyriologique Internationale, London, 7–11 July 2003*, vol. 2, ed. Dominique Collon and Andrew George (London: British School of Archaeology in Iraq, 2005), 121–32, 93–102, and 115–20.

45. It is not difficult to find examples throughout ancient history of what we now call atrocities, but Hirtius, a legate of Julius Caesar writing in the first century BCE, articulated in an uncommonly forthright manner the callous logic behind acts of extreme violence as follows:

> Nor could he (Caesar) foresee any successful outcome of his strategies if more of the enemy in other areas acted similarly. . . . For this reason he decided upon making an example of the townspeople in punishing them, so as to deter the rest. He allowed them to live, therefore, but cut off the hands

of all those who had carried arms against him. This made the punishment
for wrong-doers plain to see. (Caesar, 8.44)

See Carolyn Hammond, trans., *Caesar's Gallic Wars* (Oxford: Oxford University Press, 1996), 217.

46. See, for example, A. T. Olmstead, "The Calculated Frightfulness of Ashur Nasir Apal," *Journal of the American Oriental Society* 38 (1918): 209–63; H. W. F. Saggs, "Assyrian Warfare in the Sargonid Period," *Iraq* 25 (1963): 145–54; and more recently, A. Fuchs, "Waren die Assyrer grausam?" in *Extreme Formen von Gewalt in Bild und Text des Altertums*, ed. M. Zimmermann, Münchner Studien zur Alten Welt 5 (Munich: Herbert Utz, 2009), 65–119. A very large body of scholarship deals with Assyrian ideology and propaganda. See especially Mario Liverani, "The Ideology of the Assyrian Empire," in *Power and Propaganda: A Symposium on Ancient Empires*, ed. M. T. Larsen, Mesopotamia 7 (Copenhagen: Akademisk Forlag, 1979), 297–318; Paul Garelli, "La propaganda royale assyrienne," *Akkadica* 27 (1982): 16–29; and H. Tadmor, "Propaganda, Literature, Historiography: Cracking the Code of the Assyrian Royal Inscriptions," in *Assyria 1995*, ed. S. Parpola and R. M. Whiting (Helsinki: Neo-Assyrian Text Corpus Project, 1997), 325–38.

47. Liverani, "The Fall of the Assyrian Empire," 389–90; Reade, "Why Did the Medes Invade Assyria?" 155.

48. Liverani, "The Fall of the Assyrian Empire," 390.

49. Nathan P. Freier, *Known Unknowns: Unconventional "Strategic Shocks" in Defense Strategy Development* (Carlisle, PA: Strategic Studies Institute, U.S. Army War College, 2008), 5.

50. Brent Strawn, "Shalmaneser III: The Black Obelisk"; Sarah C. Melville, "Sennacherib: The Bavian Inscription"; and Sarah C. Melville, "Ashurbanipal: Civil War and Elamite Campaigns"; all in *The Ancient Near East: Historical Sources in Translation*, ed. Mark W. Chavalas (Oxford: Blackwell, 2006), 292, 349, and 367.

51. This is not to say that no fighting ever took place in the Assyrian heartland, for Assyria suffered sporadic raids from nomadic peoples and a number of civil wars and rebellions, although these seem to have had little effect on the country's population centers. Some revolts are mentioned in letters or in the eponym chronicles (e.g., 762 "revolt in the citadel" or 746 "revolt in Calah"), but otherwise, we know little about them. For the eponym lists, see Allan Millard, *The Eponyms of the Assyrian Empire*, State Archives of Assyria Studies 2 (Helsinki: Helsinki University Press, 1994). For the Neo-Assyrian letter corpus, see the series State Archives of Assyria, vols. 1–18 (Helsinki: Neo-Assyrian Text Corpus Project / Helsinki University Press, 1987–2003).

52. Both the Middle Assyrian and Late Assyrian coronation prayers include the mandate to enlarge the country. See Benjamin R. Foster, *Before the Muses: An Anthology of Akkadian Literature* (Bethesda, MD: CDL Press, 2005), 334, 815.

53. Altaweel, "The Land of Assur," 157; Tony J. Wilkinson et al., "Landscape and Settlement in the Neo-Assyrian Empire," *Bulletin of the American School of Oriental Research* 340 (2006): 26–27.

54. One hectare equals 10,000 square meters, or about 2.5 acres.

55. The figure for Nineveh's population given here represents the very limits of possibility, but it does indicate the city's unique position in Assyria and the wider Near East. By comparison, Nimrud was about 380 hectares and Dur-Sharrukin 315. See Altaweel, "The Land of Assur," 41, 154.

56. Zawadzki, *The Fall of Assyria*, 18.

57. For the ideology of Neo-Assyrian cities, see, for example, Louis D. Levine, "Cities as Ideology: The Neo-Assyrian Centres of Ashur, Nimrud, and Nineveh," *Canadian Society of Mesopotamian Studies Bulletin* 12 (1986): 1–7; Laura Battini, "Un exemple de propagande néo-assyrienne: Les défenses de Dur-Sharrukin," *Contributi e materiali di archeologia orientale* 6 (1996): 217–31; Mirko Novák, "From Assur to Nineveh: The Assyrian Town Planning Programme"; Stephen Lumsden, "The Production of Space at Nineveh"; and Marta Rivaroli, "Nineveh: From Ideology to Topography"; all in *Nineveh: Papers of the XLIXe Rencontre Assyriologique Internationale, London, 7–11 July 2003*, vol. 2, ed. Dominique Collon and Andrew George (London: British School of Archaeology in Iraq, 2005), 177–86, 187–98, and 199–206.

58. Andreas Fuchs, *Die Inschriften Sargon II aus Khorsabad* (Göttingen: Cuvillier Verlag, 1994), Zyl 34–37.

59. Stronach, "Notes on the Fall of Nineveh," 310; Novák, "From Assur to Nineveh," 181; and Battini, "Un example de propaganda neo-assyrienne."

60. Ariel M. Bagg, "Irrigation in Northern Mesopotamia: Water in the Assyrian Capitals (12th–7th Centuries BC)," *Irrigation and Drainage Systems* 14 (2000): 316.

61. Stronach, "The Fall of Nineveh," 311–13; M. Louise Scott and John MacGinnis, "Notes on Nineveh," *Iraq* 52 (1990): 63–73.

62. Oates, "The Fall of Assyria," 179.

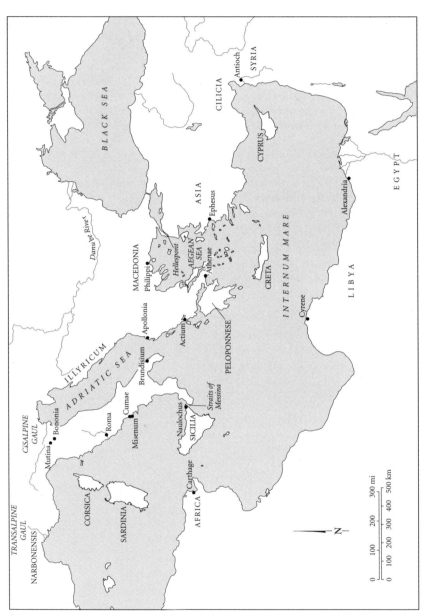

The Central Mediterranean during the Late Roman Republic

Disciplining Octavian

A Case Study of Roman Military Culture,
44–30 BCE

LEE L. BRICE

Roman armies dominated the Mediterranean world for more than six centuries, contributing to the creation and maintenance of an empire that spanned three continents and encompassed millions of inhabitants. Although Roman arms did not always triumph, such a record remains a remarkable achievement. This success also made the Roman military popular as a topic for later military historians and professionals seeking the recipe that they could draw on to improve contemporary efforts.[1] There was, of course, no recipe. Success for any military was always more complicated than any reductive formula, especially one focused simply on tactics or weaponry. Rather, the Roman army would be better considered for its military culture. That there was a distinct culture within the legions of the late Republic is not doubted, but it is important to remember that that military culture was part and product of the broader Roman culture.[2]

Culture has always affected how an army wages war. While examples of the connections between culture and war can be easy to identify in modern armies, it is much more difficult to locate specific instances in the ancient world. The primary reason for this problem is the nature of the available evidence. Ancient sources have not survived evenly. Those sources that remain usually lack the kinds of information required to develop definitive examples of a commander making operational and combat decisions that are directly linked to the society's culture. Perhaps the clearest aspect of Roman military culture for which we do have examples is discipline. It was an important component of that military culture, and we have good examples of a commander making operational decisions based on discipline.

It is not possible in one chapter to cover all facets of military discipline (*disciplina militaris*), and other works have explored it fully.[3] Instead, in this chapter I examine some of the ways in which military discipline broadly expressed Roman culture, using a case study of a commander heavily influenced in his planning and his combat decisions by features of military discipline. Because of the uneven quality and the limited quantity of our sources, my discussion focuses primarily on the Roman military of the late Republic and early Empire (first century BCE), the period of this case study.[4]

Discipline and Culture

Although in the modern world we tend to think of discipline as ubiquitous in successful armies, the routine discipline in the Roman military was new in the ancient Greco-Roman world.[5] In the past, historians assumed that Roman discipline was always rigid, brutal, and absolute, similar to that in some modern militaries. More recent work, however, has questioned this view, as historians found a great deal of indiscipline during the Republic and continuing into the Empire. There certainly is evidence that discipline in the Roman military was not as rigid as has been believed. J. E. Lendon, particularly, argues that we should see *disciplina* as a tool that commanders used to curb their soldiers' zeal (*virtus*) rather than as "a system of imposed or felt rules."[6] Moreover, we should see it as one of two military "ethics," along with *virtus*, that were in conflict but critical to military success.[7] Although plausible, Lendon's interpretation ignores certain historical features, including the typically negative outcomes of indiscipline and excessive *virtus*, the positive side of discipline, and, especially, the rhetorical nature of this type of Roman literature. A more likely interpretation of *disciplina* would be somewhere between Lendon's and the traditional view. Military discipline of the middle to late Republic was not so consistently enforced as to be called a system but was regularized to an extent by law and custom and was key to maintaining order on and off the battlefield. Regardless of the approach, scholars do not deny that discipline was critical to Rome's military success and was grounded in the broader culture.

The reality of *disciplina militaris* was much more complicated than the two-dimensional image in novels and films of a well-honed war machine famous for victory and brutal punishments.[8] Rather, it was a network of control whose purpose was to maintain military order at all times, thus enabling the commander to manage his soldiers in combat situations as well as controlling them outside combat, in camp and in the rest of society. Indeed, Roman soldiers' training, cohesion, and weapons could have made them a threat to the rest of society if they were not kept in order.

Managing the soldiers in a fight was not limited to keeping them in line but also was a means to encourage and reward great acts of bravery and endurance.[9] Cultural grounding was what made the network of "control" so successful. Two key ways in which *disciplina militaris* reflected the broader culture were in its ties to religion and its connection with status and hierarchy.

Sacramentum

The institution of Roman military discipline was made up of mental components (obedience and cult) as well as physical elements (training, drill, and daily tasks).[10] A significant mental component of the *disciplina militaris* was the military oath (*sacramentum*). During the Republic, when men were enlisted for service, they took the *sacramentum*. Initially, they swore to serve the commander (and thus the state) obediently for the duration of the current campaign. When, however, wars became so numerous that men served continuously for years, the new recruits swore to serve the commander for as long as necessary, usually not more than ten years, renewing the oath whenever a new commander arrived. When or under what circumstances the oath was instituted is not known, but as with the rest of *disciplina militaris*, it was in place by the time of the Second Punic War (218). After Marius's reforms (107–103), when the connection between legions and commanders became more personal, the oath to serve the commander took on a new, more individual flavor but seems to have retained much of its original purpose. During the early empire (properly called the Principate), Augustus adapted the *sacramentum* to suit evolving political and military demands, and he included explicit language to protect the emperor and his family. The military oath continued to evolve, and its use persisted in some form into late antiquity.[11] Its evolving in tandem with the culture was what made the oath so effective over such a long period of time.

The purpose of the oath was to maintain military order. Although the full text of the *sacramentum* is unknown, references in literary sources suggest that it carried religious and legal sanctions for maintaining order: obedience to commands, discipline, and military law. Violation of the oath originally was a religious crime resulting in the offender's being called "accursed." Over time, though, even as violation became less religiously significant, it still held the offender liable to punishment under military law. Typical charges were for specific violations of military law, such as desertion, indiscipline, and disloyalty.[12] The oath thus closely bound soldiers to the army for the duration of their service. Swearing the oath to the commander, and renewing it when a new commander took over, shows that during the Republic the *sacramentum* was not a vague oath of loyalty to the state but a specific bond of obedience to the commander. While the personal nature of the oath was necessary in order to enforce military requirements, it eventually had the unintended consequence of contributing to instability. That is, individual commanders were able to take political and economic advantage of their military strength in part because of the personal connection between soldier and commander embodied in the *sacramentum*. The success of such commanders illustrates in part the strength of the bond inherent in the oath.[13]

Clearly, the *sacramentum* had more than personal connections, as it was an important component in the matrix of discipline. The *sacramentum* was sufficiently effective and ingrained that a reminder of its sanctions was enough to help restore stability in restive units. During the early stage of the civil war between Pompey and Caesar, C. Scribonius Curio's references to the *sacramentum* were sufficient to quell a near mutiny and defection in 49.[14] Similarly, Caesar's reported reference to the oath in an assembly during the mutiny of 47 was what contemporaries thought restored order to his legions.[15] One especially famous instance took place in 14 CE when mutinying soldiers in Pannonia reacted superstitiously to a lunar eclipse. Religious concern about breaking their oath, however, persuaded them to return to ranks.[16] Nonetheless, although such instances demonstrate the oath's potential disciplinary authority, they were uncommon.

The *sacramentum* was, therefore, effective but was not a panacea. Soldiers were occasionally held in order by religious sanctions despite their restive mood, but an examination of more events shows that the notoriety of such outcomes was a result of their rarity. In these cases, the oath was sufficient to restore order because of the lack of incentive for soldiers to act further. In many instances, though, the oath alone failed to retain the soldiers' loyalty. Nevertheless, despite occasional breakdowns in military stability, the longevity of the *sacramentum* reflects more than institutional conservatism; it also indicates the oath's value in maintaining internal order.[17] The *sacramentum* was effective in part because it was grounded in the religious and hierarchical nature of Roman society and because it functioned as one element among several with the combined purpose of maintaining order.

The physical component of Roman discipline included the daily acts designed to instill and maintain a high standard of discipline and associated punishments. Training, drill, and the regimentation of daily routine all were facets of military discipline working to make soldiers obedient to orders, efficiently aggressive and steadfast in battle, and orderly in camp—the norms of behavior in the Roman military.[18] Training, drill, and the military camp itself helped ensure not only that the legion remained effective but also that discipline did not slacken; consequently, they were supposed to be maintained throughout the year. The role of training and drill should be obvious, but the standardization of the military camp layout, regardless of the region in which the legions marched and the necessity of regularly building new forts, also helped maintain order.[19]

In addition to these features of military life, daily tasks kept the men occupied. These regimented tasks included everything from foraging to building infrastructure like roads, bridges, and canals. For example, while preparing his legions for campaign against the Teutones and Cimbri (103/102), Gaius Marius had his legions build a canal in Gaul; indeed, it was expected that soldiers would bridge rivers and cut roads. Each of these duties and tasks kept the soldiers active and exercised, not only to encourage unit cohesion, but also to enforce military norms.[20] Training, drills, and tasks alone would not, however, have been sufficient to maintain good order without penalties and rewards.

Punishments and Rewards

These mental and physical components of discipline were reinforced by an array of penalties and incentives. As already noted, violation of the *sacramentum* carried legal and religious sanctions (indeed, drawing the modern distinction between legal and religious is artificial, as they were completely intertwined). As both Polybius, writing in the second century, and the late imperial *Digest* of Roman law make clear, "All are military crimes, which are committed against the common discipline," and any violations were subject to punishment, ranging from death to varieties of shame.[21] Officers had complete authority in citing soldiers for both crimes and acts of valor, but these citations had to be confirmed and the resulting reward or punishment assigned by the legionary commander (usually the consul or legate) by virtue of his *imperium* and the *sacramentum* that the soldiers had taken to obey their commander.

Just as the society and the military were hierarchically organized, so too were these punishments and rewards. All the penalties carried decline of status and prestige, a blow that would have affected citizens as well as their families. In a status-conscious culture like Rome's, this loss would have been equally or even more serious than physical pain for the punished. Capital punishment was the most serious penalty for military crimes, and it applied to a wide variety of offenses, including murder, mutiny, cowardice, treason, and a host of other crimes.[22] The most famous form of capital punishment was the decimation (*fustuarium*), usually applied to a unit that had shown cowardice, in which members of the guilty unit beat to death a percentage of their comrades, chosen by lot.[23] Capital punishment was merely one among many options. Other penalties were dishonorable discharge, disbandment, demotion, temporary expulsion, flogging, various types of humiliation, and fines. Numerous examples of their employment during the late Republic and early Principate reveal the extent to which these penalties reflected traditional military law.[24]

The disciplinary matrix included rewards as well as punishments. Just as it is necessary in the maintenance of military norms to punish those men who commit crimes, a disciplinary regime seeking to appear fair to its subjects also requires the means to encourage and reward valor. The Romans recognized that combat operations sometimes required acts of unusual bravery to stimulate others to action or save comrades from difficulties. In Rome, rewards for these acts were called *dona militaria*.[25] As a measure of how seriously these rewards were regarded, in his discussion of officers' duties Polybius related that commanders sat on horses or on high points in a battle in part so that they could see their men clearly and know who deserved recognition after the engagement. A second measure of the rewards' importance appears on military tombstones, especially those of common soldiers. Although carving a relief on a tombstone could be expensive, it became more common in the late Republic. Military men's tombstones almost invariably included either a reference to or a depiction of their *dona militaris* and promotions and sometimes also the place or reason for the award.[26]

A full hierarchy of awards were available to commanding officers and the state. Although during the Empire, military rewards eventually were granted according to the recipient's status, during the late Republic, the rewards still depended on the deed and could be won by any soldier or officer. As with punishments, numerous rules regulated the specific awards. The highest honor for commanders was a triumph or ovation awarded by the senate, which was a grand military parade in Rome during which soldiers would also be able to show off their *dona*. Men of any rank could win crowns of oak or laurel or fashioned from precious metal for great individual deeds such as saving a comrade or being the first over an enemy wall. In addition, individual soldiers could win all sorts of items made of precious metals, most commonly including spears, neck rings (*torques*), arm bands (*armillae*), decorated discs (*phalerae*), and cash.[27]

Such rewards were not limited to individuals, however. Extraordinary collective rewards helped balance brutal collective punishments like *fustuarium*. Units could win such special decorations as castles, ship prows, and crowns that were placed on their standard in recognition of valor. A legion could also earn special titles or honorifics like *victrix* (victorious) or *martia* (of Mars, god of war), in recognition of special achievement in combat. Units could also win temporary awards like cash payments or a larger share of the plunder from a conquered settlement. Collectively they even could win promotion to a new status, with privileges such as double pay, double rations, or even release from certain duties. During the late Republic, although most awards were limited to citizens, noncitizen (*auxilia*) units, too, could win awards and even citizenship.[28] If the rewards were only temporary or monetary benefits, they would not have been so effective as incentives, but because many of these awards improved the recipient's status and prestige in a culture that valued these above all else, awards and promotions provided strong incentives for competition among men and units while also helping maintain order.

Over time, although various laws and regulations emerged to augment the customs governing the conditions under which a commander could give out particular awards or impose particular punishments, their implementation remained inconsistent. The extent to which any one legion trained and drilled, and the degree of consistency with which punishments and rewards were meted out, depended entirely on the local commander (and his subordinate officers).[29] This "inconsistency" in enforcement and reward, apparent in both the *Digest* and historical accounts, was not limited to the military but was standard at all levels of Roman administration. Despite the inconsistencies, fear of punishment provided a regular means—along with training, drills, and regimented tasks—of maintaining discipline. The following case study looks at the effectiveness of these, in combination with the *sacramentum*.

A Case Study: Octavian's Early Career

Even though military discipline was one of Rome's keys to success in combat and was grounded in Roman culture, surviving examples of its role in a commander's operational decisions are rare. This dearth of examples is, however, more a function of limited sources and the commonality of military discipline than of any disregard for its importance. In other words, maintaining discipline was such a normal military activity that writers usually saw no need to draw attention to it. Instead, they usually focused on cases of indiscipline. The early career of Octavian Caesar was an exception. He was a commander who made various operational decisions based on discipline and then had to deal with the consequences.[30]

When senators assassinated Gaius Julius Caesar on March 15, 44, they created a power vacuum that could have led to the dissolution of the empire controlled from Rome. Although the empire did not break up, there was an ensuing period of internal wars among various parties who sought to dominate the state between 44 and 30. Octavian's first military experience was during these internal wars, and his success proved key to keeping the Roman world from collapsing permanently. Although at the start of this case study, he had no military experience and even seemed to disdain traditional military culture, his appreciation of the importance of discipline subsequently evolved. His choices and the results reveal the nature of discipline, its importance to the Roman army, and its grounding in Roman culture and society.

Octavian's part in the events after Caesar's assassination would not have been apparent to anyone in March 44. Aged only eighteen, he had had no opportunity for combat experience, although this was not unusual.[31] He was in Macedonia at this time, training with the troops assembled for Caesar's intended campaign against Dacia and Parthia. After learning of the assassination, Octavian returned to Italy, arriving in April. Only then did he find that Caesar had adopted him posthumously as a son and had made him his principal heir.[32] Once in Rome, while Octavian tried to secure his inheritance and his adoption, his relationship with Mark Antony (Marcus Antonius) emerged as the most threatening problem.

First Command

Over the next six months as Octavian and Antony struggled for support and supremacy in Rome, their relationship fell apart, and it became clear to everyone that military conflict was becoming increasingly likely.[33] In this context Octavian made his first decisions on how to prepare for the upcoming conflict. He decided to undermine the discipline of Antony's soldiers stationed near Brundisium by means of propaganda and bribery, with the goal of, at least, causing his opponent difficulty and, at best, persuading the soldiers to change sides. His agents created a sense among the veterans that

Antony had been easy on the assassins and now was blocking the efforts by Caesar's heir to avenge the murder.[34] Undermining discipline in this situation was not difficult, but it took time to achieve meaningful results.

Subversion was not the only way in which Octavian showed disdain for traditional military order; his approach to recruitment was just as unorthodox. When he broke with Antony in October, Octavian began raising a legion made up of demobilized veterans in central Italy, promising each man a cash-signing bounty worth two years' pay.[35] This maneuver was highly irregular and contrary to military culture, as soldiers normally were called up after authorization from the senate and then took the *sacramentum*, as discussed earlier. Moreover, in 44 Octavian was still a private citizen and had no authorization from the state to raise troops, so he was gathering soldiers who were not bound by traditional institutions to either the state or him. In fact, sources refer to them as mercenaries instead of soldiers and point out that they were beholden to money rather than the law. Octavian was aware of this unorthodox position and referred to his men as "private guards."[36]

Octavian's decision to undermine discipline among the legions near Brundisium worked, but it later affected his own troops. Soon after Antony joined his soldiers in the south, some of them mutinied and refused to march north under his leadership. Only after several speeches and more conciliatory measures was he able to restore order and start marching north after executing some of the ringleaders.[37] When he learned of this incident, Octavian led his own recruits to Rome to get senate authorization. Any pleasure he may have taken from Antony's difficulties was short-lived, however, as his own men then became unruly, and many deserted. Some were uncomfortable taking the field against Antony instead of the assassins. Others had learned of the bribes offered to Antony's men by Octavian's agents and sought an opportunity to enrich themselves further by holding out for more cash. Because he was still a private citizen and had used cash to subvert traditional institutions, Octavian could not resort to the same measures of restoring discipline as Antony had used. Despite several speeches about Caesar's death, Octavian was able to resolve the problem only by paying out additional bonuses.[38] He thus brought the incident to a peaceful if expensive close and demonstrated his willingness to use money to maintain military order.

No sooner had Octavian purchased the discipline and loyalty of his own men than two of Antony's legions (Martian and IV) defected to him near Rome. Octavian's subversive strategy had worked again: he acquired two experienced legions and put his enemy off balance. Octavian welcomed the two legions by distributing bounties equal to those he had paid his own men and promised all the men serving him that at the end of the war against the assassins, he would pay them each a bonus of 5,000 *denarii* (an extraordinary sum, equivalent to more than twenty-two years' pay). The senate then granted Octavian the position of propraetor, thereby legalizing the soldiers' status and paying the promised benefits out of state funds.[39] In this way, he finally achieved a state-sanctioned magistracy with command authority (*imperium*), thus ensuring him a legal base from which to pursue his ends. Nonetheless, although Octavian's contempt for the traditional military culture of discipline had paid dividends for the present, it also had laid the foundation for difficulties over the next eight years.

In the aftermath of the battle of Mutina (April 43), Octavian continued to manipulate military discipline as a means to his goals. Earlier the senate had ordered him to take his force north with the consuls Hirtius and Pansa to defeat Antony and relieve the siege of Mutina. Antony lost the battle and fled north, but both consuls died.[40] Octavian then wanted the senate to name him consul to fill one of the vacant posts. When the senate responded by denying the promised bounties for his men, requiring him to give some of his eight legions to other commanders, and ignoring his appeal for a consulship, he stalled for time, communicated intermittently with other legions, and gradually incited his own soldiers to resist the senate's directives.[41] Octavian thus decided to follow a familiar, seditious path consisting of appeals to Caesar's memory and reminding his men of the senate's refusal to pay the promised bonuses. He continued this strategy for several months, marching around the region but ignoring requests from the senate or other commanders for assistance. Events reached a climax in July when his eight legions marched on Rome. Although he claimed that the soldiers were violent, out of control, and had forced him to accompany them, it is clear that he had incited and was now directing them.[42] The senate was powerless, and Octavian secured a consulship. This post gave him constitutional authority to enact a number of measures, including formally ratifying his adoption, securing the benefits for the troops, and moving against the assassins, as well as a strong position from which to negotiate with Antony and Lepidus, who had joined their forces in May.[43] Once Octavian and his men had obtained what they wanted, the indiscipline ceased. He had again successfully manipulated discipline to further his own ends.

Sicily Campaign, 36

Five years later, in late 37, Octavian again was making operational and combat decisions based on his understanding of the *disciplina militaris*. The years since he became consul had been eventful. He had created the triumvirate in 43 by allying with Antony and Marcus Lepidus at Bononia. Then together with Antony in 42, he had defeated the remaining army led by Caesar's assassins at Philippi. The aftermath of that battle took Antony east and left Octavian with his hands full trying to demobilize the veterans and restore peace in Italy. This process took two years to resolve, and even after it was completed, peace was not a constant. Beginning in 38, Octavian had to contend with Sextus Pompey, the youngest son of Caesar's rival, who had grown strong enough to establish control over Sicily and the seas around Italy. Indeed, Pompey was powerful enough that when he wanted a share of power, he was able to blockade the sea trade route into Italy and thus cut off much of the food supply for Rome. Antony and Octavian thus were forced to recognize his power and make an alliance with him, though it remained uneasy.[44] In his final campaign against Pompey, sources report that Octavian again considered using discipline in his operational planning, whose results reveal some evolution in his appreciation of traditional institutions.

Italy remained relatively peaceful until 38, when hostilities broke out yet again between Pompey and Octavian. After losing one of his fleets that year, Octavian began to rebuild and make plans for a new campaign against Sicily. With the assistance of his longtime friend Marcus Agrippa, Octavian built ships and gathered crews. Realizing that his crews had been no match for Pompey the previous year, he started a training program and constructed a new harbor for that purpose. The crews took the oath upon their enlistment and thus were subject to traditional discipline. These measures took time; not until 36 did Octavian launch his final campaign against Sextus Pompey in Sicily. He used his own ships plus some on loan from Antony, all under Agrippa's direct command. Octavian also had his legions work together with those of his triumviral colleague Marcus Lepidus, who invaded the island from his bases in North Africa. After an initial setback, Octavian's forces captured several ports and then defeated Pompey's navy at Naulochus.[45] Although this victory eliminated Pompey's threat, hurdles remained in Sicily before the campaign could end.

Suddenly seizing an opportunity to assert himself in the aftermath of Pompey's flight, Lepidus made an enormous miscalculation in the dynamics of power and underestimated Octavian. He besieged the Sicilian port city of Messana after the battle at Naulochus and planned to give it to his men for plunder. When Pompey's commander in the city surrendered, Lepidus added the units to his command, thereby raising his force to twenty-two legions. Originally a fully equal triumvir, Lepidus's status had declined in the aftermath of the battle at Philippi so that he now controlled only the territory in North Africa and was equal only in name. Now he seemed prepared to insist on a fully equal triumvir status. Thus when Octavian arrived, Lepidus took sole credit for the victory and made demands of his colleague.[46] Added to this was a strong current of dissention within the two commanders' military camps.

Octavian took advantage of the unsettled mood of Lepidus's troops to complete his victory in Sicily by resorting to an old tactic. He decided to try resolving the crisis peacefully by once again undermining the discipline of an opponent's army. Once he learned of the troops' disaffection, he sent agents to infiltrate Lepidus' camp, initially concentrating on Pompey's former soldiers, sowing doubt and suspicion. Octavian also entered Lepidus's camp unchallenged and, after speaking with Lepidus, shouted appeals to some of the disaffected troops. The appeals led to a brief outbreak of violence during which Octavian was assaulted, but he was able to get back to the remainder of his escort with nothing more than injured pride. Over the next few days, he moved his troops closer to Lepidus's camp. With the camps now so close, his soldiers did not need to infiltrate their opponent's camp; they could just call over to and exchange messages with Lepidus's men, making offers and creating even more dissent. Soon afterward, Lepidus's soldiers began to defect to Octavian's side. Then, during the next few days and nights, Lepidus's entire army gradually changed its allegiance so that according to sources, he woke up one day to find all his men gone. Now that Octavian had control of all the legions, he dismissed Lepidus, a broken man with no further public role, and distributed a victory grant (*dona*), promising more cash later.[47] Octavian again had undermined an opponent's discipline to gain an advantage over his adversary. In so doing, he demonstrated that despite the lessons of the naval battle at Naulochus, his appreciation of traditional military culture was slow to mature.

Octavian's manipulation of disaffection may have been too successful, however, since unrest broke out in his own army within days of Lepidus's dismissal. The mutiny broke out suddenly and seems to have included all of Octavian's legions in Sicily, although it was limited to the island. Sources do not report any associated violence, but the episode's vigor and size made it serious. This outbreak included both soldiers and low-ranking officers—centurions and some tribunes—which was a good indication of its seriousness. Centurions were subaltern officers promoted from the ranks in accordance with their experience and ability, so their identification with the soldiers and participation was not surprising. More surprising were the military tribunes, a low-level officer's post held by men of elite social status with varying levels of experience who were learning to be upper-level officers.[48] The mutineers' demands included the payment of a bonus equal to what was given after the battle of Philippi plus immediate discharge. Their demands were not what triggered the mutiny, however; they were simply the focus of the unrest. Instead, the catalyst was the size of the army in Sicily and the prevailing climate of service and, most important, Octavian's having undermined the discipline of his opponent's legions.[49]

Because Roman commanders had a long history of problems with large assemblages of men, experience dictated avoiding such gatherings when possible as a means of heading off sedition. Velleius Paterculus, an experienced officer who served under Augustus, corroborated this view in his report of this mutiny: "There followed a sudden outbreak of mutiny in the army; for often when they consider their own numbers, soldiers resist discipline and do not restrain themselves from demanding what they think they can compel."[50] As a result of the successful campaign and the removal of Lepidus, Octavian officially had an army of forty or so legions with cavalry and support units in the area of Messana. Such a great number of men would have put great stress on the available food, water, and sanitation—a strong catalyst for military unrest.[51]

The climate of service that Octavian and the other triumvirs had created with bonuses and unending conflict added impetus to the mutiny. The extraordinary cash distributions previously awarded were one aspect of the problematic atmosphere. In 44, opportunistic leaders of all varieties had used cash bonuses to raise armies only loosely subjected to the traditional matrix of discipline. After the triumvirate began and the soldiers took the service oath, their loyalty continued to be more to their individual leaders and their promised bonuses than to the state. After Philippi, the triumvirs had to fulfill their earlier promises by granting substantial lands and rewards for service, including bonuses of five thousand *denarii*. This practice was well established by 36. Having already seen how comrades benefited through land and cash from internal war, it is hardly surprising that these soldiers decided to try cashing in on the instability.[52] Octavian's manipulation of military order through the grants of land and awards now had caught up with him in Sicily.

An additional stimulus for the soldiers' demands was the length of service. The typical length of continuous service in the military before the internal wars was six to ten years, although in an emergency, men could be called to serve for sixteen years. As noted previously, soldiers took the oath to serve for as long as the conflict lasted.[53] For men enrolled in 44, this could have meant discharge after Philippi, and certainly not after late in 36. The internal wars already had lasted for more than eight years, much longer than anyone might have expected in 44 when Caesar's heir recruited his first army. For those men who joined Octavian in 41/40 and took the oath for the duration of the conflict, the end of the Naulochus campaign could be justified as the end of their obligation. Although they could sign up for more time, they did not have to do so. In this case, it is not surprising that the legions revolted on account of their length of service.

While these demands indicate the soldiers' dissatisfaction, they are less important as triggers for the unrest than Octavian's manipulation of discipline. The underlying causes of their demands had been present before the campaign and still were present after Sextus Pompey had been defeated. Yet the legions did not mutiny until after Lepidus's men changed sides. In undermining his enemy's loyalty and discipline, Octavian thereby weakened the discipline of his own men. It was not a secret that he offered a bonus to Lepidus's men and encouraged them to break their oath, but no source indicates that Octavian had planned to give his own men a bonus. In addition, because he appeared to disregard or devalue the oath of service taken by Lepidus's men, his own men could reasonably conclude that their oath was of equally little value to their commander. The actual trigger of the mutiny that Octavian now faced was the atmosphere of indiscipline and unrest that he created by undermining Lepidus's troops. Octavian had demonstrated once again that the *sacramentum* could be disregarded, and his soldiers remembered the lesson. Once he had created that mood, his legions, encouraged further by their numbers and their not unreasonable grievances, had an opportunity to make demands, and Octavian's options for response were limited by his earlier actions.

Octavian's resolution of this crisis did indicate that he had begun to see the need for a stronger relationship with his legions, one that was grounded in the traditional military culture. In the years before this military unrest, he had used propaganda and cash freely and frequently to settle dissent within his legions. Ever since he first raised troops, he had resolved the worst problems of indiscipline by bowing to the soldiers' demands and providing them with the cash or land they demanded. Although he certainly was reliant on his soldiers to have come so far, such cash-based strategies created the breakdown in discipline that Octavian confronted in 36.

In Sicily Octavian's initial response was to resort to military law and take a firm line with the soldiers, reminding them of their oaths.[54] The appeal to traditional discipline is noteworthy because it was a completely new tactic for Caesar's heir. The attempt to enforce traditional discipline in the face of dissention demonstrated his effort to change his relationship with the military. The change of tone evidently was not successful, however, and he had to back down from rigorously enforcing discipline. As already observed, the fact that Octavian had stirred up the unrest evident in Lepidus's legions only weakened his position as a strict disciplinarian. His army was not ready for a return to traditional military culture and a new relationship, and it was obvious that Octavian had little choice but to acquiesce to some of their demands.

As he sought to divide the opposition by breaking up into segments both the army and their rewards, Octavian then revealed the extent to which his planning had evolved. In an assembly of troops, he made sundry promises concerning rewards and future service. He then tried to separate the centurions and tribunes from the common soldiers by offering them superior honors and status, including "purple-bordered garments" and membership in their local assemblies.[55] These were novel rewards, *dona militaris*, based directly on Romans' attachment to status and prestige. According to one source, however, one tribune complained loudly in the assembly about the insufficient scale of the honors, at which point Octavian became angry and walked out when other discontented soldiers applauded the tribune's remark. During that night the dissenting tribune disappeared,[56] a strong message that Octavian was determined to force a quick settlement. Additional conciliatory offers included a promise not to employ the soldiers in any other civil wars. He discharged all of his soldiers who had served since 44 and any men who had served for ten years or more. Furthermore, Octavian promised the veterans of Mutina that he would fulfill all the promised rewards. He released the men, nearly twenty thousand, and sent them off the island in order to reduce further disruptions among the remaining troops, and he settled the veterans on land held or purchased for that purpose. He then promised a *dona* of five hundred *denarii* to each remaining soldier.[57] With this grant, the unrest dissipated, and the army resumed its obedient role. Note, however, that Octavian's initial offers of future rewards were insufficient by themselves. Only after he had discharged those who wanted to leave was he able to resolve the situation. Although at Messana, Octavian had manipulated an opponent's discipline for his own benefit for the last time, it was not the last time that sources report that discipline figured into his military planning.

Wars in Illyricum, 35–33

After the events in Sicily, Octavian began preparing for the next conflict. While in hindsight it might seem that conflict between Antony and Octavian was inevitable, it is important to remember that in late 36 such a war was only a possibility, not a certainty. In any event, the defeat of Sextus Pompey and the dismissal of Lepidus did demonstrate that Octavian was the preeminent power in the western Mediterranean. Nonetheless, despite his continued residence and relationship with Cleopatra, Antony was still the more experienced and popular general, and he still had many friends in the Roman senate. The triumvirs also were still tied through Octavia, sister of Octavian, to whom Antony was still legally married, even though he already had several children with Cleopatra. Although the campaign in Sicily made Octavian popular in Rome, it did not bring about war between the triumvirs, yet. There is little doubt, however, that Octavian expected to eventually fight Antony for dominance. He began to plan accordingly.

Realizing that he was disadvantaged by both his military reputation and the quality of his legions, Octavian undertook a series of campaigns in the province of Illyricum to improve his legions' skill, self-confidence, and discipline. The campaigns, which began in 35 and lasted for three seasons, held only slight strategic significance, since there was no current threat in the region, but they were publicized as chastising local tribes.[58] The combat was not easy, however, and the army received extensive exposure to difficult fighting as well as a strong dose of discipline.

During this campaign, Octavian encountered problems with insubordination and desertion but dealt with them more in line with traditional military culture than he had in the past. Unlike previous incidents of indiscipline that seemed to grow out of the soldiers' ambitions, these were the direct result of combat rather than opportunism. What little we know of these episodes is that he reacted to them with traditional brutal discipline, including barley rations in one case and decimation in an instance when men abandoned their positions.[59] This punishment was a continuation of the practice that Octavian had initially tried to pursue after the battle at Naulochus when he moved to quell unrest according to military law and custom. In this manner, he continued the process of changing his army from the loose band of mercenaries he had led in 43 to an army bound by the full range of traditional institutions for maintaining order, from oath to whip.

Along with the renewal of discipline and the increase in his troops' battle experience, the campaigns gave Octavian an important opportunity to rehabilitate his own reputation as a battlefield commander. During the war, he led attacks, was wounded, defeated a barbarian people close enough to Italy to represent a vague threat to the populace, and even recovered a set of legionary standards lost in 48. His successful campaign there gained him a triumph, although he deferred it to a more opportune time. Octavian found the campaigns valuable as opportunities to improve his overall military standing, particularly compared with Antony's.[60]

Actium Campaign, 31–30

The final conflict between the triumvirs began as an exchange of bitter accusations that blossomed into a declaration of war. Octavian was able to whip up sufficient opposition to Antony's actions with Cleopatra to have her declared an enemy of the Roman people in 32, even though Antony clearly was the target. Since 39, Antony had remained in the east, where he followed his own course of action separately from Octavian. His behavior had been such that each year after 35, a war between the two became increasingly likely. By 32, military reverses, coupled with the discharge and settlement of his Philippi veterans, had diminished Antony's military reputation as well as his hold on other soldiers' loyalty, but he still presented a real and considerable threat.[61] The war was an enormous potential test of the discipline and loyalty of Octavian's legions, the very aspects that he had been working on as he prepared for this conflict. Every indication is that he was successful in this regard.

Octavian used a mixture of traditional and expedient measures to reduce the chances that he would encounter unrest within his military. Chief among these were the discipline he had ingrained in his legions and his personal relationship with them. By the time he moved into this war, he had made sure his legions were disciplined and loyal, by forging a strong relationship with the legions, now rooted in the traditional matrix of discipline.

As the hostilities intensified, Antony tried to disrupt his opponent by dispatching gold and agents to Italy to undermine the legions. Octavian fended off this attempted subversion, in part by falling back on the expedient of promising his men extra rewards (*dona*) in advance.[62] Although hardly traditional as such, given the established internal war practice of giving soldiers extra cash bounties and gifts in the event of victory, it is unlikely that Octavian would have been able to avoid doing so in this important campaign. Since victory would mean that his men would push on to invade Egypt, he could be certain of acquiring the necessary cash. Little wonder then that they were so enthusiastic for the combat to begin.[63] His various preparations went a long way toward ensuring that military dissent played no role in the naval battle that Octavian won at Actium in 31.[64]

Once the engagement ended, Octavian had to contend with Antony's surviving soldiers and consolidate his own force in preparations for moving against Cleopatra in Egypt. The naval fight at Actium had not affected Antony's still numerous nearby land forces, and they remained a serious threat. Although Antony's legionary commanders tried to withdraw into Macedonia, eventually the bulk of the land army surrendered after their officers fled. Octavian then combined the former opposition army with his own.[65] Having repeatedly experienced the way that mass gatherings of soldiers led to eruptions of unrest, he moved quickly to defuse the potential for unrest by discharging honorably and dispersing to Italy as rapidly as possible all of his superannuated veterans as well as all of Antony's veterans. In this instance, Octavian acted so swiftly that men were discharged without any rewards. He took a calculated risk that the resulting unrest arising from a lack of discharge bounties would be smaller than if all the soldiers remained assembled together. Sources make clear that this discharge was successful in defusing any unrest among the troops still assembled in Greece. This accomplishment illustrates the significant change in the relationship that Octavian had forged with his army since 36. The active legions remained disciplined and were confident enough in his leadership to wait for the promised rewards.[66] With these various measures born of experience, Octavian was secure enough to move east.

During the final push into Egypt, Octavian's preparations to secure discipline among his men again proved superior. Antony tried to detach men from his opponent, and he and Cleopatra sent bribes to Octavian's legions. He also distributed broadsides in Octavian's camp with offers of larger bounties for any who defected. In these instances, the strong discipline that Octavian had built up in his soldiers paid off as they remained patient for the spoils of war. After the death of Antony and Cleopatra, Octavian made a point over the years of both 30 and 29 of keeping his promises to the soldiers and veterans by paying all outstanding bonuses and continuing to settle them on land purchased for the purpose in Italy and overseas.[67] This final settlement of the soldiers after the campaign proceeded peacefully, and the period of internal wars was at an end. Regardless of how important war may have been to Roman culture, the people were tired and wanted peace. Maintaining the peace would require dealing with the military.

Octavian had learned well the lessons of the triumvirate and sought culturally consistent solutions, particularly to the enlarged military. In 27, he claimed to have restored the republic to the people, and thus he received a new name, Augustus, and title, *princeps*. In fact, however, this "restoration" marked the emergence of the Roman Empire, a period during which control of the army remained critical to the maintenance of authority.[68] As uncontested leader of the Roman world, Augustus continued to direct military campaigns large and small for more than a decade after the "restoration," and he personally selected or approved all the legionary commanders throughout his reign. He also enacted a series of military reforms that reduced the size of the military to twenty-eight legions (down from more than one hundred in 31); institutionalized or created new types of units, including the Praetorian Guard and the Urban Cohorts; made it an all-volunteer force (except in emergencies); regularized the terms of service so that legionnaires had to serve for twenty years and an additional five as veterans eligible for recall; and even created a special treasury to pay for it all.[69] Although these reforms were wide-ranging, they worked primarily because they were consistent with Roman military culture.

In the context of this chapter, Octavian's most important reform was restoring discipline as part of a reestablished military culture. Although referred to later as the "discipline of Augustus," its precise tenets remain unknown. It seems, however, to have been a document or set of rulings that standardized military discipline in line with traditional military culture.[70] Augustus's reign was replete with both generous military awards and brutal discipline, by either his order or the order of his commanders. He thus set the norm for his successors. Although it may seem that he simply reestablished norms after the triumvirate's lack of discipline, he regularized it to a much greater degree than had been the case previously. His attitude toward these reforms was a far cry from what he showed in 44 and was a result of his evolving relationship and experience with his soldiers during the triumvirate. Indeed, Augustus's reforms established the Roman army as a fully professionalized military that contributed much to the empire's success.[71]

Octavian's early career provides a good case study for not only how a Roman commander used discipline in planning and in combat but also how *disciplina militaris* functioned as part of the broader culture. At no point during his tenure as commander and then triumvir was Octavian able to ignore military discipline in his planning and preparations. During this period, his appreciation of the Roman traditional system of discipline developed as his experience matured. He began by inciting and manipulating unrest and ended by imposing a more traditional balance of reward and punishment and then institutionalizing it. He learned to deal with the results of his own expedient attitude toward discipline, and it was in these encounters that he formulated much of his later attitude. His military reforms succeeded mainly because they were grounded in the broader Roman culture. Octavian's career is a case study for seeing how an inexperienced commander learned the importance of traditional institutions through sometimes bitter experience.

NOTES

1. Adrian Goldsworthy, *The Roman Army at War, 100BC–AD200* (Oxford: Oxford University Press, 1996), 3–10. Abbreviations of ancient works are from the *Oxford Classical Dictionary*. All translations are my own.

2. Ramsay MacMullen, "The Legion as Society," *Historia* 33 (1984): 440–56; reprinted in Ramsay MacMullen, *Changes in the Roman Empire* (Princeton, NJ: Princeton University Press, 1990), 225–35; Richard Alston, "The Military and Politics," in *The Cambridge History of Greek and Roman Warfare*, ed. Philip Sabin, Hans van Wees, and Michael Whitby (Cambridge: Cambridge University Press, 2007), vol. 2, 177–80. For background on the Roman military, see Pat Southern, *The Roman Army: A Social and Institutional History* (Oxford: Oxford University Press, 2007); and Jonathan Roth, *Roman Warfare* (Cambridge: Cambridge University Press, 2009), 59–72. Readers seeking an extensive discussion of research on the Roman military should see Sara Phang, "New Approaches to the Roman Army," in *Recent Directions in the Military History of the Ancient World*, ed. Lee L. Brice and Jennifer T. Roberts (Claremont, CA: Regina Books, 2011), 105–45.

3. Gerhard Horsmann, *Untersuchungen zur militärischen Ausbildung im republikanischen und kaiserzeitlichen Rom* (Boppard am Rhein: Harald Boldt, 1991); John E. Lendon, *Soldiers and Ghosts: A History of Battle in Antiquity* (New Haven, CT: Yale University Press, 2005), 177–231, 312–13; and Sara Phang, *Roman Military Service* (Cambridge: Cambridge University Press, 2007).

4. All dates in this chapter are BCE unless otherwise noted.

5. The origin of *disciplina militaris* was not a topic that exercised Roman authors; see Horsmann, *Untersuchungen zur militärischen Ausbildung*, 1–4, n. 4; and Goldsworthy, *The Roman Army*, 1–2.

6. Lee L. Brice, "Holding a Wolf by the Ears: Mutiny and Unrest in the Roman Military, 44 BC–AD 68" (PhD diss., University of North Carolina at Chapel Hill, 2003); Lendon, *Soldiers and Ghosts*, 177–78, 194, 197; Phang, *Roman Military Service*, 26–36.

7. Lendon, *Soldiers and Ghosts*, 177–78, see also 312–13. The Latin word *virtus* does not easily translate into English and could be understood as meaning a combination of qualities, including courage, zeal, and virtue.

8. Lee L. Brice, "Fog of War: The Roman Army in *Rome*," in *Rome, Season 1*, ed. Monica Cyrino (Malden, MA.: Blackwell, 2008), 61–64.

9. Valerie Maxfield, *The Military Decorations of the Roman Army* (Berkeley: University of California Press, 1981), 1–21; Goldsworthy, *The Roman Army*, 279-82; Brice, "Holding a Wolf," 22–24, 60–65; and Lendon, *Soldiers and Ghosts*, 177–78, 194, 200, 207–8.

10. Horsmann, *Untersuchungen zur militärischen Ausbildung*, 2–3, 102–9, 189–97.

11. Polyb. 6.21.2; Dio. Hal. *Ant.Rom.* 10.18; Livy 22.38; Plut. *Sulla* 27.4; and App. *BCiv.* 1.66. See also Brian Campbell, *The Emperor and the Army 31BC–AD 235* (Oxford: Clarendon Press, 1984), 19–32; Arthur Keaveney, *The Army in the Roman Revolution* (New York: Routledge, 2007), 71–77; and Phang, *Roman Military Service*, 115–20.

12. Polyb. 6.21.2; Dio. Hal. *Ant.Rom.* 10.18, 11.43; Aul. Gell. 16.4; Livy 22.38.2–5; Epict. 1.14.15; Veg. 2.5; Servius *ad Aen.* 7.614, 8.1; and *Digest* 49.16.6. See also Campbell, *The Emperor and the Army*, 19–21, 23–25; John Lendon, *Empire of Honor: The Art of Government in the Roman World* (Oxford: Oxford University Press, 1997), 152–53; Phang, *Roman Military Service*, 26–27, 117–23; and Roth, *Roman Warfare*, 61–66.

13. App. *BCiv.* 5.17; and Brian Campbell, *War and Society in Imperial Rome, 31BC–AD 284* (London: Routledge 2002), 24. See also Lukas de Blois, "Army and General in the Late Roman Republic," in *A Companion to the Roman Army*, ed. Paul Erdkamp (Malden, MA: Wiley-Blackwell, 2007), 164–79.

14. Caes. *BC* 2.32–33.

15. Stephan Chrissanthos, "Caesar and the Mutiny of 47 B.C.," *Journal of Roman Studies* 91 (2001): 63–70.

16. Tac. *Ann.* 1.28; and Cass. Dio 57.4; Brice, "Holding a Wolf," 150–63, 230–34.

17. Campbell, *The Emperor and the Army*, 19–32.

18. Horsmann, *Untersuchungen zur militärischen Ausbildung*, 109–86, esp. 164–86; Goldsworthy, *The Roman Army*, 251–52, 279–82; Phang, *Roman Military Service*, 13–72.

19. Polyb. 6.39.11; Suet. *Calig.* 44.2, *Galba* 6.2–3; Jos. *BJ* 3.73–75, 102–3; Tac. *Ann.* 12.12.1, 13.35; and Dio-Xiph.61.30.6; Veg. 1.1, 8–27, 2.23–24; *Digest* 49.16.12. See also E. Roy Davies, "The Daily Life of the Roman Soldier under the Principate," in *Aufstieg und Niedergang der römischen Welt. Geschichte und Kultur Roms im Spiegel der neueren Forschung* (*ANRW*), vol. 2, no. 1, ed. H. Temporini and W. Haase (Berlin: W. de Gruyter, 1974), 299–338. Reprinted in *Service in the Roman Army*, ed. Roy W. Davies, David Breeze, and Valerie Maxfield (New York: Columbia University Press, 1989), 33–70; and Phang, *Roman Military Service*, 37–72.

20. Vell. Pat. 2.78.3; Jos. *BJ* 3.85–86; Suet. *Aug.* 18; Tac. *Ann.* 1.20, 11.20, and 13.35 and 53; App. *BCiv* 3.43; Cass. Dio 51.18.1; Dio-Xiph. 61.30.6; and Veg. 3.3. See also Davies, "The

Daily Life of the Roman Soldier," 328–32 and nn. 64–67; and Jonathan Roth, *The Logistics of the Roman Army (264B.C–A.D.235)* (Leiden: Brill, 1999), 140–41, 216–19; and Phang, *Roman Military Service*, 73–110, 221–26.

21. *Digest* 49.16.6. See also Polyb. 6.38.2.

22. A long list of citations could follow, but see esp. Polyb. 6.38.2; Livy 8.7.16; Front. *Strat.* 4.1; and *Digest* 48.4, 48.19.8.2–3, 19.14, 19.38.1 and 11–12, and 49.16. For a modern discussion, see Clarence Brand, *Roman Military Law* (Austin: University of Texas Press, 1968); Andrew Lintott, *Violence in Republican Rome*, 2nd ed. (Oxford: Oxford University Press, 1999), 41–43; and Phang, *Roman Military Service*, 125–29.

23. Polyb. 6.37–38.4; Dion. Hal. 9.5; and Livy 2.59. It was not always imposed on one-tenth of a military unit, but some ancient sources still call it *decimation*.

24. There are too many sources to cite all the examples, but see Lendon, *Empire of Honor*, 243–46, 248–52; Brice, "Holding a Wolf," 58–62; and Phang, *Roman Military Service*, 120–51.

25. Polyb. 6.22 and 39; Caes. *BG*, 5.44; Maxfield, *The Military Decorations*, 19–21, 55–57; Goldsworthy, *The Roman Army*, 276–82.

26. Polyb. 6.22 and 39; Maxfield, *The Military Decorations*, 67–100 and plates 2–14; Lawrence Keppie, "'Having Been a Soldier,' The Commemoration of Military Service on Funerary Monuments of the Early Roman Empire," in *Documenting the Roman Army: Essays in Honor of Margaret Roxan*, ed. John J. Wilkes (London: Institute of Classical Studies, 2003), 31–49.

27. Maxfield, *The Military Decorations*, 67–109; Goldsworthy, *The Roman Army*, 276–79; and Mary Beard, *The Roman Triumph* (Cambridge, MA: Harvard University Press, 2008).

28. Maxfield, *The Military Decorations*, 218–35.

29. Campbell, *The Emperor and the Army*, 301, 305–7.

30. Gaius Julius Caesar's grand-nephew, Gaius Octavian, took Caesar's full name once he learned he was adopted (in April), but historians still call him Octavian instead of his proper Roman name so as to distinguish him more easily from his adoptive father.

31. There was no military academy; instead, elites learned military leadership through experience. See Brian Campbell, "Teach Yourself How to Be a General," *Journal of Roman Studies* 77 (1987): 13–29; and Goldsworthy, *The Roman Army*, 121–23.

32. Cic. *Att.* 14.5.3; Nic. Dam. 8–16, 22–25, 41–55, 108–9; *RGDA* 15.1; Vell. Pat. 2.59.3–6; Suet. *Aug.* 8.1–2; App. *BCiv.*, 3.9–12, 21–23, 43; and Cass. Dio 43.41, 45.3–7, 51.7–8. See also Pat Southern, *Augustus* (New York: Routledge 1998), 16–21.

33. Nic. Dam. 107–31; *RGDA* 1.1, 15.1; Livy 117; Vell. Pat., 2.60–61.1; Plut. *Ant.* 16.1–2; Suet. *Aug.*, 10.2–3; Tac. *Ann.* 1.10.1; App. *BCiv.* 3.13–39; and Cass. Dio 45.5–11. See also Helga Botermann, *Die Soldaten und die römische Politik in der Zeit von Caesars Tod bis zur Begründung des Zweiten Triumvirats* (Munich: C. H. Beck, 1968), 26–35; Southern, *Augustus*, 22–38; and Pat Southern, *Mark Antony* (Charleston, SC: Tempus, 1998), 56–58.

34. Cic. *Att.* 15.5.3; *Fam.* 11.2, 12.3.2; App. *BCiv.* 3.39–40; see also Southern, *Augustus* 30–31, 37–38.

35. Nic. Dam. 115, 131–34, 136–38; Cic. *Att.* 16.8.2, 16.9; *Phil.* 3.3, 5.23; Vell. Pat. 2.61.2; Livy *Per.* 117; Suet. *Aug.* 10.3; App. *BCiv.* 3.40–42; Cass. Dio 45.12.2–4; and Tac. *Ann.* 1.10. The promised signing bonus (*praemia*) of 500 *denarii* was generous, as the annual pay for a legionnaire was 225 *denarii*. See also Dominic Rathbone, "Military Finance and Supply,"

in *The Cambridge History of Greek and Roman Warfare*, ed. Philip Sabin, Hans van Wees, and Michael Whitby (Cambridge: Cambridge University Press, 2007), 158–61.

36. App. *BCiv.* 3.40. See also Botermann, *Die Soldaten*, 36–45; and Campbell, *The Emperor and the Army*, 21–23.

37. The mutiny was not limited to the soldiers but also included the centurions. Nic. Dam. 139; Cic. *Att.*16.8, 16.10.1, 12 and 13a.1; Cic. *Philippics*; App. *BCiv.* 3.31, 39–44; Cass. Dio, 45.12.2–13. See also Botermann, *Die Soldaten*, 45-46; John Patterson, "Military Organization and Social Change in the Later Roman Republic," in *War and Society in the Roman World*, ed. John Rich and Graham Shipley (New York: Routledge Press, 1993), 102–6; Goldsworthy, *The Roman Army*, 251–58; Southern, *Augustus*, 38–40; Keaveney, *The Army in the Revolution*, 85–86.

38. Nic. Dam. 138–39; Cic. *Att.*, 16.15.3; App. *BCiv.* 3.40–42; Cass. Dio 45.12.4–5; Botermann *Die Soldaten*, 43–45; Samuel Finer, *The Man on Horseback: The Role of the Military in Politics*, 2nd ed. (Boulder, CO: Westview Press, 1988), 5; Keaveney, *The Army in the Revolution*, 86.

39. Cic. *Fam.* 10.28.3, 11.7.2, 12.23.2, 12.25a.4; *Brut.* 1.3.1, 2.5, *Philippics*; Vell. Pat. 2.61.2–3; Suet. *Aug.* 10.3; Tac. *Ann.* 1.10.1; App. *BCiv.*, 3.45–48, 50; and Cass. Dio 45.13.4, 46.29.2–3, 35.4. See also Botermann, *Die Soldaten*, 55–63; Southern, *Augustus*, 40–42; and Keaveney, *The Army in the Revolution*, 86.

40. Southern, *Mark Antony*, 60–63.

41. Cic. *Fam.* 10.23 and 24; 11.10, 14, 19, and 20; 12.25.2; *Brut.* 1.4.3, 10, 14, 15.6–9, 18.3–4; Vell. Pat. 2.62.1 and 3–4, 65.1; Suet. *Aug.* 12.1; App. *BCiv.* 3.74–81, 86; and Cass. Dio 46.40–41. See also Botermann, *Die Soldaten*, 114–54; and Southern, *Augustus*, 45–49. Although he was too young and had not yet held the required preliminary magistracies, he could justify his request on account of precedents set by Scipio Aemilianus Africanus and Gnaeus Pompey Magnus, as well as his control of more than eight legions just outside the city.

42. Cic. *Fam.* 12.25a.2; Livy *Per.* 119; Suet. *Aug.* 26.1; App. *BCiv.* 3.86–88; and Cass. Dio 46.42–44.1; and Keaveney, *The Army in the Revolution*, 86.

43. Vell. Pat. 2.62.2 and 5; Livy *Per.* 119–20; Plut. *Ant.* 19–20; Tac. *Ann.* 1.10.1App. *BCiv.* 3.89–98; Cass. Dio 46.44–52; Richard Weigel, *Lepidus* (New York: Routledge, 1992), 63–70; Southern, *Augustus*, 47–53; and Southern, *Mark Antony*, 66–70.

44. Weigel, *Lepidus*, 71–80; Southern, *Augustus*, 53–80; Southern, *Mark Antony*, 71–99; Brice, "Holding a Wolf," 96–103; Carsten Lange, *Res Publica Constituta: Actium, Apollo and the Accomplishment of the Triumviral Assignment* (Leiden: Brill, 2009), 18–38.

45. Vell Pat. 2.79; Livy *Per.* 128–29; Suet. *Aug.* 16.1–3; App. *BCiv.* 5.77–121; Cass. Dio 48.45–49.11; and Southern, *Augustus*, 81–84.

46. Vell. Pat. 2.80.2; Suet. *Aug.* 16.4; App. *BCiv.* 5.122; Cass. Dio 49.11.2–4; and Weigel, *Lepidus*, 88–89.

47. *RGDA* 25.1; Vell. Pat. 2.80.3–4; Livy *Per.* 129; *ILS* 108; Suet. *Aug.* 16.4; App. *BCiv.* 5.124–27; and Cass. Dio 49.12.3–4; Weigel, *Lepidus*, 88–93; Southern, *Augustus*, 84–85; Keaveney, *The Army in the Revolution*, 88–90.

48. B. Dobson, "The Centurionate and Social Mobility during the Principate," in *Recherches sur les structures socialè dans l'antiquité classique*, ed. Claude Nicolet (Paris: NRS, 1970), 99–115. Reprinted in *Roman Officers and Frontiers*, ed. M. Speidel, *Mavors* 10 (1993):

201–17; and D. Saddington, "Military Tribunes in the Roman Military and Administrative System in the Pre-Flavian Period," in XI congresso internazionale di epigrafia *Greca e Latina, Roma 18–24 settembre 1997* (Rome: Quasar, 1999), vol. 2, 297–314.

49. Vell. Pat. 2.81.1; App. *BCiv.* 5.128; and Cass. Dio 49.13.1. See also Finer, *The Man on Horseback*, 5–6; and Brice, "Holding a Wolf," 103–12.

50. Vell. Pat. 2.81.1. See also Veg. 3.4.1.

51. Southern, *Augustus*, 84–85. The majority of these legions were under strength, but this was still a large force.

52. App. *BCiv.* 5.17; and Keaveney, *The Army in the Revolution*, 53.

53. Lawrence Keppie, *Making of the Roman Army* (Norman: University of Oklahoma Press, 1998), 147–48; Keaveney, *The Army in the Revolution*, 71–77; Phang, *Roman Military Service*, 115–20.

54. Vell. Pat. 2.81.2; App. *BCiv.* 5.128; and Cass. Dio 49.13.2–14.1.

55. App. *BCiv.* 5.128; and Cass. Dio 49.14.3. See also Patterson, "Military Organization," 101–3; Southern, *Augustus*, 84–85; and Blois, "Army and General," 165–66, 173–75.

56. App. *BCiv.* 5.128.

57. Vell. Pat. 2.81.2; App. *BCiv.* 5.128–29; Cass. Dio 49.14. Ancient authors drew a clear distinction in referring to these grants as *dona* (rewards) and not *praemia* (bounties).

58. Vell. Pat. 2.78.2; App. *Ill.* 12–13, 15, 18; App. *BCiv.* 5.145; and Cass. Dio 49.36.1. See also Southern, *Augustus*, 87–90; Danijel Dzino, *Illyricum in Roman Politics 229 BC–AD 68* (Cambridge: Cambridge University Press, 2010), 102–16; and Velleius Paterculus, *The Caesarian and Augustan Narrative (II.41–93)*, ed. Andrew Woodman (Cambridge: Cambridge University Press, 1983), 192–96.

59. Vell. Pat. 2.78.3; and Cass. Dio 49.34.2–3 and 35–38.

60. *RGDA* 29.1; Pliny *HN* 7.148; Suet. *Aug.* 20; App. *Ill.* 16 and 27; and Cass. Dio 49.35.2 and 38.3–4. See also Dzino, *Illyricum*, 116–20; and Southern, *Augustus*, 87–90.

61. Vell. Pat. 2.82–83; Plut. *Ant.* 54–60; Suet. *Aug.* 17.1–2; and Cass. Dio 49.41–50.6.1. See also Southern, *Augustus*, 92–97; and Southern, *Mark Antony*, 128–35.

62. Cass. Dio 50.7.3 and 9.1; Southern, *Mark Antony*, 140–41; and Keaveney, *The Army in the Revolution*, 53.

63. Vell. Pat. 2.84.1; Cass. Dio 50.11.4.

64. Vell. Pat. 2.84–85; Plut. *Ant.* 63–68; Cass. Dio 50.12–51.1; Lange, *Res Publica Constituta*, 73–93.

65. Vell. Pat. 2.85.4–6; Plut. *Ant.* 68; Cass. Dio 51.1.4–3.1; Keppie, *Making of the Roman Army*, 128.

66. Suet. *Aug.* 17.3; Cass. Dio 51.3.1–5.1; Brice, "Holding a Wolf," 117–21.

67. *RGDA* 3.3, 15.2, and 16.1; Suet. *Aug.* 44.1; and Cass. Dio 51.6.5–10.3; 17.6–8, and 21.3.

68. *RGDA* 34; Southern, *Augustus*, 100–115; Lange, *Res Publica Constituta*, 159–90.

69. *RGDA* 16.2 and 34; Suet. *Aug.* 49.2; Cass. Dio 54.25.5–6; Kurt Raaflaub, "Die Militärreformen des Augustus und die politische Problematik des Frühen Prinzipats," *Saeculum Augustum*, vol. 1, *Herrschaft und Gesellschaft*, ed. Gerhard Binder (Darmstadt: Wissenschaftliche Buchgesellschaft, 1987), 246–50; Phang, *Roman Military Service*, 92–93, 163–66; and Kate Gilliver, "The Augustan Reform and the Structure of the Imperial Army," in *A Companion to the Roman Army*, ed. Paul Erdkamp (Malden, MA: Wiley-Blackwell, 2007), 183–200.

70. This reform seems to have been formalized, since the "Discipline of Augustus" shows up as in an inscription from the reign of Tiberius Caesar (*Senatus Consultum de Pisone Patre*) and in the *Digest* of Roman law (49.16.12). See Werner Eck, Antonio Caballos, and Fernando Fernández, *Das senatus consultum de Cn. Pisone patre*, Vestigia 48 (Munich: C. H. Beck, 1996); and the translation and discussions in *American Journal of Philology* 120 no. 1 (entire volume).

71. Lendon, *Soldiers and Ghosts*, 231–32; and Phang, *Roman Military Service*, 13–36.

Seventeenth-Century Ming China

4

Of Bureaucrats and Bandits

*Confucianism and Antirebel Strategy at
the End of the Ming Dynasty*

———— KENNETH M. SWOPE ————

Civil-Military Dichotomies in Traditional China

Chinese military history is, I am pleased to note, in the midst of something
of a golden age. For a long time, scholars in the West have too easily accepted
overgeneralizations about the complete domination of the military by the
civilian sector in traditional China. As a result, they have neglected China's
military past in favor of studies emphasizing other aspects of Chinese culture
and society. Fortunately, though, over the past decade, scholars have presented increasingly sophisticated works covering all eras of China's military
past.[1] While acknowledging that traditional Chinese literati culture certainly
valued the brush over the sword and sought to marginalize military and
martial achievements in written documents, this new generation of scholars is using China's voluminous historical record to reevaluate its military
past in both a comparative sense and on its own terms.[2] This has produced
not only studies of particular battles and campaigns but also more systematic
examinations of the relationship between war and society in China. These
efforts serve to delineate China's "military culture," which, according to Nicola Di Cosmo, entails an effort "to understand the relationship between war,
society, and thought beyond the empirical level and to recognize the ways in
which intellectual, civilian, and literary developments intervened to shape
the nature of military institutions, military theory, and the culture of war."[3]

Moreover, while comparative studies of China's military past certainly are
useful, Di Cosmo also cautions against simply trying to shoehorn Chinese
military history into a Western framework of development, observing that

> any advancement in theoretical sophistication can only be attained by pay-
> ing greater attention to the specific evolution of the culture and practice of

war in China and therefore cannot be sought purely from the application of Western-derived theory, which is naturally based on the study of societies very different from China's.[4]

An example is the stimulating recent effort along these lines by political scientist Iain Johnston. Drawing on the concept of strategic culture, Johnston identified two dominant strands in traditional Chinese strategic thought.[5] The first, which he calls the "Confucian-Mencian paradigm," is based on the underlying premise that warfare should be used only as a last resort and that officials should first try to transform the people and appease their potential enemies through benevolence and nonviolent means such as trade agreements and even bribes. The second strand, which Johnston calls the "*parabellum* paradigm," assumes a much more negative worldview of war as inevitable and argues for constant preparation and aggressive military action whenever circumstances are favorable. Perhaps surprisingly for students of Chinese (and, for that matter, Western) history, Johnston found, through study of a corpus of strategic works known as *The Seven Military Classics* (*Wu jing qi shu*) that the Chinese tended to favor the latter approach to grand strategy, particularly during the Ming dynasty (1368–1644), the period on which he focuses.[6] This is doubly surprising, since the Ming dynasty has long been seen as a nadir of Chinese military power and a time when military might was "stultified" and "generals and soldiers were regarded with fear, suspicion, and distaste."[7]

Nevertheless, Johnston's reading of Ming memorials on defense policy concerning the Mongols indicates that the Ming were generally aggressive, noting the degree to which military affairs occupied the attention of civil officials. Certainly when reading the *Veritable Records of the Ming Dynasty* (*Ming shilu*) or almost any other annalistic histories from this period, one is struck by the prevalence of military concerns, even in times of relative peace. What is particularly interesting, given Johnston's arguments, is that one can identify different approaches to military problems according to the preferences of particular emperors and specific constellations of officials. In short, while I would agree that the Ming often took an aggressive approach to military threats, the Ming system, like all imperial Chinese dynasties, was extremely personal, and decisions were more contingent on personal preferences and personalities than any other factor.[8]

Furthermore, although Johnston's assertion that the *Seven Military Classics* was the major corpus of Chinese strategic thought is somewhat problematic, it is true that all Chinese civil officials (and many military officials) would have been familiar with these texts, along with a significantly large additional body of philosophical literature generally identified as "Confucian," for lack of a better term.[9] These texts emphasized virtues like benevolence, righteousness, filiality, and loyalty, contending that the government should treat the common people in the same way that parents treat their children.[10] In times of famine, relief needed to be distributed. When popular revolts broke out, only the ringleaders were to be punished, as their followers simply did not know any better. Because humans were innately good, at least according to Mencius, they would naturally respond to such gestures and seek to do good when given the opportunity.[11] Forced to memorize these texts during their long years of study for the civil service examinations, many officials did indeed come to believe in their implicit values and tried to govern and manage military problems in accordance with such ideals. Still others may have chosen the nonviolent path owing to their own ignorance of military affairs and therefore sought to limit the damage they caused to the people. This choice, however, could come at the expense of their own careers.

The reason that such proclivities could sometimes become problematic for imperial governments was the practice of providing civil oversight and command of military operations, which became standard in China after the Tang dynasty (618–907) in response to the phenomenon of widespread warlordism attending the decline and fall of that empire.[12] While such reforms represented an admirable attempt to balance the civil (*wen*) and the military (*wu*) in accordance with the prescriptions outlined in the ancient classics, such measures in fact often led to disaster. Many civil officials understandably lacked a military aptitude and practical experience. Therefore, the emperors and their advisers had to appoint officials who worked well with their military counterparts and who deferred to their judgment in critical military matters. Needless to say, perhaps, this ideal was exceedingly difficult to achieve in the imperial Chinese governmental system, which, like imperial systems everywhere, was prone to factionalism and favoritism. Under vigorous and intelligent emperors with a grasp of military strategy, such arrangements could work reasonably well.[13] Unfortunately, however, this was seldom the case, and competing interests at court and in the bureaucracy often worked at cross-purposes. Perhaps even more important to this study, many of these civil officials were accomplished writers with a deep knowledge of Chinese history. They thus were quite capable of drawing up proposals that seemed workable on paper, were couched in the proper tones, and made due reference to the prevailing philosophical ideals. Presented to cloistered emperors, who often were their former students, these officials' plans could receive the imperial seal of approval, only to lead to disaster.

Nonetheless, it was part of the emperor's responsibility as the Son of Heaven to listen to his officials' advice and to approve plans based on a rational and sober assessment of the strategic situation and an awareness of cultural values and ideals that we might equate with the modern sense of public opinion. This in turn fostered a competitive culture of conspicuous displays of merit in which officials constantly submitted memorials to the throne, arguing not only for their own positions but also against the positions of others. Arguments were the basis for policy decisions and also were instrumental in career advancement within the official hierarchy. This maneuvering was just as important—indeed, often more important—than the actual policy debates and their outcomes. Contested standards of "proper" Confucian behavior and promotions of the public good thus became a sort of screen for more opaque and self-serving behavior. In short, arguments about military policy and strategy couched in Confucian terms were a currency to be spent in the factional competition. Although underlying cultural values certainly were important, we should consider, too, the multiple levels on which such values operated and to keep this in mind when analyzing specific campaigns and the debates surrounding them.[14]

Bringing Brushes to the Battlefield

This chapter looks at just such a campaign, in which a father and son were hamstrung by their adherence to Confucian ideals in the face of harsh military realities. In particular I will examine the most detailed plan for the extermination of the peasant rebellions that raged at the end of the Ming dynasty. What were the plan's strengths and weaknesses from strategic, tactical, and ideological perspectives? How did this campaign fit into the broader context of court-civil-military relations at the end of the dynasty? This case is illuminating because it demonstrates how factional politics, philosophical and cultural ideals, and strategic culture intersected to create the military climate and to shape actual campaigns in late imperial China. In the end we will see that contemporary officials subscribed to a range of strategic preferences and that it is too easy to characterize imperial Chinese officials as "Confucian" or pacifistic, even when the dominant philosophical and cultural ideals appear to embody such ideas. Finally, this study shows how imperial patronage affected the decision-making process for better or worse and how, when dealing with national crises, emperors, too, were bound by what we might call public opinion.

The final decades of the Ming dynasty were fraught with military threats that often were exacerbated by factional politics, cronyism, and incompetent leadership. Upon his accession to the throne in 1628, the last Ming emperor, Chongzhen (r. 1628–1644), tried to end the political squabbling by selecting his own men for important posts and giving them considerable military and civil authority.[15] Unfortunately for the Ming, though, Chongzhen proved even more susceptible to public opinion than the very men he sought to oust, and he often made snap judgments without allowing credible plans to reach fruition. One of his most controversial appointments was naming Yang Sichang (1588–1641) as the minister of war and making him responsible for simultaneously guarding the northeastern frontier against the Manchus and suppressing the great peasant rebellions that raged in central and western China in the late 1630s. Deeming the latter more important to the dynasty's ultimate survival, Yang devised what he called a "ten-sided net (*shi mian zhi wang*)" strategy to encircle and annihilate the peasant rebels. Funding was to come from a temporary increase in land taxes, and Yang promised that the rebels would be pacified in a mere three months. The plan initially was successful, as several prominent rebel leaders voluntarily submitted after they had been surrounded by Yang's subordinates. But within a year, the surrendered bandits rebelled again, and the weaknesses of Yang's strategy were exposed. Yang took the field against the rebels only to die ignominiously, most likely by his own hand.

This is a brief account, but there is a great deal more. In fact, Yang Sichang's story, properly told, has its origins in the career of his father, Yang He. In the second year of his reign, facing what were then still nascent peasant rebellions, Chongzhen appointed Yang He to be the supreme commander of Shaanxi and the three border regions.[16] Earlier Yang He had earned some fame quelling aboriginal uprisings in southwest China, and he had been a very vocal critic of the Ming commanders who had been defeated by the Latter Jin (later known as the Manchus) in the northeast. Yang He's aggressive hard-line stance and recommendations for instilling discipline and loyalty won him the favor of the emperor and the support of many officials at court.

The peasant uprisings Yang He was called on to suppress had many causes: widespread famine; flooding, desperation over an inability to pay taxes; cutbacks in the Ming's postal service, which employed large numbers of young men in the northwest; and anger over the state's laxity in delivering military salaries and rations. The last problem was aggravated by corrupt local officials who embezzled funds sent for salaries and neglected military training.[17] The first notable peasant rebel leader was Wang Jiayin, who assembled a band of starving peasants to raid the environs of the Great Wall in 1628.[18] At first, local officials did not report the uprising for fear of being reprimanded. Army deserters then joined the ranks of another disaffected peasant leader who linked up with Wang, and before long, all of Shaanxi was in an uproar.[19] The local pacification commissioner, Hu Yan'an, was so ineffectual the rebels called him their "host at the capital," and they stepped up their activities, aided by the province's rugged mountain terrain with its many hideouts. Shortly thereafter, the mounted bandit Gao Yingxiang, who became the rebellions' most important early leader, joined forces with Wang Jiayin, styling himself "the dashing prince" (*chuang wang*). By late 1630 Wang was powerful enough to take several isolated fortresses and kill a local mobile corps commander.[20] Over the next few years, several more noted leaders emerged, eventually prompting the government's appointment of Yang He.[21]

Upon assuming his post in 1630, Yang He identified a number of key problems in the region, including supply issues, the constant threat of border raids by the Mongols, and the dereliction of duty by local officials. He saw restoring the vitality of the local populace by improving administration as crucial to stabilizing the military situation, and he believed that a conscientious official could effect these changes from within. Yang assumed that government relief and transfer of peasants to areas that had presumably been less affected by natural disasters would be sufficient. Impressed with Yang's sincerity and commitment, Chongzhen made him supreme commander of the three border regions of Shaanxi, giving him the kind of power that had seldom been delegated to frontier officials since the heyday of the Wanli (1573–1620) era.[22] But Yang was faced with many challenges, some of them institutional in nature. In many cases, salaries for the troops were seriously in arrears. In fact, in 1629 the vice-minister of revenue noted that the salaries of Yansui, Guyuan, and Ningxia were thirty-six months in arrears.[23]

Thus despite his lofty rhetoric, because he recognized some of the challenges he faced, Yang expressed misgivings about the power with which he had been invested. Moreover, because he was a staunch advocate of traditional Confucian statecraft who disdained the use of troops and had little practical military experience, Yang embarked on a plan of soothing and pacifying the rebels, encouraging them to surrender to the state in exchange for food and an opportunity to return to agricultural pursuits.[24] Yang strictly forbade executing surrendered rebels and seems to have been very gullible in assuming that all who accepted pardons would return to peaceful pursuits. He even argued for leniency for some rebels who had killed officials.[25] Thus the very qualities that had made Yang a good censorial official made him a terrible military commander.

Matters were made worse by the fact that just after Yang took office, the Latter Jin raided inside the Great Wall in the northeast. Because Yang had to dispatch troops under his jurisdiction to defend Beijing, he lacked the numbers needed to quell the peasant rebels, and his only recourse was the policy of peaceful suasion (*zhaofu*) that, in any event, he favored.[26] But because natural disasters and famine persisted in the region, the number of bandits swelled. There also were allegations that even the meager relief funds sent from Beijing were being skimmed by covetous local officials. Nonetheless, Chongzhen decided to make pacification a priority over extirpation of the rebels.

In the first month of 1631, the emperor convened a palace audience to discuss the wandering-bandit problem. When a local surveillance commissioner complained that the lack of military supplies was hampering efforts to contain them, the emperor replied, "Previously you reported that the bandits were pacified. How is it that they now have multiplied?"[27] The official responded that "the riverine area between Shanxi and Shaanxi cannot be pacified; therefore Hequ alone has been encircled." He added that although the bandits were not skilled in battle, they had the help of starving peasants, and since the earlier plan to suppress them had not been implemented, the Ming were now facing a disaster. Worse, those Ming units that had been successful in the initial suppression effort had already been demobilized.[28]

Identifying with Yang He's position, Chongzhen stated, "The bandits are my children. They should be soothed and pacified. I cannot punish them. If [the former bandit] Wang Zuogua has already surrendered, how could we have killed him?" His official replied, "Because he surrendered and then started looting again. We had to kill him to set an example."[29] A few days later, the emperor ordered famine relief for Shaanxi, expressing his sympathy at the plight of the people and noting that he knew that they all were really good at heart, driven to their actions by desperation. Thus it appeared that at least the emperor was still in Yang He's camp. His resolve was strengthened by reports that suggested sending relief funds to the countryside could "turn bandits into peasants" again. A few days later, Chongzhen released 100,000 taels from the treasury to pacify the "wandering bandits," as they already were being called.[30]

The emperor's support did not silence Yang's critics, however. Many distrusted the sincerity of rebel leaders who surrendered under duress, not believing that their chants of *wansui* (long life) addressed to Yang outside his *yamen* (official compound) walls was sufficient evidence to assume that they were once again loyal subjects. In fact, adopting a strategy that the rebel leaders used throughout the last days of the Ming, many disguised themselves as Ming troops in order to gain access to towns and their resources.[31] Even after some military campaigns succeeded in stamping out local uprisings, Yang stopped his subordinates from pursuing rebel remnants, giving those who surrendered certificates of pardon and letting the ringleaders return to the countryside, where many then joined other bands.[32] Consequently, Yang's critics became increasingly vocal, perhaps best exemplified by Censor Wu Sheng, who contended that even if pacification was a policy found in the historical record, it was exceedingly difficult to be soft first and then adopt a harsher policy later.

The rebellion of a bandit leader named Shen Yikui who had previously submitted to Yang proved to be the last straw. In the wake of Shen's initial submission, the Ming had scored a series of victories, killing hundreds of rebels, including Wang Jiayin, and obtaining the surrender of many others. But then Shen Yikui rebelled again, and when he was joined by more surrendered rebels unfurling the flag of insurrection, Yang He was impeached.[33] As more impeachments attacking the pacification policy rolled into Beijing, Chongzhen eventually agreed and ordered Yang's arrest and interrogation by the Ministry of Justice.[34] Ironically enough, the emperor also approved Wu Sheng's request to retain local funds to stimulate agriculture and the local economy in lieu of sending them to Beijing.[35]

Enter the Son

As soon as Yang He was summoned to Beijing, his son, Yang Sichang, petitioned the court to replace his father so as to atone for his mistakes, but Chongzhen refused for the time being.[36] Following in the footsteps of his father, Yang Sichang was a *jinshi* (a presented scholar; the highest civil service degree) in 1610.[37] After earning his degree and aside from a brief "retirement" between 1621 and 1628, he served many years as a bureaucrat in various posts. Subsequently, after serving in midlevel positions for several years, he was transferred to Shanhaiguan in 1631 to oversee military supplies.[38]

For the rest of 1632, newly appointed more aggressive officials enjoyed a fair measure of success in battling the rebels. In fact, by the middle of 1633, Ming commanders reported that they had killed 36,600 rebels.[39] Such achievements appeared to indicate that a more forceful policy was warranted. Still, we must treat such figures with caution. Ming armies remained plagued by supply, pay, and equipment shortfalls. In addition, military officials tended to focus on body counts, which formed the basis for reward and promotion. These counts therefore also served to demonstrate tangible proof of successes, although as any student of modern warfare knows, mere body counts, especially when difficult to verify, tell little of the full story.

Although his plea to replace his father was rejected (as was his offer to serve his father's sentence of exile), Yang was promoted to censor in chief of the right[40] and touring pacification commissioner of Shanhaiguan, Yongping, and the surrounding areas in 1633. Later he was elevated still further to vice-minister of war of the right and, concurrently, vice-censor in chief of the right and supreme commander of military affairs of Xuanfu, Datong, and Shanxi. Because banditry was still spreading across the central plains, Yang recommended opening up mines to raise additional revenues.[41] He then sent to the throne a series of memorials discussing border affairs, impressing Chongzhen with his talents, though later critics have charged that Yang was a better wordsmith and calligrapher than a policymaker or tactician.[42] Nonetheless, because of these very skills, which traditionally marked an able and upright official and human being, the emperor implicitly trusted Yang, and Yang became perhaps the most influential official in the empire over the next several years.[43] It is said that Chongzhen thought no one else had Yang Sichang's grasp of the big picture with respect to military affairs.[44] And it had long been part of the Chinese imperial tradition for monarchs to entrust favored officials with sweeping powers to deal with military crises, even if such arrangements often did not work out as anticipated. So in supporting Yang, Chongzhen was executing one of his major responsibilities, namely, giving military authority to a subordinate, which was in the emperor's purview as supreme military commander of the armed forces. But just as Yang was to assume his posts, his father died in exile, and Yang retired to observe the customary mourning period. Before the mourning period was up, Minister of War Zhang Fengyi committed suicide, and the emperor himself recalled Yang to service.

Casting a Ten-Sided Net

Upon resuming office in 1637, Yang stressed that suppressing internal dissent should take precedence over dealing with the Manchus in the northeast. By this time, the scope of the peasant rebellions had greatly expanded, and the center of rebel activity was shifting south and east, closer to the capital and the agricultural heartland of the empire. In a recommendation that later caused him no small amount of trouble, Yang proposed negotiating with the Manchus in order to buy time to quell the peasant rebels. He believed that if adequate supplies were provided, then the soldiers could be fed and would fight, which in turn would strengthen protection of the local populace. Moreover, once the people felt safe, they would redirect their allegiance to the Ming government and be less inclined to join the rebels.[45] Yang also targeted his fellow officials, calling for the punishment and even the execution of officials who were derelict in their duties.[46] It was at this point that Yang unveiled his master plan for quelling the rebellion, known as the "ten-sided net" strategy.

Yang stated that Shaanxi, Henan, Huguang, and Jiangbei (the area north of the Yellow River) would be the four main lines of defense (*zheng*). Four touring pacification commissioners would be assigned to defend each line. Then Yansui, Shanxi, Shandong, Jiangnan, Jiangxi, and Sichuan would be established as the six auxiliary lines of defense. The six pacification commissioners in command of these posts would oversee both defensive and offensive operations, the idea being that the net would gradually close around the peasant rebels' positions until all were trapped and either killed or submitted.[47] But defense was to be their primary function. As the net closed, the Ming would use the classic strategy of "clearing the fields and strengthening the walls."[48] With stoutly defended cities and no supplies available, the rebels eventually would have no other recourse but to surrender.[49]

Two supreme commanders (*zongli/zongdu*) were to smash the enemy wherever they encountered them, and the other officials were to act locally, presumably in a more defensive capacity.[50] The forces under the supreme commanders were to be made up of elite troops and would be assisted by others dispatched from Beijing and from neighboring regions. Meanwhile, Xiong Wencan, who had gained a reputation for dealing with rebels through having persuaded the Ming pirate lord Zheng Zhilong to surrender, boasted that he could wipe out the rebels in no time, so he was appointed as one of the supreme commanders, along with Hong Chengchou.[51] Xiong immediately alienated the people, and he even tried to replace General Zuo Liangyu (1598–1645), one of the few Ming commanders who had enjoyed some success against the rebels, in favor of men that Xiong had brought from Guangdong.[52] Xiong also complained that he lacked cavalry, so the emperor ordered another three thousand war horses be sent to him immediately.[53]

Yang proposed increasing his troop strength by 120,000, approximately two-thirds of whom would be infantry. To outfit and supply these extra troops, Yang estimated needing an extra 2.8 million taels of revenue.[54] While many other court officials balked at further aggravating an already angry tax base, Yang argued that the land tax was vastly underreported anyhow.[55] He also contended that the extra special taxes levied in Liaodong had already raised 5 million to 6 million taels to defend that region, so there was no reason that the presumably more productive areas of central China could not assume this lesser burden.[56] Simply increasing the land tax by twelve ounces of grain per *mu* would bring in 1,929,000 taels. Another 406,000 could come from special taxes on surplus land. They could expect 200,000 from postal revenues, and the rest could perhaps be raised by selling *jiansheng* (the lowest civil service–level government student) degrees.[57] Despite the heated opposition of many of his officials to this plan, Chongzhen reasoned that one more year of hardship for the peasants outweighed the long-term risks, so he approved Yang's proposal. He then told local officials to look for ways to raise the funds and to proceed with further famine relief measures.[58] Later scholars heavily criticized Yang for this policy, some even going so far as to charge that he "killed the country with a single word" through this plan.[59] Conversely, it is said that Chongzhen appreciated that at least Yang appeared to have a concrete plan for dealing with the empire's military problems. Whereas most of his other officials vacillated, Yang was confident, forceful, and visionary.[60] To a ruler desperate for solutions (and always eager to absolve himself of blame), Yang was the perfect loyal minister.

Among Yang's more notable contemporary critics was Sun Chuanting (d. 1643), the grand coordinator of Shaanxi. A veteran official with much experience combating the rebels in his own jurisdiction, Sun submitted a memorial on border affairs in which he highlighted ten problems with Yang's ten-sided net. First, Sun believed that Yang's requests for funds and manpower were highly unrealistic. "How can the state raise an extra 2.8 million taels when they've already spent more than 1 million taels in extra revenues?" asked Sun.[61] Deeming Yang totally impractical and unversed in military affairs, Sun further questioned where the troops would come from. He also questioned Yang's timetable, supposedly a mere six months, and the issue of when the troops would be mobilized in regard to the upsurge of bandit activity. Sun noted that the planned campaign seasons for the troops did not correspond to those when the bandits were active. On top of this was the problem of geography. The terrain greatly favored the highly mobile peasant rebels who lived off the land and escaped into the mountains, gorges, and forests. But the large Ming armies had to rely on fixed positions and needed to maintain long supply lines. Jurisdictional problems exacerbated matters still further, as the rebels could easily move from province to province while the Ming defenders belatedly exchanged information or wrangled over whose responsibility it was to apprehend given rebels. In essence, Sun asserted that in addition to its high costs, Yang's plan was too static.[62] It was, in his words, no more than an "empty net" strategy.[63]

Still another shortcoming, Sun insisted, was the nature of the rebel groups. There was no real way to determine exactly how many peasant rebels were operating at any given time because they easily blended in with the local populace and often had local support. And despite frequent reports of government victories, invariably accompanied by body counts, it seemed as if their numbers were endless.[64] Sun added that the Ming needed far more troops if a coherent policy of extermination were even to be considered. With respect to what Sun meant by "extermination" (*jiao*), in the case of peasant uprisings and outbreaks of banditry it was standard government practice to kill the ringleaders and disperse the followers. But in some cases when matters reached a critical point, it was deemed useful to exterminate the entire group so as to set an example.[65] Sun Chuanting seemed to favor such an extermination policy, but as a military commander with far more field experience than Yang Sichang, he recognized the inherent difficulties of properly implementing a harsher suppression policy.

Moreover, Sun was highly critical of the government's general lack of consistency in pursuing either pacification or extermination, noting that such vacillation served only to create more confusion and distrust among the people.[66] Finally, Sun stressed the importance of appointing experienced and competent commanders at all levels. The men in charge needed to be familiar with local people and conditions and to take a more graduated, cautious, and localized approach to quelling the uprisings. In the end, Sun's recommendations were ignored, and later he even was jailed for his opposition to Yang's policies.[67]

Sun's critiques appear reasonable to a modern eye, but they did not constitute a fully fleshed-out alternative plan, and no other plan seemed forthcoming at the time. As the modern scholar Fan Shuzhi noted, if properly administered, Yang's plan had a reasonable chance of success, and in several previous meetings no official had offered anything better.[68] But there was also the problem of taxing the peasantry even more. As the emperor himself noted, "Leadership and money needed to come from the gentry, not the masses. Suppressing the bandits requires a big campaign, which requires lots of troops. The money cannot come from the people, but should come from the treasury, but the treasury is empty." So the emperor ordered the ministries to investigate all possible sources of revenue and report to him within two months.[69] In effect, Chongzhen called his gentry to the mat. When they refused to help out, he replied in disgust that he had no recourse but to raise taxes, so in the fourth month of 1637, taxes were raised across the empire.[70]

Meanwhile, back in the field, Xiong Wencan continued to clash with local commanders as his handpicked outsiders continued to clash with the local troops. He also incurred the emperor's wrath after additional troops dispatched from the capital still made little headway. Hong Chengchou and Zuo Liangyu virtually ignored Xiong's orders, and no significant victories were gained through the remainder of 1637. In addition, Xiong also tended to favor surrenders and less coercive policies, despite his bold pronouncements the previous year. This drew no small measure of criticism from his fellow officials, who argued that the wandering bandits were nothing like the pirates that Xiong had dealt with in the past.[71] But few were as straightforward as Sun Chuanting in suggesting alternatives. So again we see the interplay of court politics and Confucian sensibilities as various parties lobbied against incumbent officials often seemingly for the sake of argument, in essence to keep themselves in the discussion and in the emperor's mind, regardless of whether they offered concrete alternatives for consideration.

The most serious problem with Xiong's appeasement policy came when Zuo Liangyu was ordered to accept the surrender of the notorious Zhang Xianzhong (1606–1647) after surrounding him in the spring of 1638.[72] Zuo was furious and wanted to kill Zhang on the spot but deferred to Xiong's orders.[73] Insult was added to injury when Xiong provided Zhang with supplies for twenty thousand men to maintain local order! This prompted Yang Sichang to become more personally involved in the campaign, and he vowed to the emperor that he would close the net in the winter of 1637/1638 and crush the rebels within three months.[74] Among other things, Yang noted the need for commanders in the field to obey the authority conferred on officials such as himself, concluding that "if everyone exerts their strength to the utmost, how can the rebels not be pacified?"[75]

Yang also defended Xiong Wencan, pointing out that despite his many ardent supporters, Hong Chengchou had been battling the rebels for seven years with no real results, whereas Xiong had been at it for only three months and already had accomplished more.[76] But memorials poured in criticizing Xiong's apparent willingness to appease and co-opt the rebels rather than execute them. Incidentally, Hong Chengchou also came under attack, but he insisted that the reason he had not engaged the rebels more forcefully was that because his troops had such a fearsome reputation, the rebels always fled before he could engage them, so he could not be blamed.[77] At this point, Chongzhen chastised Yang for divisive talk, and Yang stopped attacking Hong. But after another three months passed with no results, Yang asked to be replaced. The emperor refused, in effect telling Yang to find a way to succeed. Yang then sent up another memorial, criticizing Hong Chengchou's handling of matters while praising Xiong Wencan's adroit mixture of aggressive and conciliatory measures in Jiangbei and Jiangnan. Yang then provided a list of officials who deserved merit or punishment for their actions, most notably calling for the arrest of Hong Chengchou, whom he may have resented because Hong had replaced his late father.[78] The emperor followed Yang's recommendations.

The Failure of Appeasement

Despite his support of Xiong Wencan, or perhaps because of it, Yang no longer seriously discussed the implementation of the ten-sided net. As originally presented, the strategy combined elements of extirpation and pacification, with an emphasis on the former that seemed designed to silence the more vociferous critics. But Xiong Wencan never seriously considered the more offensive options at his disposal, and he made no real attempt to implement Yang's plan as originally outlined. Moreover, in the initial glow after the presumed surrender of Zhang Xianzhong, Xiong's policy of pacification was verified in Yang's eyes. In a meeting with Chongzhen, Yang talked about the primacy of military action and how these successes demonstrated the virtue of imperial justice. But even the emperor balked at such hyperbole, chiding Yang that the Ming was not the Warring States era of ancient China, during which virtue allegedly caused the people to bend before the ruler like grass before the wind.[79] This happened even though Zhang had obtained quite a deal for himself, including control of a town, supplies for his men, and other privileges.[80] There even was rapturous talk of how the surrendered bandit chieftains (some had followed Zhang in submitting) were now willing to turn swords into plowshares.

Yet even while this was taking place, Sun Chuanting and Hong Chengchou were pursuing, with some success, a policy of annihilation against the peasant rebels in their midst.[81] Zuo Liangyu also scored some victories in Sichuan, and Xiong Wencan reported to the throne that ultimate victory appeared imminent.[82] So while he was trying to cash in on his own policies of pacification, Xiong had no qualms about also taking the credit for the achievements of others, even when they directly countered his orders and policies.

In effect, some of the commanders were carrying out the more aggressive aspects of the "ten-sided net" on their own, ignoring the coordinative aspects that might actually have enabled it to succeed if properly executed. But as was too often the case in the late Ming period, these officials spent more time pursuing their own ends and framing their decisions in moralistic terms than in unified actions that actually helped the people and the state.

In addition, as had happened to his father a few years earlier, Yang's ambitions were undone by another Manchu incursion. In fact, Yang already had incurred the enmity of several high officials when he interpreted certain astronomical phenomena as justifying his negotiations with the Manchus. Accordingly, he sent out some feelers, but their recent military successes left the Manchus disinterested in talking.[83] Already being criticized for conducting negotiations, negotiations that led nowhere anyway, in mid-1638 Yang's responsibility and potential culpability for the situation were signaled by his being made grand secretary, minister of rites, and minister of war, in addition to his other titles. He then proceeded to demote several of his key foes just as the invaders broke through the Great Wall's defenses, prompting another round of infighting. Yang consequently was impeached for errors of state, was demoted three grades for his failures, but managed to survive, owing to the emperor's continued support.[84] Other officials were cashiered and prominent officials, including Sun Chuanting and Hong Chengchou, were transferred to the northeast, thereby allowing the rebellions in the northwest to fester once more. But now, even Yang was forced to direct his interests to securing the northeast before turning back to deal with the peasant rebels.[85] Although his plans for bolstering the northwest's defenses are beyond the scope of this chapter, suffice it to say that they bore Yang's hallmark of being expensive and impressive on paper but difficult to implement and somewhat out of touch with reality. For example, he expressed hopes that he could raise an additional 7.3 million taels through new taxes.[86]

Yang Sichang Takes to the Field

As of late 1638, the court mistakenly believed that the peasant rebellions had largely been quelled, but within a few months, Zhang Xianzhong rebelled again. Zhang had been preparing for such a move for quite some time, extorting money from local officials as part of a transit tax, reinforcing the walls of the town where he was settled, and drilling his troops. He also systematically bribed Ming officials to ignore his activities. Enraged, Yang Sichang took to the field himself to deal with the problem. So in the eighth month of 1639,

Yang Sichang was reappointed minister of war, grand secretary, and supreme commander of bandit pacification and received the double-edged sword of authority. The emperor approved Yang's request to raise an additional five million taels to wipe out the rebels and gave him the authority to select his own army inspectors, following Yang's earlier suggestion that he needed more unified field authority.[87] The emperor gave Yang generous funds for the troops and offered personal encouragement. He even personally served Yang wine at a banquet and gave him a poem in his own handwriting. As Yang set out on his assignment, Chongzhen gushed, "With officials like this, what can we have to worry about? With you in charge, it is as if I am going myself."[88]

Yang reached Xiangyang on the Han River on the twenty-ninth day of the ninth month of 1639. He entered Xiong Wencan's headquarters and immediately took control of the army, sending Xiong forward to Beijing and refusing to defend him any longer.[89] He then met with his commanders and devised another strategy of containment. Yang again advocated bringing in troops from neighboring regions and encircling the rebels, thereby returning to the more aggressive strategy that was at the core of the original ten-sided net plan. Funds would again come from new taxes and from revenues retained in the provinces.[90] Zuo Liangyu was invested with the title of Bandit-Pacifying General, and his early Ming successes brought liberal rewards from Yang.[91]

But within a short while it seemed to Zuo that Yang wanted to keep him inactive and in defensive positions, thereby denying him the chance to earn merit or to exact revenge on his old rival, Zhang Xianzhong. They also clashed over military policy. Yang wanted to divide the troops into smaller strike forces, whereas Zuo favored larger commands whose numerical superiority would give the Ming the advantage.[92] Yang's public whippings of military officials who failed to hold towns or capture rebels did little to improve morale or firmly establish his command authority over his military subordinates. Still, a few victories in 1639/1640 delighted the emperor and brought Yang more rewards as well as a promotion to junior guardian of the heir apparent.[93]

Subsequent victories piled up, and it looked as if the Ming were finally turning the tide. In the early months of 1640, Zhang Xianzhong fled to Sichuan, hotly pursued by Zuo Liangyu. Ignoring Yang's orders to cease the pursuit, Zuo eventually surrounded Zhang near Mount Manao and scored a major defeat, killing 3,500 and capturing several commanders.[94] Chongzhen was delighted and rewarded the commanders responsible for the victory with cash and bolts of cloth. Although subsequent operations were moderately successful, the Ming eventually found themselves overextended and hampered by terrain, weather, and inferior numbers. They pulled back, and Zhang himself escaped to western Sichuan.[95]

Nonetheless, Yang saw the victory at Mount Manao as problematic because Zuo Liangyu had subverted his authority to gain it. Seeking to counter Zuo's growing reputation and authority, Yang made the serious mistake of recommending that another general, He Renlong, be given Zuo's title of Bandit-Suppressing General. When his recommendation was not approved, Yang succeeded only in alienating both men.[96] This in turn caused Zuo to vacillate in pursuing Zhang Xianzhong and allowed the rebel leader to recover his strength through the summer months. Zuo also may have deliberately allowed Zhang to survive because totally eradicating him would have removed the justification for Zuo's own lofty position and given him a pretext for squeezing local officials for supplies and funds.[97] In such actions, we see in action the ongoing problem of civil-military relations and command authority. Although Yang Sichang was technically the supreme commander of these operations, he lacked the power to enforce his orders on his military subordinates, and when he clumsily tried to circumvent the influence of the powerful general Zuo Liangyu, he ended up both enraging Zuo and alienating the man he had hoped to use in Zuo's stead.

Fearing that the rebels in the west were growing stronger, Yang moved his headquarters south to Yiling on the Yangzi River and suggested a new policy of holding strong points. Then a few timely Ming victories and key defections seemed to turn the tide again, and Yang prepared to close his net around Sichuan, where most of the remnants had gathered. Continuing his heavy-handed mode of command, he invoked the authority of the double-edged sword to execute one official at Wushan and then moved to Chongqing in the eleventh month of 1640 as Zhang Xianzhong rampaged throughout Sichuan.[98] Yang also requested more officials and aid from the court, which were granted.[99] He now maintained that because he lacked the numbers for encirclement, defense and ambush became his preferred tactics. Soon all of Sichuan was in tumult as cities were taken or abandoned to the rebels' depredations, although He Renlong did manage to defeat Luo Rucai, killing more than a thousand insurgents and driving Luo back east toward Yang Sichang.[100]

Nonetheless, the badly disciplined and undersupplied Ming troops were prone to desertion when they camped too long. And with famine forcing the peasants into cannibalism, the bandits had no shortage of recruits. Increasingly frustrated, Yang requested to be relieved of his post, but the emperor responded by sending him 50,000 taels for medicine and another 200,000 for famine relief.[101] Chongzhen refused Yang's continuing requests to retire, despite reports that the rebels were taking sites in Shaanxi, Sichuan, and Huguang. The Ming did, however, gain the surrender of several notable rebel commanders in the late summer of 1640, prompting Yang Sichang to send troops west into Sichuan on the advice of one of his subordinates, although some felt that he did this in part to protect Yang's native province of Huguang from further depredations.[102]

Yang's subordinates continued to defy his orders. In the tenth month of 1640, Zhang Xianzhong's forces took one town because the local commander had split up his forces to defend multiple sites. Zhang's spies found the weak point and attacked there. Hearing of the defeat, fighting in Sichuan continued through the fall of 1640. Even though the Ming units won several skirmishes, they subsequently were routed, and the rebels moved east again.

This prompted Yang to relocate his headquarters to Chongqing, Sichuan, where he would be closer to the thick of the fighting. At this point, Yang also put a 10,000-tael price on the head of Zhang Xianzhong, along with a hereditary marquis post. The next day a note appeared on the wall of Yang's office headquarters in Chongqing, reputedly from Zhang Xianzhong, stating that the rebel leader had put a bounty of a mere three taels on Yang's head![103] Yang now feared that Zhang had spies in his own entourage, and he sent several complaints to the emperor. But other reports trickled into Beijing charging that Yang was spending most of his time drinking wine and composing poems in his tent and that he knew nothing about Sichuan or its customs.

Yang even was accused of reciting Buddhist incantations to ward off locusts, a serious charge to level against a proper official, since it implied superstition.[104] It is interesting to see references to such behavior in light of the prevailing official culture of the late Ming period. If Yang had been more successful, then his eccentricities certainly would have been ignored, perhaps even lauded. But because he had acquired many enemies over the years and because everyone knew that the emperor was sensitive to criticism and rightly concerned about the spread of the peasant rebellions, such charges served to advance the positions of Yang's foes and constituted a sort of negative capital for his plans. Not only did Yang fail as a military commander, he also was a superstitious bully. Surely, reasoned such critics, the emperor could see this and would take appropriate actions to rectify the situation. That most of these officials presented little in the way of concrete alternatives is noteworthy but not unsurprising. After all, the immediate goal for many such officials was as much to discredit Yang and advance their own agendas—couched in Confucian rhetoric—as it was to actually stop the rebellions.

The court became increasingly frustrated with Yang's inability to achieve results and with his disputes with his subordinates, against whom Yang railed incessantly for their supposed incompetence. But many of the new troops were green and unfamiliar with Sichuan's terrain. They therefore were prone to falling into the traps and ambushes of the wily and experienced Zhang Xianzhong.[105] Yang's inactivity even elicited a mocking poem from Zhang Xianzhong:

> Before we had coordinator Shao
> Who often came forth and danced with me
> Then came the armies who would not fight
> But followed me around
> But now we have good commander Yang
> Who graciously leaves me a three-day road![106]

The rebels took the key town of Luzhou in the twelfth month of 1640 but fled before the Ming troops could trap them there.[107] Meanwhile, Yang feared that the rebels would be able to strike east again, perhaps threatening the Ming prince at Luoyang. Although Yang ordered Zuo Liangyu to head east, Zuo refused, not wanting to open an escape route for them into Shaanxi. To one of Yang's commands, Zuo replied, "Was it not by disobeying you that I gained the victory at Mount Manao?"[108] More memorials detailing Yang's failures as a commander flooded the capital, and he realized that his time as commander might soon be over.

So Yang ordered all his commanders to assemble at Yunyang to mount one more campaign to crush the rebels. But by this time, He Renlong had already moved west, and others simply ignored Yang's orders. The only officer who came to Yang's aid was the doughty Meng Ruhu (literally, "fierce as a tiger"), who had fought the rebels at Kaixian and Huanglingcheng in eastern Sichuan but was badly beaten. Even though Meng escaped his first encirclement, he later was captured and executed. Yang still desperately pressed for an offensive campaign against the recommendations of his military advisers, who suggested taking defensive positions.[109] Yang argued that because there was too much terrain to cover, offense was better. But as the rebels turned back east and flanked the Ming forces, Yang regretted his directive. He then returned to Yiling and sent an urgent dispatch to Zuo Liangyu. But the rebels severed their lines of communication, even capturing a lone messenger dispatched to spread the word of the rebels' movements.[110]

Yang's fears were realized when Zhang Xianzhong captured the Ming prince of Xiang at Xiangyang. On the eleventh day of the second month of 1641, using the seals of office they had recovered from the Ming messengers, Zhang's men entered the town with the help of fifth columnists. Upon taking the town, Zhang occupied the prince's seat in his palace and had the prince brought before him. He offered the prince a cup of wine and then addressed him, saying,

> I wish to have the head of Yang Sichang, but he is far away in Laikou, so now I'll have to borrow the prince's head in his stead. This will cause Sichang to suffer the full penalty of the law for having lost this princely fief. Now the prince should use all his strength to finish his wine.[111]

The prince was tied to the top of the palace walls, and the whole structure was set alight. The prince's corpse was lost in the flames, and all his concubines were killed. Zuo Liangyu rushed to the town but arrived too late. The rebels then moved east, taking several more towns, including Guangzhou.

By the time he got word of all these developments, Yang was in despair and believed that he had no chance of success. He sent a letter to the emperor asking to be executed for his failures. Upon hearing that Luoyang had fallen to Li Zicheng and that the prince of Fu had been killed, Yang stopped eating and died sometime early in the third month of 1641, although some versions of the story maintain that he committed suicide by taking poison.[112] Ding Qirui was appointed to replace him. Even though many officials recommended a posthumous punishment for Yang, the emperor pointed to his achievements and instead raised him to the ceremonial rank of grand guardian of the heir apparent. Yang was buried at his ancestral home of Wuling, although afterward when Zhang Xianzhong took the town, he dug up the family graves, burned Yang's wife's coffin, and desecrated Yang's corpse.[113]

Wen, Wu, and Rulership in Late Ming China

Yang's tragic saga is, unfortunately, representative of late Ming politics and illustrates the many problems confronting the late Ming military and its commanders. The empire had no dearth of men of martial ability and real experience. But too often, significant and sweeping authority was invested in purely civil officials who lacked real military experience. Moreover, the

Chongzhen emperor had a mercurial temperament and frequently changed his mind about everything from policy to strategy to appointments.[114] Having grown up in the poisoned atmosphere of the Tianqi (r.1621–1627) court, he was highly sensitive to the dangers of factionalism, so he often overreacted to any hints of factional favoritism or allegiances. This resulted in so many changes of personnel that no plan could ever properly be implemented, no matter how sound. Very competent officials were executed for real or imagined offenses, and the empire effectively, and in many cases literally, cut off its own administrative head.

In this sense, Chongzhen's reign offers an interesting contrast with that of Wanli (r. 1573–1620), who, for most of his reign, actively patronized and protected key military officials and supreme commanders from baseless or petty accusations so that they could do their jobs. As one seventeenth-century source notes, after Yang's death, the court no longer appointed civil officials as supreme commanders of the army.[115] Although the Ming dynasty lasted just three more years, even this late realization is a telling indictment of the practice.

It is very difficult to believe that Yang's ten-sided net strategy could have succeeded except under the best of conditions. The main problem was that of resource allocation. Had the state been able to effectively contain the Manchu threat in Liaodong, perhaps it could have mustered the necessary manpower. Indeed, we see time and again that manpower or other resources had to be shifted just as government forces seemed on the verge of triumph. This also speaks to the issue of prioritization. High officials always were divided over whether the peasant rebels or the Manchus constituted the more serious threat to the dynasty's survival. The majority of officials seemed to view the peasant rebels as a more serious threat to the state's short-term survival, a "disease of the heart," to borrow Chiang Kai-shek's famous phrase. While they were undoubtedly more formidable in the conventional military sense, the Manchus seemed more likely to be contained or·accommodated in some fashion, even though they had raided widely in north China since the 1620s.

Whichever threat was deemed greater, the main difficulty confronted by all late Ming military officials was obtaining sufficient provisions and military supplies. Yang Sichang's rosy projections notwithstanding, the devastation wreaked by drought and floods, and the peasant rebellions themselves made it unlikely that sufficient provisions could have been extracted from the affected areas. Yang's forces were consistently undersupplied, by their own accounts generally obtaining only about half the supplies they needed.

These logistical problems were made worse by Yang's lack of military experience and poor evaluation of military talent. Nonetheless, the Ming achieved many local victories against the peasant rebels right up to the end of 1643. When properly led and outfitted, Ming troops almost always bested peasant rebel units. They also proved adept at holding cities and towns. Here, however, lay the strength of the rebel movements themselves: their mobility, as noted by Sun Chuanting, among others. Victory would have required a multilayered suppression strategy that combined offense, defense, and the reclamation of lost agricultural lands to resettle former bandits. Then maybe someone less dogmatic and heavy-handed than Yang might have been able to close the net.

Finally there is the matter of warfare and culture. Even though ancient Chinese culture emphasized the complementary nature of civil and military authority, in practice the pendulum generally swung toward one side or the other. Traditional histories, written by civil officials and their ilk, would have us believe that the civilian side rightly dominated the military, particularly in dynasties such as the Song (960–1279) and the Ming. But the reality was far more complicated. In times of peace and prosperity under vigorous emperors, civil and military officials worked well together. Policies of pacification and suasion, especially with respect to quelling internal unrest, thus had a much better chance of succeeding. For if the state had been able to offer adequate famine relief without raising taxes to pay for other things, it also could have resolved other issues before they became problems.

But times of strife, invasion, and rebellion required a stronger imperial hand, which too often was missing. In these cases, the classic Confucian approach based on suasion and benevolence had much less chance of working. As I have pointed out here, contemporary officials were well aware of this fact. But because men like the classically educated Yang had the ear of the emperor, they were allowed to pursue their policies of pacification and suasion. Their hearts might have been in the right place, but their minds were not. Had they heeded some of the ancient classics' other lessons and had a firmer grasp of military strategy, then perhaps their tragedies, and that of the Ming state, might have been avoided.

The emperor's self-perception bound him to listen to such suggestions. His own deeply embedded sense of propriety and the extent to which his legitimacy rested not only on managing the crisis but also on doing so in a acceptable way pressured him to implement the Yang's plans. Because the Mandate of Heaven could be revoked and the emperor replaced, his position, particularly in this time of crisis, was as precarious, if not more so, as that of men like Yang in the Ming hierarchy. When we understand these realities, we are more likely to sympathize with the position of a supposedly absolute ruler within this imperial bureaucratic structure and see how the culture of the system could sharply influence, if not always dictate, decisions involving the pursuit and prosecution of war.

NOTES

1. Indeed, even some Chinese scholars had decried traditional China as having an "a-military" (*wu bing wenhua*) culture. See, for example, Lei Haizong and Lin Tongqi, *Zhongguo wenhua yu Zhongguo di bing* (Changsha: Yuelu shushu, 1989). For an example of the uncritical acceptance of such characterizations by Western military historians, see Geoffrey Parker, ed., *The Cambridge Illustrated History of Warfare: The Triumph of the West* (Cambridge: Cambridge University Press, 1995). Although there are too many recent monographs to enumerate here, four edited collections are worthy of mention: Hans van de Ven, ed., *Warfare in Chinese History* (Leiden: Brill, 2000); Peter Lorge, ed., *Warfare in China to 1600* (Burlington, VT: Ashgate, 2005); Kenneth Swope, ed., *Warfare in China since 1600* (Burlington, VT: Ashgate 2005); and Nicola Di Cosmo, ed., *Military Culture in Imperial China* (Cambridge, MA: Harvard University Press, 2009). The seminal earlier volume is Frank A. Kierman Jr. and John King Fairbank, eds., *Chinese Ways in Warfare* (Cambridge, MA: Harvard University Press, 1974).

2. For a discussion of the antimilitary bias of Confucian officials, see Di Cosmo, *Military Culture*, 2–3. For a critique of essentialized notions of Chinese martial culture, see Peter Lorge, *War, Politics, and Society in Early Modern China, 900–1795* (London: Routledge, 2005), 1–5.

3. Di Cosmo, *Military Culture*, 4, esp. 3–4 for his definition of military culture.

4. Di Cosmo, *Military Culture*, 5.

5. For Johnston's overview of strategic culture, see Alastair Iain Johnston, *Cultural Realism: Grand Strategy and Strategic Culture in Chinese History* (Princeton, NJ: Princeton University Press, 1995), 1–29; and for his discussion of strategic culture in China in particular, see 61–108.

6. See Johnston, *Cultural Realism*, 248–55, for his discussion of the suitability of this approach for the communist era. The *Seven Military Classics*, which include Sunzi's *Art of War*, have been translated into English. See Ralph D. Sawyer, trans., *The Seven Military Classics of Ancient China* (Boulder, CO: Westview Press, 1993).

7. Lynn A. Struve, *The Southern Ming, 1644–1662* (New Haven, CT: Yale University Press, 1984), 6.

8. Lorge makes this point as well. See Lorge, *War, Politics, and Society*, 177–83.

9. For a detailed study of the imperial civil service examination system in late imperial China, see Benjamin A. Elman, *A Cultural History of Civil Examination in Late Imperial China* (Berkeley: University of California Press, 2000).

10. Of course, the texts are not uniformly pacifist. In a chapter entitled "Benevolence the Foundation," the military text *The Methods of the Sima* notes that "if one must kill men to give peace to the people, then killing is permissible." See Sawyer, *The Seven Military Classics*, 126.

11. On Mencius, see Herrlee G. Creel, *Chinese Thought from Confucius to Mao Tse-tung* (Chicago: University of Chicago Press, 1953), 68–93. For excerpts from the traditional Confucian classics in translation, see William Theodore de Bary et al., eds., *Sources of Chinese Tradition*, vol. 1, 2nd ed. (New York: Columbia University Press, 1999).

12. On the Tang, see David A. Graff, *Medieval Chinese Warfare, 300–900* (London: Routledge, 2002). On the evolution of civilian oversight of the military, see Lorge, *War, Politics, and Society.*

13. An example of this would be the first half of the reign of the Ming Emperor Wanli (r. 1573–1620), who patronized military officials and used them to counteract the power of civil officials and certain factions within his government. See Kenneth M. Swope, "Bestowing the Double-Edged Sword: Wanli as Supreme Commander," in *Culture, Courtiers, and Competition: The Ming Court (1368–1644)*, ed. David M. Robinson (Cambridge, MA: Harvard University Press, 2008), 61–115.

14. I am indebted to the comments of Stephen Morillo on an earlier version of his piece for helping me sharpen these points.

15. For a recent Chinese biography that emphasizes the tragedy of Chongzhen's reign and difficulty of his position, see Zhang Dexin and Tan Tianxing, *Diguo zhongxing de beige: Chongzhen huangdi qi jiang* (Beijing: Zhongguo guangbo dianshe daxue chubanshe, 2009).

16. Zhang Tingyu et al., comps., *Mingshi*, 12 vols. (Taibei: Dingwen shuju, 1994), 6727 (hereafter cited as *MS*). Incidentally, Yang He's biography is not in the same chapter of the *Mingshi* as that of his son.

17. On the origins of the late Ming rebellions in the northwest, see Gu Yingtai, *Mingshi jishi benmo*, in *Lidai jishi benmo*, 2 vols. (Beijing: Zhonghua shuju, 1997), 2448 (hereafter *MSJSBM*); Peng Sunyi, *Liukou zhi* (Hangzhou: Zhejiang renmin chubanshe, 1983), 1–4 (hereafter *LKZ*); Wu Weiye, *Suikou jilue*, 4 vols. (Taibei: Guangwen shuju, 1968), 1.2a–2b (hereafter *SKJL*); and Dai Li and Wu Qiao, *Liukou changbian*, 2 vols. (Beijing: Xinhua shudian, 1991), 29–42 (hereafter *LKCB*). For modern discussions of the outbreak of the uprisings, see James Bunyan Parsons, *Peasant Rebellions of the Late Ming Dynasty* (Ann Arbor, MI: Association for Asian Studies, 1993), 1–21; and Li Guangtao, *Mingji liukou shimo* (Taibei: Zhongyang yanjiuyuan lishi yuyan yanjiusuo, 1965), 1–32 (hereafter *LKSM*). Li also notes that religious sectarians and unemployed miners swelled the ranks of the peasant rebels. For a theoretical study of collective violence in the Ming, see James W. Tong, *Disorder under Heaven: Collective Violence in the Ming Dynasty* (Stanford, CA: Stanford University Press, 1991).

18. Ji Liuqi, *Mingji beilue*, 2 vols. (Beijing: Zhonghua shuju, 1984), 96 (hereafter *MJBL*).

19. See Fan Shuzhi, *Wan Ming shi*, 2 vols. (Shanghai: Fudan daxue chubanshe, 2003), 896–97; and *MSJSBM*, 2448.

20. *SKJL*, 1.7a.

21. On the early rebel leaders, see Fan Shuzhi, *Wan Ming shi*, 897–903; and *SKJL*, 1.5a–5b.

22. Fan Shuzhi, *Wan Ming shi*, 903. On Wanli's delegation of command authority, see Swope, "Bestowing the Double-edged Sword."

23. *LKSM*, 19–20.

24. See Fan Shuzhi, *Wan Ming shi*, 903–4. On Yang He's general policies, see Chenmain Wang, *The Life and Career of Hung Ch'eng-ch'ou (1593–1665): Public Service in a Time*

of Dynastic Change (Ann Arbor, MI: Association for Asian Studies, 1999), 39–48; and Parsons, *Peasant Rebellions,* 8–16.

25. *SKJL,* 1.5b; and *MJBL,* 125–26.

26. Interestingly enough, his son, Yang Sichang, later blamed troop transfers to the northeast for his own problems in quelling the peasant uprisings. There is certainly some merit in these claims, although the Ming should have been able to handle the rebellions in these earlier stages with more disciplined policies. See *LKSM,* 13–14.

27. *LKZ,* 5.

28. Ibid.

29. Ibid.

30. See Fan Shuzhi, *Wan Ming shi,* 905–7. Late Ming and early Qing writers recognized that the peasant rebellions were caused by a complex web of social and economic woes that could not be easily managed or corrected. See the discussion in Fan Shuzhi, *Wan Ming shi,* 907–8.

31. *LKZ,* 6; and *MJBL,* 131.

32. *LKZ,* 6.

33. *SKJL,* 1.8b–9a.

34. *LKZ,* 8; and *MS,* 6728. Yang had actually asked to resign earlier, but his request was rejected by the emperor. See Fan Shuzhi, *Wan Ming shi,* 910–11.

35. *SKJL,* 1.10b.

36. *MS,* 6728.

37. Yang Sichang's official biography can be found in *MS,* 6509–21. Also see L. Carrington Goodrich and Chaoying Fang, eds., *Dictionary of Ming Biography,* 2 vols. (New York: Columbia University Press, 1976), 1538–42 (hereafter *DMB*).

38. *MS,* 6509.

39. *SKJL,* 1.11b.

40. Most upper-level ministerial positions included designations of left and right, directions corresponding to where officials sat during ceremonies and audiences in ancient times. There was little functional distinction in the directions, although the left was generally considered more prestigious.

41. *MS,* 6509. Harry Miller suggests that "opening mines" in the late Ming often was a euphemism for imposing a luxury tax on the wealthy, typically collected by imperial eunuchs. See Harry Miller, *State versus Gentry in Late Ming Dynasty China, 1572–1644* (New York: Palgrave Macmillan, 2009).

42. See Parsons, *Peasant Rebellions,* 54; and Fan Shuzhi, *Wan Ming shi,* 970.

43. For a contemporary assessment of why the emperor trusted Yang, see *SKJL,* 5.10b–11a.

44. For more on Chongzhen's trust of Yang Sichang, see Meng Sen, *Mingshi jiangyi* (Beijing: Zhonghua shuju, 2009), 286–87.

45. Fan Shuzhi, *Wan Ming shi,* 971.

46. *SKJL,* 5.11a.

47. *SKJL,* 6.3a–3b.

48. For a discussion of this practice in the context of late Ming China, see Kenneth M. Swope, "Clearing the Fields and Strengthening the Walls: Defending Small Cities in Late Ming China," in *Secondary Cities and Urban Networking in the Indian Ocean Realm, c.1400–1800,* ed. Kenneth R. Hall (Lanham, MD: Lexington Books, 2008), 123–54.

49. *SKJL*, 6.3b.

50. *MS*, 6510.

51. *MS*, 6510; *MSJSBM*, 2459; and *LKZ*, 47. For biographies of Xiong Wencan, see *DMB*, 562–66; and *MS*, 6733–38. Also see *SKJL*, 6.1a–1b. On Zheng Zhilong, see Arthur O. Hummel, ed., *Eminent Chinese of the Ch'ing Period.* 2 vols. (Washington, DC: Library of Congress, 1943), 110–11 (hereafter *ECCP*).

52. On Zuo, see *ECCP*, 761–62. Yang had actually favored keeping Zuo in power, at least initially, on account of his reputation and prior achievements. On Xiong's appointment, see Fan Shuzhi, *Wan Ming shi*, 978.

53. *SKJL*, 5.17a.

54. *SKJL*, 5.15a–15b.

55. *LKZ*, 47. On the problems caused by increasing taxes in the late Ming, see *LKSM*, 48–49.

56. Fan Shuzhi, *Wan Ming shi*, 974.

57. See *MS*, 6510. For slightly different figures, see Parsons, *Peasant Rebellions,* 56.

58. *MS*, 6510.

59. See Fan Shuzhi, *Wan Ming shi*, 974; and *LKZ*, 47–48.

60. *SKJL*, 5.20a–21a.

61. Sun Chuanting, *Sun Chuanting shudu* (Hangzhou: Zhejiang renmin chubanshe, 1983), 1. Ironically, Sun had been recalled to the west in part because Yang had not gotten along with Hong Chengchou. See *SKJL*, 6.4b.

62. Sun, *Sun Chuanting shudu*, 1–2.

63. Ibid., 2.

64. Ibid., 2–3.

65. Incidentally, the Chinese government of the People's Republic still sometimes employs such methods, known as "striking hard," in cases of corruption and malfeasance.

66. Sun, *Sun Chuanting shudu*, 3.

67. Sun, *Sun Chuanting shudu*, 3–4; and Chen-main Wang, *The Life and Career of Hung Ch'eng-ch'ou*, 68–69.

68. Fan Shuzhi, *Wan Ming shi*, 974–75.

69. Ibid., 975.

70. Ibid., 976.

71. *SKJL*, 6.2b.

72. Parsons, *Peasant Rebellions,* 60–62; Fan Shuzhi, *Wan Ming shi*, 979–80; and *LKZ*, 53. For Zhang's full biography, see *MS*, 7969–77.

73. *SKJL*, 6.6b.

74. See Parsons, *Peasant Rebellions,* 57–58; Fan Shuzhi, *Wan Ming shi*, 978–79; *LKZ*, 53; and *MS*, 6511.

75. *MS*, 6511.

76. *SKJL*, 6.5a.

77. *SKJL*, 6.7b–8a.

78. *MS*, 6512.

79. Ibid.

80. See Fan Shuzhi, *Wan Ming shi*, 980–83.

81. For details about these campaigns, see Fan Shuzhi, *Wan Ming shi*, 983–88.

82. *SKJL*, 6.20a–20b.

83. Fan Shuzhi, *Wan Ming shi*, 991–93.

84. *MS*, 6513. Also see Fan Shuzhi, *Wan Ming shi*, 992–95.

85. See Fan Shuzhi, *Wan Ming shi*, 989–91.

86. See *MS*, 6514–15.

87. *SKJL*, 7.9b.

88. *MS*, 6515; and *SKJL*, 7.10b.

89. *MSJSBM*, 2459. Xiong was executed in the marketplace as soon as he reached the capital. See *MS*, 6738.

90. Fan Shuzhi, *Wan Ming shi*, 1012.

91. *MS*, 6516; and *LKZ*, 57.

92. See Fan Shuzhi, *Wan Ming shi*, 1014–15; and *LKCB*, 728–34.

93. *MS*, 6517.

94. Fan Shuzhi, *Wan Ming shi*, 1015; and *SKJL*, 7.14b–16b.

95. *SKJL*, 7.17a–17b.

96. *LKZ*, 58, 63–64.

97. See *LKSM*, 54–55.

98. Granting the double-edged sword (*bao jian*) was a tradition dating back to antiquity in China. The emperor would present his commanding general with a ceremonial blade symbolizing the complete delegation of command authority in the field to the officer. Ming documents note that this invested such men with the power to "kill first, then memorialize later."

99. *LKZ*, 66; and *MS*, 6517.

100. *SKJL*, 7.20a.

101. *SKJL*, 7.20b.

102. See *MJBL*, 300; and *SKJL*, 7.21a.

103. *MS*, 6718; and *SKJL*, 7.26a.

104. Fan Shuzhi, *Wan Ming shi*, 1020–21; and *SKJL*, 7.20a.

105. *SKJL*, 7.21b.

106. Cited in Fan Shuzhi, *Wan Ming shi*, 1021.

107. *MS*, 6718.

108. *LKZ*, 72.

109. *SKJL*, 7.28b.

110. *MS*, 6520. They also obtained Ming military seals of authority by intercepting this messenger.

111. *LKZ*, 74; *MJBL*, 301; and *SKJL*, 7.29a At around the same time, Li Zicheng butchered and ate the Ming prince of Fu in Luoyang.

112. See *SKJL*, 729a.

113. *MS*, 6521.

114. On Chongzhen's employment and dismissal of officials, see Meng Sen, *Mingshi jiangyi*, 277–79.

115. *SKJL*, 7.30a.

5

The Battle Culture of Forbearance, 1660–1789

JOHN A. LYNN II

The battle of Mollwitz (April 10, 1741) was far from the greatest day in the military life of Frederick the Great (r. 1740–1786). This, his first battle, was a confused affair, at first nearly lost by Prussian cavalry but finally saved by Prussian infantry, masters of that time's drill-oriented tactics.

Four months into the War of the Austrian Succession, Frederick brought to Mollwitz 21,000 troops, 17,000 of whom were infantry. Because the king was a neophyte in combat, he relied heavily on his second in command, Marshal Kurt Christoph Graf von Schwerin (1684–1757). The Austrian army that opposed the Prussians was smaller, 17,000 troops, only 11,000 of them infantry. With their advantage in mounted troops, the Austrians began the action with a cavalry charge that drove Frederick's cavalry off the battlefield and battered his infantry. At this point, Schwerin advised his king to remove himself from danger and leave Schwerin with the infantry to carry on the battle. To his later chagrin, Frederick followed the marshal's advice and rode off in the tracks of his routed cavalry. Schwerin then ordered a general advance of the superb Prussian infantry, which marched forward with its battalions arrayed in line. As an Austrian officer reported, "I can well say, I never in my life saw anything more beautiful. They marched with the greatest steadiness, arrow-straight, and their front like a line, as if they had been upon parade. The glitter of their clear arms shone strangely."[1]

Long years of drill under the strict and, at times, brutal supervision of their officers and sergeants had imbued Prussian infantry with as much perfection in maneuver and fire as was possible. The Prussians did not depend on the private soldier's initiative but on his obedience and precise execution of orders. Supported by their artillery, the Prussians endured enemy cannon and musket fire until close enough to fire, at which point they exchanged volleys with the Austrians, who could not match their rate of fire. Indeed, the Austrian officer testified, with some amazement, "The fire from them went on no otherwise than a continued peal of thunder." The Austrians broke, and "the spirits of our army sank altogether, the foot plainly giving way," suffering 1,500 dead, 3,000 wounded, and 1,000 prisoners and missing. It was a bloody day for the Prussians as well, but they held the field and, thus, the province of Silesia. On this day, tactical performance had not only won the battle; it had essentially won the campaign, although hostilities continued until a truce was agreed to in October.

This chapter attempts to explain why armies, particularly their infantry battalions, fought on the battlefield in the way that they did from the late seventeenth century through the onset of the French Revolution. Although the subject is tactics, my discussion is largely cultural and social. Descriptions of tactical practice often assume that it was simply determined by the weaponry of the day, but that is not my approach here. Physical technology obviously sets parameters; there are good reasons not to shave with an ax. But eighteenth-century weaponry could be used in different ways, and the factors shaping combat went far beyond the physical characteristics of the muskets and cannon that troops brought to the battlefield.

Seventeenth- and eighteenth-century kings and commanders like Frederick the Great crafted a form of combat that fit not only the tools of war but also the social prejudices and cultural predilections of the times. I have labeled the resulting practice, taught by drill and applied on campaign, the *battle culture of forbearance*. While this terminology was not used at the time, it expresses the most basic assumptions about life and war held by the military elites who commanded troops in combat, as at Mollwitz.

The Technological Challenge: Musket and Cannon in Battle

The gunpowder weapons carried by infantry evolved between 1660 and 1789, although their basic range and accuracy remained essentially the same. At the start of the period, the most common shoulder-fired gunpowder weapon was the muzzle-loading, smoothbore matchlock musket. This weapon used a match to ignite the gunpowder through a mechanism, or lock, that ignited the powder charge when the trigger was pulled. The match was a cord of flax or hemp soaked in a nitrate solution so that it would continue to glow at its ends, much like a modern cigarette. This match had to be removed for loading lest it set off the gunpowder prematurely, but it was reattached on the lock to a lever, or cock, for firing. When the soldier pulled the trigger, the cock snapped down, thrusting the glowing match into a small pan of priming powder mounted on the weapon's barrel. When this priming charge exploded, it flashed though the touch hole, a small hole bored into the chamber of the barrel, and set off the main charge that then propelled the lead ball toward its mark. The matchlock's complicated loading procedure limited the rate of fire to, at best, one shot per minute, and even then, the rate of misfire could be as high as 50 percent.[2] To supplement this slow-firing weapon—in particular to protect the infantrymen from charging cavalry—some of the soldiers carried pikes, spears as much as sixteen feet long, instead of muskets. Pikemen formed a foreboding, bristling barrier of spear points by bracing their pikes with the butts thrust into the ground and slanted them forward at a deadly angle to skewer man or horse.

By 1700, however, European armies had exchanged their matchlocks for flintlocks. These smoothbore weapons had the same ballistic characteristics as matchlock muskets but were fired by means of a flintlock, a mechanism that struck a piece of flint against an iron "frizzen" to create sparks that ignited the gunpowder in the priming pan. Flintlock muskets were much safer and more dependable than matchlocks and required less time to load, which doubled the rate of fire.[3] The pikes also disappeared when the French introduced an effective bayonet, which was attached to the barrel of the musket by means of a socket so that it did not interfere with loading and firing the musket. Now the infantryman carried a single weapon that served as both firearm and edged weapon. By the late seventeenth century, the adoption of the bayonet also enabled entire battalions to charge with cold steel.

But even effective smoothbore musket fire had only a limited range; that is, the ball was accurate and powerful enough only to do damage at short distances. The Prussians carried out the best contemporary scientific study of musket fire, establishing that an infantry battalion firing late eighteenth-century Prussian flintlock muskets at a huge target (100 feet long and 6 feet high, simulating part of a deployed enemy infantry line), hit the target with only about 30 percent of its fire at 160 yards. Their muskets performed better at 80 yards but still put only 50 percent of their shots on target. Firing at a man-sized target, the same musket scored hits with only 20 percent of its shots. The French model 1777 Charleville musket scored better, hitting the large target about 50 percent of the time at 160 yards and 75 percent at 80 yards.[4] The inaccuracy of these smoothbore weapons was implicit in the technology.

From 1660 to 1789, artillery improved and also increased in number, but its ballistic characteristics remained relatively constant. Like the shoulder arms, cannon were muzzle loaders. Although cannon were cast in different sizes, one of those commonly used on the battlefield was the eight pounder, which meant that the spherical iron ball it shot weighed eight pounds. The barrel of such an artillery piece weighed 2,250 pounds in the French Vallière system, adopted in 1732. Because the weight of an artillery piece limited its mobility, artillery reformers of the late eighteenth century worked to lighten cannon by casting them with shorter barrels. Thus, an eight pounder in the improved Gribeauval system of 1776 mounted a barrel that weighed only 1,275 pounds.[5] Such cannon had an effective range of as much as 800 yards on the battlefield and could mow down infantry with canister shot at 400 to 500 yards.[6] Along with lighter barrels, artillery reforms in Austria, Prussia, and France improved artillery carriages and harnessing to make them more agile, although it still required many horses to haul the guns and their ammunition caissons. A Gribeauval eight pounder was pulled by four horses in the field artillery and was supported with two ammunition caissons, each of which required two additional horses.[7]

The eighteenth century witnessed a marked increase in the number of cannon brought to the battlefield. During the late seventeenth- and early eighteenth-century, the number of artillery pieces with a field army equaled about one gun for every 1,000 men. Pierre Surirey de Saint-Rémy (1645–1716), an authority on artillery, advised fifty cannon for an army of 50,000 men (one per 1,000).[8] Marshal Claude Louis Hector de Villars (1653–1734) had sixty guns for a force of 80,000 at Malplaquet in 1709 (0.75 per 1,000). But the wars of midcentury saw larger numbers of cannon employed; Frederick the Great brought 170 guns for 39,000 troops at Leuthen in 1757 (4.35 per 1,000), and his opponents boasted 210 artillery pieces for 80,000 troops (2.65 per 1,000). Artillery improvements and multiplication amounted to the most important change in military technology between the advent of the flintlock musket and the French Revolution.

The Tactical Answer: A Battle Culture of Forbearance

The tactics used in this technological environment had to take account of the range, firing rate, and lethal effect of the weapons on the battlefield. The characteristic battle formation for infantry was the line, which became more uniform in composition and organization with the adoption of the flintlock musket and bayonet. Such a line of infantrymen stood in four, three, or, eventually, two ranks to maximize the firepower of a battalion armed with these relatively inaccurate and slow-firing muskets. By marshaling so many muskets firing forward, infantry could inflict serious damage, even with the musket's shortcomings. The line also allowed officers and sergeants to observe and closely control the men under their command, which was an essential advantage of such a stand-up formation. In order for the line to fight effectively, the musketeers had to be correctly aligned with one another, although not necessarily as "arrow straight" as the Prussians at Mollwitz. This alignment was not simply for appearance but protected the men from being injured by their comrades. The touch hole through which the flash of the priming powder ignited the main charge became a channel through which part of that major explosion exited. Therefore, when firing, a man standing to the right of another and a bit too far forward in his stance risked danger to his eye or ear from the blowback though the touch hole of his comrade's musket.

Terrain and situation determined how close armies would deploy into battle against each other. There was no general rule, but it was best to avoid deploying so near the enemy that its artillery fire could immediately ravage the line. But because artillery did not bring an infinite amount of ammunition to the battlefield, commanders withheld their cannon fire until their guns could have greatest effect on the adversary. If ordered to attack, the troops would experience an intense version of hell as they advanced. Assuming that this line of infantry began its attack a quarter mile from its adversary, it would require at least fifteen minutes to traverse this distance at a march pace, rather than at a run, to conserve their energy and maintain their order.[9] During its advance, the infantry would be subject to an increasingly deadly barrage of artillery fire and, ultimately, infantry volleys. If the attacking line chose to stop and fire, it would generally do so at a range of less than one hundred yards. During the remainder of the march forward, the men simply had to absorb the punishment and keep advancing without responding.

Unless troops were particularly adept at delivering crushing volleys of fire, as were the Prussians, most military thinkers deemed it best to attack without stopping to fire. In fact, even Frederick came to believe that troops should maintain their momentum and not halt to discharge their muskets. Ideally, "the infantry will advance rapidly but in order. I do not want it to fire. Its menace will defeat the enemy."[10] Charging without stopping to fire was a well-recognized method of attack. The accomplished French Marshal Nicolas Catinat (1637–1712) reported that at the battle of Marsaglia, on October 3, 1693, his infantry charged the enemy "with bayonets on the ends of their fusils and without firing a shot."[11] This commander explained his logic by arguing that by continuing the advance without firing, even after the enemy had fired, the attacker gained a psychological advantage. "One prepares the soldier to not fire and to realize that it is necessary to suffer the enemy's fire, expecting that the enemy who fires is assuredly beaten when one receives his entire fire."[12]

Even if a soldier did fire in the attack, the nearly universal advice was never to fire first. In a memoir dedicated to the young Louis XIV in 1663, the experienced soldier d'Aurignac advised generals that he who fired first was lost and that above all, generals must "command both cavalry and infantry when approaching the enemy to fire only after the enemy had fired first."[13] Similar advice to delay one's fire until the last moment applied to defending infantry as well. Given the inaccuracy of the musket, he who fired last, meaning closest, scored the most devastating hits. The great French military engineer Sébastien le Prestre de Vauban (1633–1707) put it succinctly: "Usually, in man to man combat the advantage lies with those who fire last."[14] Thus followed the common defensive maxim that troops should hold fire until the enemy was at extremely close range: "Don't fire until you see the whites of their eyes." Americans are most likely to associate this particular command with the Battle of Bunker Hill, but it had a long lineage before that, stretching back at least to the battle of Dettingen in 1743.[15]

Because infantry had to endure crossing the deadly, artillery-swept no-man's-land without seeking cover or firing back, artillery was the primary technological determinant of the need for forbearance. When Frederick the Great insisted that the common soldier should fear his officer more than the enemy, he explained this by pointing out, "Otherwise no one would be able to lead him in the attack as three hundred cannon thunder against him. In such danger, the goodwill of the soldier does not prevail; one must rely on fear."[16] Cannon fire not only killed and maimed; it also terrified soldiers because it inflicted such catastrophic wounds, smashing and tearing bodies.

The battle culture of forbearance emphasized not so much inflicting casualties as demonstrating that one could absorb enemy fire and continue to fight and advance without breaking or flinching. As the great French monarch Louis XIV (r. 1643–1715), explained, "Good order makes us look assured, and it seems enough to look brave because most often our enemies do not wait for us to approach near enough for us to have to show whether we are in fact brave."[17] An orderly advance under the gaze of the enemy was equated with victory; the attacker must appear to be unshakable. This emphasis on taking losses with a stoic, hit-me-with-your-best-shot mentality may seem counterinstinctual, but it was regarded as the best way to come to grips with the enemy and overthrow him psychologically. The surprising truth is that seventeenth- and eighteenth-century Europe developed a battle culture based less on fury than on forbearance.

Battle Avoidance

Forbearance demanded a willingness to pay a heavy cost in casualties as an essential preliminary to victory. Moreover, even though forbearance guaranteed that battles would be bloody, it could not guarantee that they would be decisive. During the Nine Years' War, Louis XIV explicitly ordered his finest commander, Marshal François-Henri de Montmorency, duc de Luxembourg (1628–1695), to engage in maneuvers and skirmishes and avoid pitched battle: "Make use of my cavalry rather than engaging yourself in an infantry battle, which causes the loss of a lot of men but which never decides anything."[18] In fact, the *ancien régime* provides few examples of battles that ended major wars. The presence of numerous fortified towns and the dependence on cumbersome logistics made it difficult to turn a victory into decisive military or political success. Wars tended to drag on until exhaustion settled the matter.

Given the sure cost, great risk, and risky nature of battle, Enlightenment pundits advised against it and sought alternatives. The tendency of rulers and generals to eschew battle expressed a characteristic of the age: a reluctance to accept chance and a preference for the predictable, attitudes that perfectly reflected Enlightenment concepts of reason and control. War by rules and principles disdained chaos. This was linear in the mathematical sense, since military action should produce an expected and knowable result. The impressive Marshal Maurice de Saxe (1696–1750) claimed that "war can be made without leaving anything to chance. And this is the highest point of perfection and skill in a general." He also counseled, "I do not favor pitched battles, especially at the beginning of a war, and I am convinced that a skillful general could make war all his life without being forced into one."[19] Dietrich Heinrich Freiherr von Bülow (1757–1807), repeated this sentiment: "It is always possible to avoid a battle."[20] Frederick the Great may have written early in his career that "war is decided only by battles, and it is not finished except by them."[21] But he also had more conventional opinions about combat: "Most generals in love with battle resort to this expedient for want of other resources."[22]

Seen in this light, it is not surprising that siege warfare was so important during this time. It promised a better return on the investment in money and blood. It was scientific and sure; Vauban's system of conducting sieges promised success by a calculated timetable. This scientific predictability, in addition to the regular geometry of fortress construction and siege lines, also harmonized with contemporary Enlightenment tastes.

The Vile Common Soldier

Up to this point, our analysis has combined a traditional emphasis on technology with a sense of Enlightenment culture, but there is more to consider. The battle culture of forbearance also grew out of a disparaging view of the common soldiers in the ranks as untrustworthy individuals devoid of honor and best controlled with fear. In 1747, just a few years after he was saved by the solid performance of his infantrymen at Mollwitz, Frederick the Great explained that his army was "composed for the most part of idle and inactive men."[23] This perception that soldiers were of low character was not simply a Prussian conclusion but was typical of the reigning international military culture. The Enlightenment philosopher, or *philosophe*, Louis de Jaucourt (1704–1779), writing in 1751, argued that "soldiers in the countries of Europe are truly . . . the most vile portion of the subjects of the nation."[24] The French general and renowned military reformer Jacques Antoine Hippolyte, comte de Guibert (1743–1790), wrote in 1772 that in Europe, the soldier's profession was "abandoned to the most vile and miserable class of citizens."[25] Claude Louis, comte de Saint-Germain (1707–1778), who served as the French minister of war from 1775 to 1777, dismissed his own rank and file as "the slime [*la bourbe*] of the nation and all that is useless to society."[26]

Such opinions, while certainly dominant, were not universal. Some officers recognized that either their soldiers were better men than the stereotype allowed or that the rank and file had the potential to be transformed into admirable citizens. These more positive sentiments were more likely to be expressed during the last decades of eighteenth century than earlier, as Julia Osman observed.[27] Nevertheless, seemingly more generous opinions might voice a paternalism that simply replaced condemnation with condescension. Benjamin Rush, a signer of the Declaration of Independence, reported a conversation with a British officer in America: "One of their officers, a subaltern, observed to me that his soldiers were infants that required constant attention."[28]

Given the general belief that soldiers came from the lowest elements of society, military leaders crafted a discipline based primarily on fear, designed to achieve obedience in the midst of the duress and danger of battle. In his *Military Testament* (1768), Frederick the Great famously advised, "And because officers must lead their soldiers into the greatest dangers, and the rank and file cannot be inspired by ambition, the common soldier must fear his officer more than the dangers to which he is exposed."[29] Convinced that French soldiers were "the slime of the nation," Saint-German argued, "We must turn to military discipline as the means of purifying this corrupt mass, of shaping it and making it useful."[30] During the Enlightenment, harsh views were shared not only by military officers but also by men of letters. The *philosophe* Claude Adrien Helvétius (1715–1771) commented in his *De l'esprit* (1758) that "discipline is, in a manner, nothing else but the art of inspiring soldiers with a greater fear of their officers than of the enemy."[31] The very English Edward Gibbon praised the Romans by reporting that "it was an inflexible maxim of Roman discipline, that a good soldier should dread his officers far more than the enemy."[32] With men who could not be expected to do their duty unless ordered to do so, discipline, always important, was paramount. As Maurice de Saxe testified, discipline "is the soul of all armies."[33] Even Joseph Marie Servan de Gerbey (1741–1808), a French military officer and reformer who advocated a citizen army, lamented that "our discipline is only to inspire in the soldiers more fear of their officers than of their enemy."[34]

In order for troops to be controlled by fear, they had to be constantly supervised by their officers. Frederick the Great explained his reluctance to trust his soldiers in night attacks because "the major part of the soldiery require the eye of their officers, and the fear of punishments, to induce them to do their duty."[35] This need for watchfulness began at the top. "Unless the general has a constant eye upon them and obliges them to do their duty, this artificial machine, which with greatest care cannot be made perfect, will very soon fall to pieces."[36]

The infantry battle line made a good deal of sense in technological terms when the goal was to mass fire forward. But it made even more sense as a formation that allowed officers and sergeants to closely observe and strictly control the men under their command. Sergeants usually stood in the rear, not the front, as a threat to those men who might panic in battle. The line was not simply a technological convenience but a perceived command necessity.

Not surprisingly, desertion was a major concern for commanders who led such troops. Not only were soldiers less than trustworthy, but the rigid discipline believed necessary to control them gave them an added incentive to desert. During the War of the Spanish Succession (1701–1714), the French secretary of war, Michel Chamillart (1652–1721), exhorted one of his agents in the field to increase his diligence because "I know that desertion is great everywhere and it is a major evil and that after so many efforts and infinite care, one can count on nothing for certain!"[37] Desertion rates varied from army to army, regiment to regiment, and peacetime to wartime. Historian André Corvisier's calculations put the desertion rate for the entire French army between 1716 and 1749 at nearly 23 percent. In the Vivarais regiment, for example, the average desertion rate was twice as high during wartime as during peacetime.[38] The Russians, who were particularly hard on their men, are supposed to have lost twenty thousand soldiers to desertion in 1732 alone.[39] Military textbooks often charge the Prussians with very high desertion rates as well, but more recent scholarship argues that desertion rates were fairly low for the Prussians, at least in peacetime. Between 1713 and 1739, the rate averaged only 1.9 percent.[40] And yet Frederick was constantly concerned with stopping desertion. His instructions to his generals state that "one of the most essential duties of a general officer . . . is to prevent desertion." This is followed by a list of fourteen principles to follow, such as not camping close to woods—lest the soldiers disappear into the trees—and not marching at night—because deserters can use the dark for cover.[41]

At one point, Frederick hit on something profound when he contrasted three sources of military motivation: fear, reward, and honor. "For the officer, honor is reserved. . . . Nothing therefore must incite the officer but honor, which carries its own recompense; but the soldier is driven and restrained and educated to discipline by reward and fear."[42] Modern social science talks of behavior in terms of compliance: ways in which individuals are induced to "comply" with the demands of military authority.[43]

In an immediate sense, enduring the discomfort, suffering, and danger of a military campaign is hardly an obvious choice. Better to avoid the risks. Something, therefore, had to be put on the other side of the balance to tip the scale in the right direction. Historically, this was physical coercion, material reward, or symbolic reward, termed *coercive compliance, remunerative compliance*, and *normative compliance*. *Coercion* compels compliance by force and fear. The soldier obeys because he has no choice or because disobedience guarantees a sure and severe punishment. *Remuneration* is held out as a benefit that compensates the soldier for his effort and risk. This could be the hope of plunder gained from the defeated, a cash reward, or, as in medieval Europe, the bargain of land and labor in exchange for military service. *Normative compliance* is the most complex. Here the rewards are not material but psychological: praise, respect, or a sense that one has done the right thing. This last turns out to be the most effective, but it requires the soldier to identify with the state, the military, and/or his unit; he must see his efforts as measured by something greater than his own immediate interest. Because the so-called vile slime and scum who made up the rank and file were presumed to be incapable of such lofty sentiments, officers believed that they had to convince them to perform their duties by means of the stick of physical coercion and the carrot of material reward. Honor as a standard of normative compliance was reserved for a higher-minded sort of human being—the aristocratic officer—who was compelled by the standards set by his social class.

Social Prejudice: Honor as an Aristocratic Monopoly

To grant aristocrats a nearly exclusive monopoly on honor was more than simply a compliment; it was a defense of noble prestige, privilege, and power. As the social class uniquely qualified to provide the army's officer corps and to command the common soldiers who could not function properly without its direction, the aristocracy deserved its special status. Its own social prejudices simultaneously justified and reinforced their social privilege. Consequently, aristocrats' class attitudes shaped military culture and, ultimately, tactical practice.

The privileges enjoyed by continental European aristocratic elites included land, wealth, and political and social preeminence. Among their specific advantages, aristocrats enjoyed tax breaks, including outright exemptions, and dominance over political and military offices. Although such privileges varied considerably from place to place and evolved over time, they were important both materially and symbolically. In general, birth determined aristocratic status, although it was possible, as in France, to purchase government positions that accorded noble status to the individual and his descendants. In England, the highest nobles were known as peers, and there were relatively few of them. However, the wealthy and influential landed gentry served as a meeting ground for families of old lineage and the rising new rich. Even though the French nobility was larger and more inclusive than the British peerage, it still amounted to only about 1 percent of the French population.

The roots of the military aristocracy extended back to the Middle Ages. Although medieval armies contained large numbers of commoners, particular as foot soldiers, the more elite, heavily armed cavalry included landholders and their retinues, men we usually call *knights*, who were culturally elevated as the paragon warriors of their day. They served monarchs and great lords as fighters in expectation of rewards—usually confirmation of or increases in their lands and their authority over the peasants who worked the soil—and so the military aristocracy increasingly became ideologically, economically, and socially ensconced as a privileged class.

With the waning of the Middle Ages, aristocrats evolved from individualistic fighting knights to officers who served their rulers by leading troops composed of lower-class combatants. Military service nevertheless remained the fundamental justification for the privileges and powers that aristocrats enjoyed. Defending their tax privileges, French nobles pointed to the fact that they paid an *impôt de sang*, a tax in blood. Thus both interest and self-image led the nobility to clamor for military service. In the sixteenth century, the aristocratic philosopher Michel de Montaigne (1533–1592) wrote, "The proper, sole and essential life for one of the nobility of France is the life of a soldier."[44] Young French nobles rushed for commissions at the start of each war. One military commissioner wrote to the minister of war during the Dutch War (1672–1678) that it was "a marvel to see the quantity of people of high birth and others . . . who are eager to have employment [as officers]."[45]

Aristocrats saw themselves fundamentally as the repositories of military talents and sacrifice. The Prussian King Frederick William I (r. 1713–1740) required the sons of his aristocracy to man his officer corps, and they came to see it as their natural place. The Prussian monarchy rewarded those who served with status and gave them preference for posts. The nobilities of other states also desired military service as their proper role and one that instilled glory. In 1784, an aristocratic observer said of the Piedmontese aristocracy, "A predilection for the military life was the dominant passion among the young nobles."[46]

Aristocratic culture, and therefore the military culture that was shaped as a reflection of aristocrats' prejudices, defined men in the ranks as "vile" inferior souls who could see no further than their own short-term benefit, who lacked higher standards, and thus who could be moved only by physical punishment and material reward. They may have composed the vast majority of the army, but they had little military value without their aristocratic officers to supervise, control, and lead them. So even if men of noble and privileged birth did not constitute the entire army, its entire worth depended on them. To concede that the troops themselves might be worthy men—and thus potent on the battlefield without constant direction—would be to question the right of the aristocracy to its high social status and the rewards that flowed from it.

The historian Yuval Harari advanced another idea that stresses the officers' demand for control over the men in the ranks. He believes that consciously or unconsciously, the educated aristocratic officer regarded his relationship with the common soldier in the context of the mind/body split implicit in contemporary philosophy, as exemplified by René Descartes (1596–1650). Mind and body were two dimensions of human existence, related but distinct and often pulling in different directions. Admirable individuals imposed the superiority of the mind over the body, which Harari sees as a metaphor for the relationship between officer and common soldier: "Whereas the common soldiers were increasingly seen as automatons, and were taught to identify with the body, officers . . . were taught to identify with their minds, and to conceive their entire being in the army as that of 'minds.'"[47] Interestingly, when British officers were removed from their men while held as prisoners of war in 1781, one officer described it as "the separation of soul and body."[48]

Harari here brings the high culture of philosophy to bear on the military culture of the age. This should not come as a surprise because military thought regularly displays the imprint of the intellectual climate in which it arises. The military reforms of the late sixteenth and early seventeenth centuries can be seen as a kind of military Renaissance in that they consciously revived elements of classical Roman practice, and unquestionably the Enlightenment affected military thought. So Harari's conclusion is not at all far-fetched: "War in the early modern period was the supreme model for the victory of mind over body."[49]

Drill: Making the Body Obey the Mind

Unreliable troops were trained to submit to the will of honorable officers through drill, which could be said to be the way in which the mind of the officer exerted dominance over the body of the soldier. Drill became absolutely integral to battle culture during the seventeenth century—what the scholar Michael Roberts terms "the revolution in drill."[50] No French monarch surpassed Louis XIV's intense interest in drill. He was convinced that "many more battles are won by good march order and by good bearing than by sword blows and musketry. . . . This habit of marching well and of keeping order can only be acquired by drill."[51] Here again, he repeated the theme that the maintenance of disciplined order alone, rather than bloody combat, wins battles.

Not surprisingly, this was the age in which drill regulations came into their own. In the past, men acquired weapons skills through individual instruction and personal application and learned to be competent in group tactics through practice with their comrades. What modern drill did was to synchronize movements among soldiers by defining those movements in the precise form and sequence to be performed on command and then by compelling troops to follow them exactly by constant, supervised repetition— what Wayne Lee identified as *collective synchronized discipline*.[52] Punishment threatened those who did not make their bodies conform to command. This required a master plan of movements from individual loading and firing to company, battalion, and regimental maneuvers. A critical step along this path was the publication in 1607 of *Wapenhandlinghe van Roers, Musquetten ende Spiesson* by Jacob de Gheyn (1565–1629). This manual broke down the handling of matchlock firearms and pikes into a series of exact positions, which were illustrated by engravings. For example, de Gheyn illustrated forty-three positions for loading and firing the matchlock musket.

Drill manuals available to officers expanded to include the deployment of military units in battle. Initially, individual commanders followed their own preferences in drill. But even though not all regiments drilled exactly alike, they all drilled, and the tendency was toward increasing regularity. The first decades of the eighteenth century seem to have been central to the process of establishing obligatory, government-prescribed regulations that standardized the manual of arms and company and battalion drill; Prussian drill took form during the reign of Frederick William I. New regulations in 1753 and 1754 established armywide standards for the French. The 1754 regulation, for instance, was the first French ordinance to stipulate explicitly that troops were to march together in step.[53]

Military commanders were required to drill their men frequently. Beginning in the 1660s, Louis XIV ordered individuals to maintain their personal skills, companies to drill at least twice a week, and entire garrisons to drill weekly. During summer, training camps were required for entire field armies. At a camp near Bouquenon on the Sarre, established in the summer of 1683, Louis visited his troops. The infantry drilled within their companies from 5 to 10 a.m. and then maneuvered by battalion or brigade 4 to 7 p.m. Once a week the entire assemblage of twenty-four battalions of infantry maneuvered as a whole.[54] The camp held near Compiègne in 1698 included 53 infantry battalions and 152 cavalry squadrons with 40 cannon.[55] The camp lasted two weeks and involved not only drills but also a mock battle, an attack on entrenchments, and practice at escorting convoys. Prussian military exercises became famous during the eighteenth century, somewhat to the amusement of Frederick the Great, who seemed entertained by the way in which visiting foreign officers observing the exercises hoped to unravel the key to his victories. His field exercises also were very large, involving 44,000 troops in 1753.[56]

Drill was, of course, a way of regulating the handling of weapons in combat, but it was ultimately about conquering the men in the ranks by substituting routine for initiative. It was intended to make the private soldiers' obedience an instrument for their officers' honor.

Social Reality: Worthy Men in the Ranks

The battle culture of forbearance may have been built on assumptions concerning the nature of the men in the ranks, but were those assumptions justified? Were common soldiers, by and large, men devoid of honor and initiative, incapable of fulfilling their duty if not closely supervised and directed? If not, then the battle culture of forbearance stands as a cultural construction that reduced military effectiveness in order to protect the privileges of the elites.

Social studies by scholars such as André Corvisier, Sylvia Frey, Matthew Spring, Edward Coss, and Sabina Loriga tell a tale that differs significantly from the stereotypes embraced during the eighteenth century.[57] The myth has it that the common soldier was likely to be a man with little substance and, perhaps, a criminal past. The best research indicates, however, that eighteenth-century recruits were most likely to be castoffs of the economic system rather than outcasts from society.

In France, recruits entered service by three different routes. Peasant lads, particularly younger sons with little chance for land or employment, might sign on to serve under a local noble in what André Corvisier calls "seigneurial recruitment." This willing recruitment of solid peasant youth supplied much of a regiment's needs in peacetime. Recruiting parties scoured the towns for additional manpower, which was particularly important in wartime. When demand was high, these parties used liquor, trickery, and women to entice enlistment and, when all else failed, turned to coercion. Still, their primary targets were men down on their luck, not ne'er-do-wells. Finally, during the eighteenth century, France, as did other continental European states, instituted a form of limited conscription to create the provincial *milice*, or militia, to flesh out the army in time of war. Recruits were chosen for the *milice* by lot, *tirage au sort*, at local gatherings. This was not slanted toward undesirables but took away sons from good peasant families. Consequently, the rural population resented the *milice*, as one government minister reported, because "each *tirage* was the signal for the greatest disorders in the countryside."[58]

As an example of a soldier brought in by recruiting parties, consider Claude Le Roy. He was born in 1767 in the village of Talmay but could not remain there owing to the lack of economic opportunities.[59] Being adventurous, he spent with an uncle some years at sea as a cabin boy, but when he returned to his village, it still offered only a hardscrabble existence. He learned the trade of hatmaking from a local hatter and went to Paris to try to get a job, but this was a naïve idea, since he knew how to make only country hats and the Parisian guild blocked him from gaining employment. He was down to his last coins when he and a friend who had come to Paris with him heard the drums of a recruitment party, and they signed up in 1784. Claude served throughout the wars of the French Revolution and Napoleon, eventually reaching the rank of major.

Prussian service relied on foreign recruits, native volunteers, and conscripted peasants. An unusually high percentage of foreigners entered Prussian service, and in the mid-1750s they constituted about half the army.[60] Voluntary enlistments by native Prussians added more men, but not nearly enough, so starting in 1733 the Prussians instituted a very effective form of compulsory service, the canton system. Young men from the countryside were chosen by lot to shoulder the musket as part-time soldiers in regular regiments associated with their local areas, or cantons. After training, they returned home to carry on relatively normal civil lives for ten months of the year in peacetime, and during the other two summer months, they returned to drill with their regiments. Frederick encouraged such men to raise families "so as to populate the country, and to preserve the stock, which is admirable": the soldier as breeding stock.[61] The canton system maximized agricultural production and army size at minimum cost, since the cantonists were not paid during their ten months at home. During the eighteenth century, other German states, including Wurttemberg and Hesse-Kassel, adopted versions of the canton system.[62]

English volunteer recruitment also netted a better quality of recruit than the oft-repeated stereotypes would have us believe. It is true that British laws allowed local authorities to conscript men who were a burden on the community. The 1778 press law—that is, the law decreeing the impressment, or conscription, of men—targeted "all able bodied loose idle and disorderly persons, vagrants," which included "all persons convicted by due course of law of cheating deceiving and imposing upon their employers."[63] But even though this law netted men, they were regarded as particularly untrustworthy and liable to desert the army, so they were sent off to outposts, such as the West Indies, where desertion was difficult.[64] Studies by both Sylvia Frey, on the American Revolution, and Edward Coss, on the later conflict in Spain against the Napoleonic French, argue that pressed men were not sent to the primary war fronts. These scholars dismiss the idea that the British soldier was "the scum of the earth," as the duke of Wellington would call the men he commanded against Napoleon.[65] Rather, they had more in common with Claude Le Roy: solid men compelled by economic hard times to enlist.

Social reality, therefore, did not match the cultural perception held by the aristocracy, and there also is very good reason to question the aristocratic prejudice that there was no honor among common soldiers. In fact, there is every reason to believe that common soldiers adhered to their own codes of honor. The most prevalent reference group for establishing and enforcing soldiers' codes was the small group of comrades who shared life and its discomforts and dangers. In the French army, this was the mess group, or *ordinaire*. In other armies, this might be a similar mess group or squad. Modern military sociology labels this the *primary group*, but it can be humanized as the "band of brothers" so commonly found in armies throughout the ages. Many volumes have been written on primary group cohesion in modern armed forces, and the concept can also be usefully applied to earlier eras, such as the eighteenth century.[66]

In a historical paradox, drill—which was a reaction to a belief that soldiers had no honor—may have fostered stronger bonds between the rank and file, bonds that inspired honorable conduct among them. Historian William H. McNeill argues that rhythmical moving together in drill creates a kind of "muscular bonding" as the body affects the mind. "Prolonged drill allowed soldiers, recruited from the fringes of an increasingly commercialized society . . . to create a new, artificial primary community among themselves. . . . Men who had little else to be proud of could share an esprit de corps with their fellows and glory in their collective sufferings and prowess."[67] While Frederick the Great clearly regarded honor as a superior motivation that inspired his officers alone, he recognized that the rank and file could be moved by esprit de corps, and he welcomed its utility: "All you can do with the soldier, is to give him esprit de corps, that is a higher opinion of his regiment than of all the other troops in the world."[68] Pride in the unit set a code of behavior. One gravely wounded French sergeant made light of his wounds with the remark, "It is nothing; the regiment has shown itself well."[69]

A soldier group's elements of honor differed from the standards held by their officers. For example, it is unlikely that soldiers fought over the status of their family. But the troops surely enforced codes of bravery and responsibility among themselves. Even Frederick the Great stated in his instructions to his generals: "Besides this, the soldiers will not suffer a man to remain amongst them who has betrayed any symptoms of shyness."[70] The scholar André Corvisier found that French soldiers "often forced their officers to expel a man for 'low' behavior, perhaps for having mistreated a comrade or for having given a bad impression of the military valor of the corps."[71] A British officer serving in America issued instructions to his officers in 1780 stressing responsibility born of comradeship in the ranks: "The man who at any time behaves unfaithfully by his comrade must be despised, and he who abandon[s] his friend in danger [must] become infamous."[72]

As a parallel to the frequent dueling among their honor-conscious officers, common soldiers tested the manliness of new recruits by forcing them to fight in a kind of blood rite of passage. French soldiers reported clandestine duels of this kind in the mid-eighteenth century, when sometimes the weapon used was a bayonet.[73] Noted historian Jean Chagniot concluded that "combat with edged weapons was in effect a kind of rite of initiation for the recruit, and he dare not hide from it under penalty of being discredited."[74]

Reform?

Despite evidence to the contrary, aristocratic officers were not disposed to accept that while many rogues may have found refuge in the army, the men in the ranks often were solid men with their own sense of honor. Such men might have been trained to bring out qualities other than rigid obedience and to fight in other ways than the rigid linear warfare that dominated in Europe. But while reformers glimpsed some possibilities during the second half of the eighteenth century, particularly when experimenting with light infantry, ultimately there is no reason to believe that European military elites had any intention of tearing down the social divide between honorable aristocratic officers and a denigrated rank and file.

The second half of the eighteenth century brought some reforms that raised the professional level of the aristocratic officer corps, supplied better technology (particularly artillery), and carried out some tactical experiments (particularly with light infantry). These reforms, however, did not fundamentally alter the social, cultural, and tactical assumptions that formed the basis of European warfare. In France, military reform even moved in the opposite direction when the Ségur Law of 1781 further restricted the officer corps to the old noble families. Under this law, commissions were essentially reserved only for those men who could prove four generations of noble descent. The door to the officer corps had never been wide open to those without a noble pedigree, but some men from the middle class or from very recently ennobled families had found a place there. This law subsequently closed the door and locked it.

Necessity or Choice? Social Revolution and Tactical Innovation

The development of new tactics and a new military culture as a result of the French Revolution provides a test for the facts, findings, and speculations advanced thus far in this chapter. Given the relative stability in weapons technology from the late reign of Louis XIV through the Napoleonic wars, whatever fundamental changes in battlefield tactics affected Europe after 1789 cannot be ascribed to technological innovation but, instead, to alterations in other foundations of the battle culture of forbearance.

The tumultuous events of 1789 in Paris changed the French from subjects into citizens and soldiers from vile to virtuous. The Declaration of the Rights of Man and Citizen passed by the new National Assembly in August declared equal political and civil rights for all, ending the special status and privileges of the aristocracy. Soldiers, once feared as instruments of an old and oppressive government, were now redefined as defenders of a new and liberating regime. Only days after the fall of the Bastille on July 14, the journalist Camille Desmoulins (1760–1794) declared, "Brave soldiers, mingle with your brothers, receive their embraces. You are no longer the satellites of the despot, the jailors of your brothers. You are our friends, our fellows, citizens, and soldiers of the Patrie."[75] There was more than a little wishful thinking in these words, since the revolutionaries rightly feared that the king might still turn his troops against the people. In the name of defending itself against this possible threat, the city of Paris, followed almost immediately by other cities and towns, quickly created its own citizen militia, the National Guard. The soldier and politician Edmond Louis Alexis Dubois-Crancé (1747–1815) thus could claim with more authority in December 1789: "Is it not an honor to be a soldier, when this title is that of defender of the Constitution of his country?"[76]

War broke out in the spring of 1792, and regiments of the old royal army and battalions of the new National Guard marched off to the frontiers. On August 10, crowds stormed the Parisian palace where the king and queen resided and arrested them. France thus became a republic, and the republican soldier in the ranks came to enjoy a political cachet even greater than that of his officer. Before the Revolution, the officer was regarded positively as a man of honor, while the common soldier was considered dangerous; however, this popular vision changed with the coming of war. In 1792 and 1793 leading generals, notably the marquis de Lafayette—once a hero of the American Revolution—and Charles Dumouriez tried to use their troops to restore the monarchy in France. In the eyes of the revolutionaries, such men were traitors who demonstrated that the ambition of the officer corps could become a threat to the republic. Officers were needed, of course, but they were not entirely trusted. Conversely, the common soldier fought and died for the republic without the hope of personal gain; he sacrificed for the public welfare. Pierre Gillet, a member of the National Convention who went to the front, proclaimed in April 1794: "The soldiers are like the people, they are good."[77] In contrast to the royal minister of war, Saint-Germain, who had condemned the common soldier as "slime," the republican minister of war, Jean-Baptiste Bouchotte, testified simply, "The soldiers are good."[78]

Now that soldiers enjoyed high repute, more was expected of them, and the armies of revolutionary France developed a far more demanding, flexible, and effective tactical system, particularly for the infantry.[79] The line remained for massing firepower, most notably on the defensive. But when on the attack, the infantry now formed in columns, which, standing twelve men deep, were only one-quarter the width of lines and thus more nimble. Little concerned with parade-ground alignment and intended to take advantage of the enthusiasm of men dedicated to defending their new society and government, columns swept forward swiftly, often with the men cheering or singing in the ranks. Ideally, attacks were prepared by swarms of light-infantry skirmishers who unsettled the enemy resistance. These skirmishers fought as individuals, seeking cover and selecting targets on their own. If need be, entire regular line battalions could be trusted to fight in this fashion. This combination of line, column, and skirmishers took some time to develop, but it became known as the *ordre mixte*, or mixed order, in which regiments deployed two of their battalions in column, joined together by one in line, with the whole covered by skirmishers. This became Napoleon's favorite formation for infantry.

Other European armies had to adjust to the new French way of war. Superficially, this meant copying French tactical forms, but far more fundamentally, it meant accepting a new view of the common soldier. Different armies adopted varying levels of reform, but all had to respond. After they were defeated and humiliated by Napoleon in 1806, the Prussians went the furthest to reform their military institutions, whereas, for example, the Russians underwent a more modest reform. The English innovated tactically but kept their eighteenth-century style of recruitment and elite command.

It is important to realize that tactical innovation after 1789 did not depend on technological innovation, so it is clear that technology did not determine a single way of fighting. Although other European armies found that the more accurate muzzle-loading rifled weapons were particularly useful for skirmishers, the French retained their smoothbores. Even though the Prussian tests referred to earlier demonstrated that rifles were three times more accurate, they also took three time longer to load, because the musket ball had to fit very tightly into the barrel. Thus, if a soldier with a smoothbore had enough ammunition, he could do as much damage in a given amount of time as could a rifleman. Speaking of the Prussian case, the historian Peter Paret concluded: "This should help dismiss the argument . . . that technological deficiencies forbade the more general employment of skirmishing in the old Prussian army. On the contrary, the necessary equipment existed, but the leadership of the army was unwilling to make use of it."[80] The great Prussian general Gerhard Johann David von Scharnhorst (1755–1813) admitted,

> Good marksmanship is always the most important thing for the infantry— it always decides the action. Before the war [with Napoleon in 1806] we taught the men to load quickly, but not well, to fire quickly, but without aiming. This was very ill-considered; we must therefore work with all out might to root out this error.[81]

Conclusion

Frederick II, so often victorious and, on occasion, brilliantly so, was not a great innovator; rather, he was a consummate practitioner in the context of the battle culture of forbearance. At Mollwitz, although he was just learning the art of command, his officers already had mastered the tactics of this battle culture by mastering their men; Frederick's father, King Frederick William I, had seen to that. Frederick thus defined an age not by his genius but by his conformity.

In studying the battle culture of forbearance that Frederick exemplified, there is much to learn. First, we must examine critically the concept of technological determinacy in war. Ways of war certainly must fit within the parameters of contemporary weaponry, but the same weapons can be used differently by different battle cultures. Second, military cultures, like other categories of culture, must be put in the context of the divisions within society. Social class exerted a very great influence in shaping the battle culture of forbearance. The more complex a society is, the more competing cultural constructions vie with one another over conceptions of war and the warrior. Differences in social class, gender, and identity influence cultural conceptions, but the subcategories of analysis may also be much more nuanced than these basic splits. Third, radical changes in society are very likely to bring with them radical changes in military culture, and these often mean a greater or lesser change in the conduct of war. The greatest fractures or transformations in military thought and practice quite often are determined by changes that are not originally military, as was the case with the French Revolution.

NOTES

1. An Austrian officer, in Thomas Carlyle, *History of Friedrich II of Prussia, Called Frederick the Great*, vol. 4 (London: Chapman and Hall, 1898), 129.

2. David G. Chandler, *The Art of Warfare in the Age of Marlborough* (New York: Hippocrene, 1976), 76–77.

3. Ibid., 77.

4. Peter Paret, *Yorck and the Era of Prussian Reform, 1807–1815* (Princeton, NJ: Princeton University Press, 1966), 271–73.

5. John A. Lynn, "Forging the Western Army in Seventeenth-Century France," in *The Dynamics of Military Revolution, 1300–2050*, ed. Williamson Murray and McGregor Knox (Cambridge: Cambridge University Press, 2001), 43.

6. For details on Gribeauval cannon, see David G. Chandler, *The Campaigns of Napoleon* (New York: Macmillan, 1966), 358–59.

7. Matti Lauerma, *L'artillerie de champagne française pendant les guerres de la Révolution* (Helsinki: Akateeminen Kirjakauppa, 1956), 16.

8. Chandler, *The Art of Warfare*, 146, 171.

9. Maurice de Saxe estimates seven or eight minutes to cover 300 paces. Figuring a pace as 30 inches, 300 paces equal 250 yards. See Maurice de Saxe, *Mes rêveries* (Amsterdam: Arestée et Merkus, 1757), 70.

10. Frederick II the Great, *The Instructions of Frederick the Great for His Generals, 1747*, trans. Thomas R. Phillips, in *Roots of Strategy*, ed. Thomas R. Phillips (Harrisburg, PA: Military Service Publishing, 1940), 388–89.

11. Catinat, in Camille Rousset, *Histoire de Louvois*, 4 vols. (Paris: Didier, 1862–64), 4:524.

12. Catinat, in Jean Colin, *L'infanterie au XVIIIe siècle: La tactique* (Paris: Berger-Levrault, 1907), 25.

13. Paul Azan, *Un tacticien du XVIIe siècle* (Paris: Chapelot, 1904), 91.

14. Sébastien le Prestre de Vauban, *A Manual of Siegecraft and Fortification*, trans. G. A. Rothrock (Ann Arbor: University of Michigan Press, 1968), 123.

15. J. R. Donald, in *Journal of the Royal Highland Fusiliers* 24, no. 2 (winter 2000), quoted at http://www.phrases.org.uk/bulletin_board/18/messages/305.html (accessed September 4, 2010).

16. Frederick II, "Das militärische Testament," in *Militärische Schriften*, ed. Nikolas von Taysen (Berlin: Richard Wilhelmi, 1882), 205.

17. Louis XIV, *Mémoires de Louis XIV pour l'instruction du dauphin*, ed. Charles Dreyss, vol. 2 (Paris: Didier, 1860), 112–13.

18. Louis XIV to Luxembourg, August 1691, in Rousset, *Histoire de Louvois*, 4:510.

19. Maurice de Saxe, *My Reveries on the Art of War*, in *Roots of Strategy*, ed. Thomas R. Phillips (Harrisburg, PA: Military Service Publishing, 1940), 298–99.

20. Bülow, in Azar Gat, *Origins of Military Thought: From the Enlightenment to Clausewitz* (Oxford: Oxford University Press, 1991), 85.

21. Frederick II, *Instructions*, in *Roots of Strategy*, ed. Thomas R. Phillips (Harrisburg, PA: Military Service Publishing, 1940), 391.

22. Frederick II, in R. R. Palmer, "Frederick the Great, Guibert, Bülow: From Dynastic to National War," in *Makers of Modern Strategy*, ed. Peter Paret (Princeton, NJ: Princeton University Press, 1986), 103.

23. Frederick II, *Military Instruction from the Late King of Prussia to His Generals*, trans. Major Foster, 3rd ed. (Sherborne: Cruttwell, 1797), 5–6.

24. Louis de Jaucourt, "Déserteur," in *Encyclopédie, ou dictionnaire raisonné des sciences, des arts et des métiers*, ed. Denis Diderot and Jean d'Alembert, vol. 4 (Paris: Briasson, David, Le Breton, and Durand, 1751), 881.

25. Guibert, in Julia Osman, "The Citizen Army of Old Regime France" (PhD diss., University of North Carolina at Chapel Hill, 2010), 23.

26. Saint-Germain, in M. Delarue, "L'éducation politique à l'armée du Rhin, 1793–1794" (Mémoire de maitrise, Université de Paris-Nanterre, 1967–68), 42. In this sense, *bourbe* is the slime or mud at the bottom of a puddle.

27. See Osman, "The Citizen Army." For other examples of more positive assessments of common soldiers and talk of a citizen army in the late 1770s and 1780s, see Matthew H. Spring, *With Zeal and with Bayonet Only: The British Army on Campaign in North America, 1775–1783* (Norman: University of Oklahoma Press: 2008).

28. Benjamin Rush, in Spring, *With Zeal and with Bayonet Only*, 107.

29. Frederick II, *Militärische Schriften*, 205.

30. Saint-Germain, in Christopher Duffy, *Military Experience in the Age of Reason* (London: Routledge, 1987), 89–90.

31. Claude Adrien Helvétius, *De l'esprit: or, Essays on the Mind, and Its Several Faculties* (London: Dodley, 1759), 348.

32. Edward Gibbon, *The History of the Decline and Fall of the Roman Empire*, vol. 1 (London: Strahan and Cadell, 1776), 11.

33. Maurice de Saxe, *Reveries, or Memoirs upon the Art of War* (London: J. Nourse, 1757), 79.

34. Joseph Servan, in Osman, "The Citizen Army," 141.

35. Frederick II, *Military Instruction* (1797), 112.

36. Ibid., 5–6.

37. Chamillart, in Georges Girard, *Le service militaire en France à la fin du règne de Louis XIV: Rocolage et milice, 1701–1715* (Paris: Plon, 1915), 325–26.

38. André Corvisier, *L'armée française de la fin du XVIIe siècle au ministère du Choiseul: Le soldat*, 2 vols. (Paris: Presses universitaires de France, 1964), 2:736–37.

39. M. S. Anderson, *War and Society in Europe of the Old Regime* (New York: St. Martin's Press, 1988), 130.

40. Willerd R. Fann, "Peacetime Attrition in the Army of Frederick William I, 1713–1740," *Central European History* 11, no. 4 (December 1978): 327.

41. Frederick II, *Military Instruction* (1797), 3–5.

42. Frederick II, in Alfred Vagts, *A History of Militarism, Civilian and Military* (New York: Free Press, 1959), 72–73.

43. For compliance theory as it applies to military motivation, see Steven D. Westbrook, "The Potential for Military Disintegration," in *Combat Effectiveness: Cohesion, Stress, and the Volunteer Military*, ed. Sam C. Sarkesian (Beverly Hills, CA: Sage, 1980), 244–78.

44. Michel de Montaigne, in Maurice Keen, *Chivalry* (New Haven, CT: Yale University Press, 1984), 249.

45. Commissaire Lenfant to Louvois, in Louis Tuetey, *Les officiers de l'ancien régime. Nobles et roturiers* (Paris: Plon, 1908), 61.

46. Augustino de Levis, in Sabina Loriga, *Soldats—Un laboratoire disciplinaire: L'armée piémontaise au XVIIIe siècle* (Paris: Les belles lettres, 2007), 60.

47. Yuval Noah Harari, *The Ultimate Experience: Battlefield Revelations and the Making of Modern War Culture, 1450–2000* (Houndsmill: Palgrave Macmillan 2008), 118.

48. Ensign Thomas Anburey, speaking of the Convention Army at Lancaster, Pennsylvania, in Spring, *With Zeal and with Bayonet Only*, 108.

49. Ibid., 124.

50. Michael Roberts, *The Military Revolution, 1560–1660* (Belfast: University of Belfast Press, 1956), 10.

51. Louis XIV, *Mémoires*, 2:112–13.

52. Wayne E. Lee, *Barbarians and Brothers: Anglo-American Warfare, 1500–1865* (New York: Oxford University Press, 2011), chap. 3.

53. Colin, *L'infanterie au XVIIIe siècle*, 32.

54. Victor Belhomme, *Histoire de l'infanterie en France*, 5 vols. (Paris: Charles-Lavauzelle, 1893–1902), 2:236–38.

55. Service historique de l'armée de terre, Archives de guerre, A2c 346, piece no. 3.

56. Dennis Showalter, "Frederick the Great: The First Modern Military Celebrity," *Military History* (July/August 2007), available at http://www.historynet.com/frederick-the-great-the-first-modern-military-celebrity.htm/2 (accessed March 2, 2011).

57. Corvisier, *L'armée française*; Sylvia Frey, *The British Soldier in America: A Social History of Military Life in the Revolutionary Period* (Austin: University of Texas Press, 1981); Spring, *With Zeal and with Bayonet Only*; and Loriga, *Soldats*, all tell a tale that differs significantly from the stereotypes embraced during the eighteenth century before 1789. In addition, Edward J. Coss, *All for the King's Shilling: The British Soldier under Wellington, 1808–1814* (Norman: University of Oklahoma Press, 2010) describes a somewhat later period, but he reveals a strong continuity with eighteenth-century patterns for British forces.

58. Turgot, in Albert Duroy, *L'armée royale en 1789* (Paris: Lévy, 1888), 42.

59. Claude-François-Madeleine Le Roy, *Souvenirs du major Le Roy, vétéran des armées de la République et de l'Empire, 1767–1851*, ed. Gabriel Dumay (Dijon: Berthier, 1914).

60. Willerd R. Fann, "Foreigners in the Prussian Army, 1713–56: Some Statistical and Interpretive Problems," *Central European History* 23, no. 1 (March 1990): 82–84.

61. Frederick II, in Barton Hacker, "Women and Military Institutions in Early Modern Europe; A Reconnaissance," *Signs* 6, no 4 (summer 1981): 660.

62. See Peter H. Wilson, "The German 'Soldier Trade' of the Seventeenth and Eighteenth Centuries: A Reassessment," *International History Review* 18, no. 4 (November 1996): 757–92.

63. The 1778 press law in Frey, *The British Soldier in America*, 5.

64. Ibid., 6.

65. Wellington, in Elizabeth Longford, *Wellington: The Years of the Sword* (New York: Harper & Row, 1969), 321.

66. For a discussion of primary group cohesion in the eighteenth century, see John A. Lynn, *The Bayonets of the Republic* (Boulder, CO: Westview, 1996), chaps. 2 and 7. For a discussion of this in a seventeenth-century context, see John A. Lynn, *Giant of the Grand Siècle* (New York: Cambridge University Press, 1997), chap. 13. See also the works of Frey, Spring, and Coss.

67. William H. McNeill, *Keeping Together in Time: Dance and Drill in Human History* (Cambridge, MA: Harvard University Press, 1995), 131.

68. Frederick II, *Militärische Schriften*, 205.

69. Albert Babeau, *La vie militaire sous l'ancien régime*, vol. 1, *Les soldats* (Paris: Firmin-Didot, 1890), 192.

70. Frederick II, *Military Instruction* (1797), 6.

71. André Corvisier, *Armies and Societies in Europe, 1494–1789*, trans. Abigail T. Siddall (Bloomington: Indiana University Press, 1979), 182.

72. Major Patrick Ferguson, instruction to his American Volunteers, January 1780, in Spring, *With Zeal and with Bayonets Only*, 111.

73. See accounts of duels in Naoko Seriu, "Faire un soldat: Une histoire des hommes à l'épreuve de l'institution militaire" (PhD diss., École des hautes études en sciences sociales, 2005), 270–74.

74. Jean Chagniot, *Paris et l'armée au XVIIIe siècle* (Paris: Economica, 1985), 589.

75. Cornwall B. Rogers, *The Spirit of the Revolution in 1789: A Study of Public Opinion as Revealed in Political Songs and Other Popular Literature at the Beginning of the French Revolution* (Westport, CT: Greenwood Press, 1969), 210.

76. Theodore Iung, *L'armée de la Révolution, Dubois-Crancé, mousquetaire, constituant, conventionnel, général de division, ministre de guerre*, vol. 2 (Paris: Charpentier, 1884), 16.

77. Albert Mathiez, *La victoire en l'an II* (Paris: Alcan, 1916), 149.

78. Auguste Herlaut, *Le colonel Bouchotte, ministre de la guerre en l'an II*, vol. 2 (Paris: Poisson, 1946), 128.

79. For the most complete analysis of tactical evolution in the first years of the French Revolution see Lynn, *The Bayonets of the Republic*.

80. Paret, *Yorck and the Era of Prussian Reform*, 272.

81. Scharnhorst, in Paret, *Yorck and the Era of Prussian Reform*, 158, n. 10.

6

Success and Failure in Civil War Armies

Clues from Organizational Culture

MARK GRIMSLEY

Musketry roiled the fields and woodlands along the beleaguered Union front at Chickamauga on September 20, 1863. Surprised the previous afternoon by a massive Confederate attack, the Union Army of the Cumberland braced for a day of combat that surely would be even more desperate. With trouble brewing in his own sector, division commander Brigadier General Thomas J. Wood received an urgent message from the headquarters of army commander Major General William S. Rosecrans. "The general commanding," it read, "directs that you close up on Reynolds as fast as possible, and support him." Wood realized at once that the order made no sense. The Reynolds to whom it referred, Major General Joseph Reynolds, commanded a division to the north of the sector that Wood was supposed to hold. To "close up" on Reynolds would mean shifting Wood's own division to connect with the right flank of Reynolds's division. But between those two divisions was a third under Brigadier General John M. Brannan, so it was obviously impossible to obey this portion of the order. Moreover, to "support" Reynolds's division meant placing his own division to Reynolds's rear. That, however, would open a gaping hole in the Union line.[1]

The obvious thing to do was to remain in place. The staff officer who brought the order quickly realized that it had been badly written and did not reflect Rosecrans's intent, which was to have Wood's division close up on Reynolds *after* Brannan's division had moved back to allow this maneuver. He tried to explain this to Wood, but Wood refused to listen. The order was imperative, he said, and had to be obeyed at once. The staff officer begged him to wait just ten minutes so that he could ride back to Rosecrans's headquarters—a mere six hundred yards away—and clarify the directive. Wood shook his head and carefully placed the slip of paper in a pocket notebook. But before doing so, he waggled it in front of his division staff. "I hold the fatal order of the day," he said, "and would not part with it for five thousand dollars."[2]

Wood then withdrew his division from its sector to place it behind Reynolds's division. A few minutes later, when the Confederate assault began, thousands of rebel infantry poured through the gap created by Wood's withdrawal. In the fighting that ensued, the Army of the Cumberland was nearly wrecked.

Why on earth had Wood done such a thing? It transpired that in the days preceding September 20, Rosecrans had twice reprimanded Wood in full view of Wood's staff for failing to carry out an order promptly enough. Wood's literal obedience to an absurd order was—said many then and later—a case of payback. Wood apparently wanted to discomfit Rosecrans so badly that he did not care that it might take the loss of a battle and hundreds of lives to do so. An act of greater pettiness would be hard to imagine.

Among the units in Wood's division was the 125th Ohio Volunteer Infantry Regiment. Raised in August 1862, the regiment had never before fought in a major battle, but as the situation deteriorated, Wood repeatedly called on the 125th to shore up vulnerable sections of the Union line, in one instance ordering it to charge the enemy alone. Without hesitation, its colonel, thirty-four-year-old Emerson Opdycke, led his 314 men against superior numbers.[3] Observing them, an admiring Wood shouted to everyone within earshot, "See the Tigers go in!"[4] The charge bought time for other Union regiments to assemble for a stand at the crest of a nearby hill. The 125th soon joined them and for hours repelled one Confederate attack after another. Ordered by Major General George H. Thomas to hold the position to the last, Opdycke replied, "We will hold it, General, or go from here to heaven."[5] The colonel stubbornly remained on horseback, despite making himself an obvious target. His courage galvanized the men.

Several generals complimented the regiment on its performance, but the men of the 125th relished most the description that Wood bestowed on them, and for the rest of the war they proudly called themselves "Opdycke's Tigers." They took equal pride in the fact that although this was their first battle, not a single man broke from the line. By the time the combat ended, one of every three men had been killed or wounded or was missing in action.

It would be hard to find a greater contrast between the pettiness of General Wood and the blood-soaked sacrifice of the 125th Ohio. Yet the men of the 125th refused to see it that way. After the battle, they learned of the controversy surrounding Wood's response to the "fatal order"—a response that, viewed rationally, had caused most of the unit's losses. But the Ohioans rejected any narrative that made Wood seem less than a hero, for to do so would have tarnished the cherished regimental sobriquet: "Tigers." Thus, in the postwar regimental history of the 125th, Captain Charles T. Clark insisted that "the fault lay with the *writer* of the ambiguous order" and that Wood did right in "hastening to the point where the uproar of battle, as well as the tenor of the order, indicated that prompt assistance was required."[6]

What is going on here? One answer might be simply the idiosyncrasies of an individual general and one of the regiments under his command. But both the general and the regiment were part of organizations, and a better response would acknowledge the way in which those organizations shaped the values of the men within them. Success or failure in Civil War combat often turned on the organizational cultures that cocooned both the senior leaders and the rank and file.

A Definition of Organizational Culture

Organizational culture derives from the modern conception of culture. This is not the everyday usage of high culture, in the sense of museums or classical music, but culture as explained by anthropologist Clifford Geertz, whose definition has been enormously influential. Alluding to a famous statement that "man is an animal suspended in webs of significance that he himself has spun," Geertz declared, "I take culture to be those webs, and the analysis of it to be therefore not an experimental science in search of law but rather an interpretive one in search of meaning."[7] By this reasoning, human gestures and customs, the architecture of buildings, and a thousand other things are all manifestations of culture, artifacts of the "webs of significance" that surround us and inform our beliefs about the nature of the world around us, the value systems to which we should adhere, our notions of appropriate behavior, and so on.

Organizational culture therefore concerns the webs of significance found in specific institutions. While the concept usually is applied to modern corporations, it also applies to the modern military, although the goals of corporations and the U.S. Army obviously differ. Nonetheless, civilian managers and military officers have long noticed commonalities between the skill sets required to be a good corporate executive and to be a good commander. Retired officers, for instance, routinely find second careers as business executives.

We also might point to staff rides: military tours of battlefields that "combine a rigorous course of historical preparation with an examination of the terrain on which an actual battle occurred."[8] Once the exclusive province of military officers, in recent years business executives have used staff rides as tools for managerial development. Their reasoning is that key aspects of military leadership are analogous to the challenges of leadership in the business world. The army has enthusiastically assisted these efforts[9] and even has looked to corporate management for clues to improving management within its own vast organization.

At the U.S. Army War College, for example, the mandatory Strategic Leadership course combines three theoretical models of organizational culture.[10] The first draws on the work of social psychologist Edgar H. Schein, who argues that to understand the culture of a specific organization, it is necessary to study three components: artifacts, values, and assumptions. *Artifacts* are on-the-job behaviors and other things—such as whether employees work in offices or cubicles, individually or in teams—that can be directly observed and studied.

The overt *values* of an organization also can be observed because they are openly stated in corporations' documents like statements of purpose and rules governing such matters as attendance and employees' attire. The military counterparts are the oaths taken by officers and soldiers, injunctions such as "Duty, Honor, Country" and the moral imperative that one must never leave a buddy behind.

More elusive are an organization's subterranean values—what might be called its "lived values." Some of these actually contradict the stated values. For example, a corporation that ostensibly urges employees to think "outside the box" may in fact promote those who adhere to well-established customs and norms. This lived value is sufficiently obvious that few employees overlook it. Consequently, they will ignore hollow calls for innovative thinking in favor of conformity, which, they correctly discern, is the real way to get ahead in the organization.

Undergirding these values (both stated and lived) are *assumptions*—taken-for-granted beliefs about human nature and the way in which the world operates.[11] The Army War College considered this part of Schein's model to be valuable but thought Schein's explication of it was too "esoteric" to be an effective means of presenting the idea to officers.[12] Searching for a way to introduce the idea of assumptions more clearly, they found it in the work of a group of analysts who devised the GLOBE project, a list of nine implicit values, termed *dimensions*, that could be placed on a scale from low to high, coupled with a statistically and conceptually valid way to quantify them.[13]

Of these, the Army War College course chose five dimensions as being the most relevant to the modern U.S. Army: (1) *high performance orientation*, the extent to which an organization encourages and rewards innovation, high standards, and performance improvement; (2) *in-group collectivism*, the degree to which individuals express pride, loyalty, and cohesiveness in their organizations; (3) *institutional collectivism*, the degree to which the organization's practices encourage and reward the collective distribution of resources and collective action; (4) *power distance*, the extent to which an organization accepts and endorses authority, power differences, and status privileges; and (5) *assertiveness*, the degree to which individuals are—and are expected to be—assertive, confrontational, and aggressive in their relationships with others. When assessing Civil War field armies, it is helpful to bear in mind a sixth dimension: *uncertainty avoidance*, the degree to which an organization relies on social norms, rules, and procedures to alleviate ambiguity and the unpredictability of future events.[14]

The war college also uses a third model created by social psychologists Kim S. Cameron and Robert E. Quinn, who maintain that organizations can be placed somewhere on a quadrant with two scales of "competing values": on the vertical scale, flexibility versus control; and on the horizontal scale, an internal focus on maintenance and integration versus an external focus on positioning and differentiation. This scheme results in four types of culture: *hierarchy, clan, market,* and *adhocracy.*[15]

We will leave aside the last two cultures in favor of the ones most relevant to Civil War armies. The *hierarchy* culture corresponds to the traditional corporate model of strong top-down control. It best fits Civil War armies when assessing the interactions of the high command. The *clan* is more flexible. "Rather than strict rules and procedures," the authors explain, "people are driven through vision, shared goals, outputs and outcomes." Rules do exist "but are often communicated and instilled socially to reinforce [an organization's] commitment to its people."[16] The clan model works well when assessing the organizational culture of the regiment, which was the fundamental building block of Civil War armies.

The need to think in terms of two, not one, organizational culture types is imperative because organizations in the Civil War era differed from their modern counterparts in one crucial respect. Modern organizations have both the desire and the ability to exert their norms and values from the company president all the way down to the lowliest clerk. Their ability to do so hinges on a high degree of what business historian Alfred D. Chandler terms *administrative coordination.* In 1860s America, however, this attribute had not yet emerged, although the first modern enterprises—the railroad and the telegraph—were beginning to develop it. Railroads needed administrative coordination for traffic to move efficiently and safely. Telegraph companies needed it to transmit efficiently the thousands of messages across their wires.[17]

Even though many Civil War officers were familiar with the railroad and telegraph industries, they had little interest in extending this incipient administrative coordination to Civil War armies, and even less hope of doing so had they tried. Such armies were simply too cobbled together and too loose-jointed to permit it. Nonetheless, Civil War armies did have identifiable organizational cultures, and the most gifted leaders often displayed a sort of preconscious grasp of how organizational culture works.

How do organizational cultures originate? Schein argues that they spring from three sources: the beliefs, values, and assumptions of the founders of organizations; the learning experiences of group members as their organization evolves; and/or new beliefs, values, and assumptions brought in by new members and leaders. Once created, these cultures are remarkably static and resistant to change. Managers locked within them display considerable ability to explain away even the most blatant evidence that their cultural norms are maladaptive. Consequently, changing the culture usually requires either a relentless, well-calculated effort by a strong leader or else an "organizational shock," a crisis that brutally exposes how much the organization's self-perception departs from reality.[18]

Organizational Culture Applied to Civil War Armies

Both contemporary observers and subsequent historians have long noticed that Civil War field armies seemed to have distinctive "personalities." Some behaved with confident aggressiveness, others seemed notably cautious, and still others were riven by squabbles and rivalries that undercut both morale and effectiveness. Although historians have seldom given more than passing attention to the origins and persistence of these personalities, some have offered shrewd hypotheses. These can be roughly divided into three categories.

The first emphasizes the societal cultures that allegedly influenced the armies. In 1978, Michael C. C. Adams wrote that the apparently excessive caution of Union armies in the eastern theater could be traced back to Northerners on the Atlantic seaboard who had a pronounced image of white Southerners as barbaric but militant and warlike. But this excessive caution did not influence Northerners from western states, and therefore these armies performed better. A few years later, Grady McWhiney and Perry D. Jamieson argued that the Celtic heritage of many white Southerners fostered among Confederate armies a reflexive, ultimately ruinous cult of the offensive.[19]

The second hypothesis emphasizes the nature of the Civil War armies, which were ad hoc organizations slightly leavened by officers with experience in the prewar regular army but were dominated by citizens in uniform whose principal allegiance was to their regiments. Gerald J. Prokopowicz advanced this thesis in a 2001 assessment of the Army of the Ohio during the war's early years. "The reason that the Army of the Ohio . . . fought as it did in 1861–62," he wrote, began with

> the way in which it was recruited, trained, and organized. Assembled out of a collection of independent and fiercely clannish companies and regiments, the Army of the Ohio resembled a strong but ponderous beast whose component units could absorb enormous punishment on the battlefield without breaking, but which lacked the agility to execute the maneuvers necessary to destroy its enemies.

Although Prokopowicz restricted his analysis to the Army of the Ohio, he maintained that the same dynamic applied to all Civil War armies.[20]

The third hypothesis—and the one widely embraced by both contemporary observers and later historians—emphasizes the impact of army commanders, who were presumed to dominate the personality of the armies they led. Their mind-set influenced key subordinates, the theory ran, who in turn influenced lower-ranking officers. Thus, a timid commander fostered an army characterized by timidity, an aggressive commander fostered an aggressive army, and so on.

Although none of these hypotheses explicitly uses the concept of organizational culture, they do form a useful point of departure. The main task is to expand, refine, and sometimes reframe these insights by exploring the organizational cultures that had the greatest impact on Civil War military operations: at the top, the *hierarchical* culture that characterized relations among the senior leadership and, at the bottom, the *clannish* culture that characterized relations between officers and men at the regimental level.

This chapter examines the hierarchical culture of five field armies: on the Union side, the Army of the Potomac, the Army of the Tennessee, and the Army of the Cumberland; and on the Confederate side, the Army of Northern Virginia and Army of Tennessee. (The two Tennessee armies should not be confused. The name of the Union army derived from the Tennessee River, whereas that of its Confederate counterpart came from the state of Tennessee.) Although these were not the only Civil War armies, they were by far the largest. More important, they decided nearly all the campaigns that had the greatest influence on the war's outcome.

This chapter also recognizes that in regard to the clannish culture, each field army was a conglomeration of smaller organizations, of which the most important was the regiment. Prokopowicz, of course, explicitly makes the case that regiments, much more than armies, influenced the conduct and outcome of military operations. Although I believe this is going a bit far, his idea still has great merit. The senior leadership of the various field armies formulated and executed plans, and the level of function or dysfunction within these groups greatly affected success or failure at the *strategic* level. But at the *tactical* level, the regimental culture mattered more, for unlike modern military organizations, the hierarchical culture of the senior leadership never extended itself to dominate the clannish culture of the regiments.

Senior Leadership Culture

The senior leadership culture centered mainly on the relationships between army commanders and a small but potent group of subordinates: the generals who led the army's corps, consisting of between ten thousand and twenty thousand men. Corps constituted a field army's major strike force and therefore exerted a critical influence on its operations. While these cultures varied widely from one army to another, all had to contend with four factors that also shaped these cultures. All four were subsets of a single, overriding reality, for in nineteenth-century America, the interplay between the military and the political worlds was great.

First, both presidents—Abraham Lincoln and Jefferson Davis—routinely involved themselves not just in major decisions about strategy, allocation of resources, and so on, but also in personnel matters. They frequently forced army commanders to retain a subordinate that the commanders disliked. Worse, the presidents often allowed some subordinates to have direct personal access to them, which made it possible for disgruntled corps commanders to complain about their army commanders.

Second, professionally trained generals constantly worked alongside amateur generals who owed their rank to political prominence. In those days, it was commonly believed that any man of strong character could make an effective general, and since being a general already was a reliable road to the presidency—examples are George Washington, Andrew Jackson, William Henry Harrison, and Zachary Taylor—powerful politicians coveted commissions as generals. Although most political generals were corps commanders, in a few instances they actually commanded armies. Either way, professional and political generals frequently did not get along. Professionals tended to see the war solely as a military problem; political generals tended to be much more aware of its political contours. This disparity not only generated much friction, but it also made it particularly difficult for an army commander to control a corps commander who was at the same time a powerful politician.

Third, despite a partial professionalization of the prewar U.S. Army, it was not yet professionally unacceptable to overtly use political patrons. Indeed, most senior commanders had them. Major General Ulysses S. Grant had Congressman Elihu P. Washburne of Illinois, and Major General Joseph Hooker had Secretary of the Treasury Salmon P. Chase. In fact, having a powerful political patron was very much the norm. Only a few high-ranking generals—Major General George H. Thomas, for instance—lacked such a patron (in the case of Thomas, largely because he was a native Virginian who had remained loyal to the Union. Thus the Virginia politicians who normally would have been his patrons were in the Confederacy).

Finally, seniority was important. It was not uncommon for generals with the same rank to delay key decisions while comparing dates of rank in order to determine which of them should be in command. In several instances, a general resigned rather than accept an order placing a general junior to him in a position of greater responsibility. At a critical point in the Atlanta campaign, for example, Hooker abruptly resigned rather than accept a decision to appoint a junior officer to army command while he himself remained a mere corps commander.[21]

Although influenced by these permanently operating factors, senior leader cultures still differed widely and were generated in different ways. Of potentially great significance was the character of the army's "founding commander." The Union Armies of the Tennessee and the Potomac demonstrate the founder's role in shaping organizational culture, in part because the two armies were such a study in contrasts. The Army of the Tennessee had an unusually healthy organizational culture, but that of the Army of the Potomac was notoriously problematic.

The Army of the Tennessee had the good fortune to have as its founding commander Ulysses S. Grant, who led the army for about twenty months, one of the longest tenures of any army commander on either side. Although the army was not formally established until October 1862, for all practical purposes it operated as an army from the time of the Fort Donelson campaign in February 1862. It enjoyed repeated success; even its drubbing on the first day at Shiloh (April 6, 1862) was redeemed the next day by a counterattack that recaptured the lost ground and sent the Confederate army in full retreat. Its next major campaign, against the Mississippi River fortress city of Vicksburg, required nine months. Although punctuated by one setback after another, Grant displayed a consistent policy of maintaining the initiative and doggedly pursuing one effort after another to seize the city until, in a brilliant spring offensive, he succeeded in capturing not just Vicksburg but also its entire defending army of thirty thousand men. By then, writes historian Steven E. Woodworth, the Army of the Tennessee had "completely imbibed [Grant's] quiet, can-do attitude, and this spirit continued to characterize its operations even after Grant had moved on to higher command."[22]

Grant's success would have been unlikely without his ability to forge close partnerships among key commanders, mostly notably Major General William T. Sherman but also Major General James B. McPherson and two naval flag officers, Andrew Foote and David Dixon Porter. These last two partnerships were especially significant because riverine operations were crucial to Grant's victories in the western theater, although he never had direct command of either naval officer. Instead, he gained their cooperation through the careful cultivation of relationships based on regarding them as peers.[23]

In such instances, the power distance between Grant, Sherman, McPherson, Foote, and Porter was minimal. Nonetheless, the hierarchy culture is the most appropriate lens through which to view Grant's generalship because he had other corps commanders, most notoriously Major General John McClernand, who actively challenged Grant's leadership. Grant therefore had to insist on his prerogatives as an army commander. Consequently, when necessary he did maintain a firm power distance between himself and his subordinates. If that distance diminished, it was because a subordinate earned Grant's trust, not because Grant was helpless to prevent it.

Even so, Grant's style of command, characterized by a steady promotion of gifted leaders who also exhibited loyalty and the ability to work as a team, became a hallmark of the Army of the Tennessee's top command. He encouraged assertiveness among his subordinates, so that they felt safe in offering advice, their in-group collectivism was unusually high, and the distribution of resources among the various corps was equitable enough that it would be fair to say the same of the army's institutional collectivism. And one final point must be emphasized. The Army of the Tennessee displayed a low degree of uncertainty avoidance, a trait derived from Grant, who had an unusually high degree of tolerance for the ambiguity and limited information characteristic of combat operations. In other words, he focused far more on what he wanted to do rather than on what his adversaries might attempt.

Very different was the Army of the Potomac, notwithstanding the fact that of all Civil War armies, it was the first to be formed and the most meticulously organized. Its component regiments spent nine months encamped together before its maiden campaign, so that it carried out its initial training together. That training was unusually systematic, with new regiments assigned to a special provisional division specifically designed to hone their military skills. It had examining boards to weed out incompetent officers and large-scale troop reviews—sometimes numbering more than sixty thousand men—that graphically underscored to the soldiers both the power of the army and their place within it. Most important, its founding commander was Major General George B. McClellan, an officer acknowledged even today as having charisma and outstanding organizational ability.

McClellan remained in command for seventeen months, and his hallmark traits—a suspicion of the Lincoln administration, a strong involvement in Washington politics, a cautious approach to military operations, and a tendency to overestimate the size and prowess of the enemy forces—characterized the organizational culture of the Army of the Potomac throughout its history. This was exacerbated by the fact that each of McClellan's successors—Major Generals Ambrose E. Burnside, Joseph Hooker, and George G. Meade—was promoted from within the army and steeped in its organizational culture.

The culture of the Army of the Potomac's senior leadership was characterized by high power distance. McClellan really trusted few commanders and many he did not trust at all. The army's in-group collectivism and institutional collectivism both were low, since many corps commanders believed that the army's resources were unevenly distributed. This dynamic was heightened by President Lincoln, who at numerous points interfered in the army's senior leadership issues as well as its military operations. Lincoln's and McClellan's mutually suspicious relationship is notorious and is usually blamed on McClellan. But Lincoln contributed to the strained relationship as well. Incredibly, it was he, not McClellan, who on the eve of the Army of the Potomac's first campaign selected its four corps commanders. Lincoln's principal criterion was that they were generals known to *disagree* with McClellan's military judgment.[24]

In addition, Lincoln tolerated, and often seemed to encourage, disgruntled subordinates who approached him and other Washington officials to criticize McClellan behind his back. This in turn made even more corrosive the bickering that characterized the Potomac army's senior leadership. One example is that after the army's severe defeat at Fredericksburg in December 1862, a number of top-ranking commanders tried to get rid of Major General Ambrose E. Burnside by going to Washington and laying their case before several politicians, including Lincoln himself.[25]

Furthermore, even the audacious Grant discovered he could do little to change the enduring impact of McClellan's caution. He certainly tried. Well aware of its hard-luck reputation, as general in chief he located his headquarters with the Army of the Potomac from April 1864 until the end of the war. Time and again, he was astonished by the skepticism that army's senior leaders harbored about one another's ability compared with the awe in which they held the army's nemesis, Confederate General Robert E. Lee. "Some of you," Grant once snapped at a Potomac army general, "seem to think that [Lee] is suddenly going to do a double somersault, and land in our rear and on both of our flanks at the same time."[26]

Grant realized that he could not supervise all the Union armies and at the same time exert direct command over the Army of the Potomac, but it sometimes seemed that he tried. He practically looked over the shoulder of George G. Meade, its nominal commander, micromanaged Meade's decisions, and sometimes issued orders directly to Meade's corps commanders. Meade tolerated this arrangement with surprisingly good grace and clearly attempted to do everything Grant asked of him.

The problem with the Potomac army's command structure was not Grant's and Meade's personal relationship but their contrasting command styles. By temperament and experience, Grant had a *coping* style of generalship, that is, a style aimed at shaping any outcome toward a desired objective. A coping style shows greater tolerance for uncertainty and less fear of improvisation and encourages a faster reaction time.

Meade's essential command philosophy was based on uncertainty avoidance. For him, good generalship consisted of *control*, using resources and manipulating variables so as to guarantee success. Because that is impossible in war, since the enemy will systematically seek to undermine the effort to gain control, the next best thing is to avoid losing. This mentality was squarely in the McClellan tradition. Grant perceived the grip of this tradition on the army but underestimated its strength. He thought that simply by guiding Meade, he could force the army to adapt to his style. It is often said that Grant was the de facto commander of the Army of the Potomac. But it was Meade, not Grant, who remained the principal influence on the army's organizational culture. And Meade perpetuated the emphasis on control. He never caught Grant's vision. Although he obeyed Grant's orders like a good soldier, he was never a true partner in the way that Sherman had been.[27]

Grant was impressed by not only the Army of the Potomac's chronic timidity regarding Lee's army but also Lee's pugnacity, which Grant had never witnessed in his previous opponents. Midway through the Overland campaign, he conceded that after such an engagement as ferocious as the Wilderness, Confederate generals Braxton Bragg or Joseph E. Johnston "would have *retreated!*"[28]

The Army of Northern Virginia is the principal, and arguably the only, example of a Civil War commander who changed an army's organizational culture. General Robert E. Lee did not create the Army of Northern Virginia; it had existed for nearly a year before he assumed command in June 1862. But its previous commander, General Joseph E. Johnston, was notably defensive in his thinking. Not until the Army of the Potomac got within a few miles of Richmond did Johnston attempt his first and only counterattack, the battle of Seven Pines. In it, his army had fought stubbornly, but in a confused fashion and without the fire of a truly offensive spirit.

On the battle's second day, Johnston was wounded, and President Jefferson Davis appointed Lee to replace him. What followed was a startling reversal in the campaign's momentum. From the outset, Lee thought not in terms of holding McClellan at bay, as Johnston had done, but of organizing a counteroffensive that would destroy McClellan's army outright. Within a month, he unleashed a campaign, known as the Seven Days' Battles, that shoved the Army of the Potomac away from Richmond and into a defensive crouch along the banks of the James River. It was a brilliant achievement but disappointed Lee. "Under ordinary circumstances," he complained in his after-action report, "the Federal army should have been destroyed."[29]

Lee believed that if the Confederacy were to win the war, it would have to do so in the short run, before the U.S. government could fully exploit its massive advantages in population, manufacturing capacity, and wealth. The Confederates therefore could not afford to stand on the defensive. They must attack—early, often, and aggressively—and damage the Union army so severely as to convince Northern public opinion that victory was impossible and thus to accept Confederate independence. It was "a very bold game," Lee conceded after the war, "but it was the only one."[30]

To carry out such a vision given inferior numbers and resources, Lee realized that he must compensate by producing an army that was aggressive to its core. To create it, Lee followed a consistent policy of promoting commanders who showed aggressiveness and quietly but ruthlessly weeding out those who proved cautious or incompetent.[31] No officer in the army could fail to notice that the key to advancement was aggressiveness and the key to oblivion was excessive caution.

Lee's bias in favor of aggressiveness was so great that he forgave much from officers who displayed it and little from those who did not. Lee's handling of two of his corps commanders, Lieutenant Generals Ambrose P. Hill and Richard S. Ewell, illustrates this. Hill attracted Lee's favorable notice in the Seven Days' Battles, even though on its first day, Hill's aggressiveness led him to launch a rash attack on his own initiative that not only failed but also destroyed the operational surprise Lee had tried hard to ensure. Hill's subsequent performances at Antietam and Chancellorsville, however, persuaded Lee to elevate him to corps command. After the death at Chancellorsville of the corps commander, Lieutenant General Thomas J. "Stonewall" Jackson, Lee's closest operational partner, Lee selected Ewell as his replacement, also on the basis of Ewell's track record of bold leadership.

Both commanders proved a disappointment. At Gettysburg, Ewell was cautious and Hill exerted scant influence on the battle (apparently because of an illness). Moreover, an error in Hill's deployment of his corps nearly resulted in disaster at the battle of the Wilderness in May 1864. Although Ewell showed much greater competence in the Wilderness fight, neither he nor Hill distinguished themselves in the remaining battles of the Overland campaign. Eventually both men became seriously ill and temporarily relinquished command, in each case to Major General Jubal A. Early, an officer whose aggressiveness as a brigade and division commander Lee had long admired.

The crucial difference in the fates of Hill and Ewell illustrates Lee's bias toward aggressiveness. When both officers reported themselves fit to resume duty, Lee disingenuously insisted that Ewell was sicker than Ewell believed— despite Ewell's fervent assertions to the contrary—and flatly refused to let him return to corps command. Instead, he made Early the permanent commander of the corps. In contrast, despite deficiencies in Hill's subsequent performance, Lee restored him to corps command and retained him until Hill's death a week before the surrender at Appomattox. The reason for Lee's differential treatment of Hill and Ewell is obvious: whatever Hill's shortcomings, Lee could count on his aggressiveness, whereas in Ewell's case, he had lost that confidence.[32]

But perhaps more than any single factor, it was Lee's generalship in the Maryland campaign that cemented the Army of Northern Virginia's style and gave it the psychological mastery over the Army of the Potomac that eventually frustrated and baffled Grant. Despite inferior numbers, deficient equipment, and an army weary from ten weeks of nearly continuous campaigning in Virginia, Lee invaded Maryland in September 1862. He soon suffered a series of setbacks that would have led most generals to abandon the campaign. Instead, Lee chose to make a stand at Sharpsburg, Maryland, with the wide Potomac River only a mile to his rear, so that in the event of defeat his army would almost surely be destroyed. Lee never explained his reasons for doing so. Some historians have assumed he believed that without a major battle he could not abandon Maryland for political reasons because it was a border state the Confederacy hoped to add to its republic. A few have argued that he had sound military reasons for believing he could win a victory at Sharpsburg. But most believe the decision was almost a fatal mistake.[33]

Whatever the case, on September 17 Lee managed to fend off McClellan's Army of the Potomac in the bloodiest single day in American military history, a battle of numerous hairbreadth escapes that came close to destroying the Army of Northern Virginia. Yet despite this near debacle, Lee's aggressiveness remained unabated. That evening he met with his senior leaders to consider whether a counteroffensive was possible. Reluctantly convinced that there was not, he nonetheless chose to stand his ground on the following day, openly daring the Union army to hit him again, which it completely failed to do. Lee then withdrew in his own good time. Whether or not Lee intended it, the effect was to consolidate the Army of Northern Virginia's reputation as a mortally dangerous opponent.

The success that Lee enjoyed as a result of his offensive spirit paid other important dividends. It gave him unquestioned mastery over the army. Like Grant, Lee tolerated dissenting advice, but unlike Grant, Lee never experienced outright defiance—and he had the moral authority to crush any subordinate who tried it. Moreover, his success gained him the confidence of Confederate President Jefferson Davis, who supported Lee's strategic decisions almost without question, an advantage Lee ensured through careful cultivation of the president's goodwill.

These were no small advantages. The history of the Army of Tennessee, the Confederate's other major field army, is one long lesson in what can occur when an army commander enjoys neither firm control over his subordinates nor the unqualified confidence of his superior.

For most of the war, the Army of Tennessee was led by General Braxton Bragg. Like Lee, Bragg assumed command after the army's formation. By the time he took charge, the army already had fought the Shiloh campaign under

General Albert Sidney Johnston and the Corinth campaign under General P. G. T. Beauregard. Unlike Lee, Bragg was an irascible man. But he shared Lee's aggressive instincts. Within a few weeks of taking the helm, he had organized an offensive that carried his army into Kentucky and forced the Union Army of the Ohio to retreat all the way to Louisville.

Again like Lee, Bragg's invasion of a border state proved unsuccessful. But whereas the invasion enhanced Lee's reputation for boldness, Bragg came under serious criticism, much of it emanating from one of his corps commanders, Lieutenant General Leonidas Polk. Polk was a West Point graduate who had long ago resigned from the army in order to become an Episcopalian clergyman. Unfortunately for Bragg, he was a friend of President Davis. In the wake of the Kentucky invasion, Davis summoned first Bragg, then Polk, to Richmond to confer about the operation. Polk took the opportunity to inform Davis that although Bragg had good organizational skills, he was a poor field general and ought to be replaced. Davis liked both Bragg and Polk and declined to follow Polk's advice, but his open solicitation of that advice encouraged Polk to share his critique of Bragg with the army's other corps commander, Lieutenant General William J. Hardee, and as time went on, Polk lost few opportunities to undermine Bragg with other senior leaders.[34]

As a result, Bragg could not sustain his status as the army's undisputed master. It was one thing to treat subordinates like peers if they displayed the requisite ability, temperament, and loyalty. Grant and Lee created command partnerships with great success. But it was quite another to have subordinates treat the army commander like a peer, and an unwanted peer at that. Bragg might have solved the problem by getting rid of Polk, but Davis's continued friendship with Polk foreclosed this option. On top of that, his inability to change his corps commanders blocked Bragg from promoting younger generals who showed a military ability far greater than that of the rather plodding Polk and Hardee.[35]

The result was a hierarchical culture characterized by a low power distance, but of an unwelcome, destructive kind, that is, low in-group collectivism, and low institutional collectivism. This toxic senior command relationship inevitably affected field operations. During the Chickamauga campaign, for example, two key commanders flatly refused to carry out Bragg's order to strike the Union Army of the Cumberland while it was spread out and vulnerable. They did so again the next day. Polk also balked at an order from Bragg because he felt he knew better than Bragg and was immune to retaliation. Even the successful Chickamauga attack nearly failed because Bragg's senior leaders moved sluggishly. Bragg simply did not have the practical authority to force them to accept his will.[36]

It would be fair to say that the Army of Tennessee's high command deserved to fail at Chickamauga and won the battle only because the senior-level organizational culture of its adversary, the Army of the Cumberland, was equally dysfunctional. Indeed, this dysfunction led directly to Wood's gleeful embrace of the "fatal order of the day" that did in fact prove fatal.

The sources of this culture were similar to those of Bragg's army but with some interesting contrasts. Unlike the Union Army of the Tennessee, it began in fairly amorphous form under the command of, first, Major General Robert Anderson and then Brigadier General William T. Sherman, both of whom served for brief periods and had little influence on the army's organizational culture. Thus, not only did the army have no founder as influential as McClellan or Grant, it would be fair to say it had no founder at all. It even began its career under a different name: the Army of the Ohio.

Major General Don Carlos Buell commanded that army for about nine months, but for most of that period it comprised an army only in an administrative sense. Functionally it was a number of divisions and brigades scattered across much of southern Tennessee and northern Alabama. Aside from the battle of Shiloh, it did not operate as an army except during the Perryville campaign of September/October 1862. Thus Buell had scarcely more impact on the army's organizational culture than did Anderson or Sherman.

This does not mean that during its first year of existence, the Army of the Cumberland had no organizational culture. It simply means that its culture was not the product of its commander but, rather, grew from other experiences. Prokopowicz's thesis makes sense in regard to the nature of that culture; that is, its officers and men thought in terms of a conglomeration of regiments rather than a unified army.

This was just as well, because during Buell's tenure, the senior leadership culture was utterly toxic. Repelled by his cautious generalship and generous treatment of Southern civilians, which struck them as criminally mild, at least three factions undermined Buell at every turn: a powerful bloc of Indiana generals egged on by the state's governor, Oliver P. Morton; officers sympathetic to the division commander Brigadier General Albin Schoepf, who at one point called Buell a traitor; and supporters of the corps commander Major General Alexander McCook, who openly despised Buell. It was said that after the battle of Perryville, McCook and Buell did not even speak to each other. Buell also was quietly opposed by his second in command, Major General George H. Thomas, who nonetheless refused an offer to replace Buell because he had no wish to preside over this den of vipers.[37]

Instead, Buell wound up being replaced by Major General William S. Rosecrans. Rosecrans was one of the few Civil War army commanders to come from outside an army rather than by being promoted from within it. It was during his tenure that the Army of the Cumberland acquired its name and also when it finally fought its first battle—Stone's River—as a collective whole. Rosecrans commanded the army for the longest period up to that point: twelve months exactly. But if Rosecrans effected any change in the army's organizational culture, it is difficult to see how. First, by that time the culture would have had a strong constraining effect, so that any leader would have found changing it to be a major undertaking. Second, given the absence of any concept of organizational culture and insight into how to achieve significant change, it is unreasonable to expect that Rosecrans could even have begun to do so.

What Rosecrans could and did influence was the army's "command climate," essentially though not exclusively a matter of influencing morale through the credibility of the commander and the level of communication, trust, and confidence between the senior leadership and their subordinates.[38] Although Larry J. Daniel, a modern historian of the Army of the Cumberland, does not use the term *command climate*, he describes the atmosphere during Rosecrans's tenure as an incremental improvement over that during Buell's leadership but still characterized by rampant pettiness, parochialism, and sometimes "poisonous" relationships with subordinates.[39]

Rosecrans contributed to this culture through an unusually antagonistic relationship with the Lincoln administration as well as his frequent, capricious, and savage criticism of subordinates. In doing so, he fostered the atmosphere that influenced Wood's decision to obey the "fatal order" at Chickamauga. Eventually Rosecrans's own chief of staff, Major General James Garfield, grew so disgusted that he exploited his extensive contacts with Washington power brokers to have Rosecrans relieved of command. This took place when Grant, by then chief of the Military Division of the Mississippi—which encompassed most of the Union forces between the Appalachian Mountains and the Mississippi River—and therefore Rosecrans's superior, exercised the War Department's discretionary authorization to remove Rosecrans and substitute George H. Thomas.[40]

Daniel extolled Thomas as the "catalyst that gave the army its lethal edge," which certainly sounds as if Thomas managed to influence the Army of the Cumberland's organizational culture.[41] But this overstates the case. By the time Thomas assumed command in October 1863, the army's organizational culture had long since taken on a life of its own and resisted efforts to change it. Indeed, as a commander promoted from within the army, Thomas was a product of its organizational culture and took for granted many of its values, assumptions, and norms.

Moreover, just eight months elapsed between the time Thomas took command and the time the Atlanta campaign began—a very short time for any senior leader to change an organizational culture—and it was a period of extensive organizational reshuffling. If intentional and focused toward a specific objective, this kind of reshuffling might have represented an attempt to shift the army's organizational culture. But in fact it had a somewhat random character and was caused as much by external factors as by Thomas.[42] The most that can be said is that Thomas improved the army's command climate.

During the 1864 Atlanta campaign, the Armies of the Tennessee and the Cumberland fought together under the overall command of Major General William T. Sherman. As he embarked on the campaign, Sherman emphatically believed the two armies formed a study in contrasts. Although it was the smaller of the two, he considered that the Army of the Tennessee was the more responsive and aggressive and, whenever possible, used it for the most critical maneuvers of the Atlanta campaign. The Army of the Cumberland he regarded as "dreadfully slow." Six weeks into the campaign, he complained to Grant that "a fresh furrow in a ploughed field will stop the whole column, and all begin to entrench. . . . We are on the offensive, & yet it seems the whole Army of the Cumberland is so habituated to be on the defensive that I cannot get it out of their heads."[43]

Not unreasonably, many analysts have assumed that Sherman's appraisal of the two armies reflected chauvinism more than reality. Sherman had served in the Army of the Tennessee for most of his Civil War career, had learned much from Grant as his principal partner in command, and had briefly led the army before being vaulted to command of the Military Division of the Mississippi. He had greater confidence in McPherson, his own protégé, than in Thomas, even though Thomas was tried and tested in army command, whereas McPherson was new to the job. But was Sherman correct in perceiving that the two armies had contrasting organizational cultures? If so, to what did he ascribe this? And was he correct in assuming that the contrast made a difference?

With regard to the first question, Sherman surely was correct. The Army of the Tennessee reflected Grant's impact in shaping an army characterized by aggressiveness and cordial relationships among subordinates that inspired mutual confidence. During the Atlanta campaign, the Army of the Cumberland seemed to have a very different spirit: one of slowness and seeming defensive-mindedness. Sherman placed the blame on Thomas. To emphasize the value he placed on lightness and speed, Sherman had made a point of bringing no tents along with his headquarters. He ordered his subordinates to do the same. In the nomenclature of organizational theory, the proscription on tents was an "embedding mechanism," a tangible means by which a leader signals the shift in the values he is trying to achieve. But Thomas, he told Grant, had utterly disregarded his instructions. Every one of Thomas's aides and orderlies had a wall tent, Sherman insisted, "and a Baggage train big enough for a Division." Thomas had promised to send it all back, but nothing had come of it. Sherman believed that the Army of the Cumberland's slowness "has cost me the loss of two opportunities" in the early weeks of the campaign, "which never recur in war."[44]

The literature on organizational culture, however, strongly suggests that if the Army of the Cumberland had a predilection for being slow and defensive-minded, the roots of that culture antedated Thomas, so he could not easily have changed it, no matter what he did with his baggage train or anything else. After the fall of Atlanta, Sherman's ultimate solution was to send Thomas to defend the critical city of Nashville and make his famous March to the Sea with troops drawn largely from the Army of the Tennessee.

In sum, the hierarchical senior leader culture proved very difficult to manage. Only Lee and Grant succeeded, and Grant discovered that even he could not reshape the culture of the Army of the Potomac, just as Sherman discovered that he could do no better with the Army of the Cumberland.

Regimental Culture

The clannish regimental culture differed starkly from the hierarchical senior leadership culture and was, on the whole, much healthier. To start with, the *power distance* between the leaders and the led was seldom very great. A Civil War regiment consisted of consisted of ten companies of one hundred men, each led by a captain. In nearly every instance, the companies were recruited by community leaders, men of established standing who could persuade other men to enlist under their command. Thus a successful businessman might announce that he was forming a company of infantry. Other men, familiar with his reputation, would join up, and frequently they would then elect their officers, starting with the community leader, who invariably was elected captain. Furthermore, because a company consisted of men from the same locality who knew one another, an officer usually was familiar to his men from civilian life and could scarcely afford to adopt an imperious attitude. Instead he had to exercise a style of leadership based on persuasion.

This dynamic carried up to the regiments and the colonels who led them. Disease, wounds, and death rapidly wore them down to anywhere from 50 to 30 percent of their original strength of a thousand men. A colonel therefore presided over a fairly compact group of men whom he knew and was known by them personally. The regimental environment greatly resembled an extended family. Soldiers routinely called themselves "the boys." They understood the need for leadership and preferred officers who were militarily competent. Nevertheless, they resented and resisted any officer who tried to put on airs. Colonels discovered that they were most effective if they behaved like benevolent parents, and one of the highest accolades a soldier could pay an officer was to say that he behaved "like a father."[45]

Although this clannishness often militated against the strict discipline that characterized a professional army, it paid huge dividends in terms of *in-group collectivism*, which military historians more commonly call *unit cohesion*. This cohesion was born partly of mutual loyalty among kinsmen and neighbors and partly from the awareness that if a man shirked his duty or showed cowardice, everyone back home would soon know it. Civil War soldiers identified very closely with their regiment, took enormous pride in it, and, in combat, fought to the death to defend the regimental colors from capture, even in circumstances when such fights were tactically meaningless.

Two other attributes, *high performance orientation* and *institutional collectivism*, are reasonably straightforward when applied to Civil War regiments. The perseverance of regiments in combat, underscored by casualty rates that in most battles ran from 30 to 70 percent, amply attests to the former—and as Prokopowicz asserted, this largely explains the enormous resilience of Civil War armies—while the equal distribution of resources within a given regiment was practically a given.

Two intermediary organizations linked the clannish culture of the regiment to the hierarchical culture of the senior leadership: the brigade, commanded by a brigadier (one-star) general and typically consisting of five regiments, and the division, commanded by a major (two-star) general and typically consisting of three brigades. Although the combat power of these units obviously trumped that of the regiment, their organizational cultures had far less impact. The reason was that the composition of brigades and divisions frequently changed as regiments or brigades were reshuffled within them. While it would be wrong to say that soldiers took no pride in the brigade or division to which they nominally belonged, their organizational identification remained firmly fixed on their regiment.

The Nineteenth Indiana Volunteer Infantry Regiment is an instructive case. Recruited primarily from Wayne County, Indiana, at the war's outset it found itself dispatched to Washington, D.C., where it formed part of the burgeoning Army of the Potomac. It was soon attached to a brigade, led by forty-year-old Brigadier General John P. Hatch, whose other regiments hailed from Wisconsin. Hatch was a West Point graduate and a career officer who effectively trained the brigade. But despite his military expertise, Hatch exerted scant influence on the organizational culture of the Nineteenth Indiana, which instead centered on its colonel, fifty-one-year-old Solomon Meredith. Meredith had an imposing personality and an impressive career, first as the sheriff of Wayne County, then as a state legislator, and finally as the U.S. marshal for the district of Indiana.[46] He was well known to all the men of the regiment and the principal authority figure in their martial universe.

In May 1862 the Nineteenth acquired a new brigade commander, thirty-five-year-old Brigadier General John Gibbon. Like Hatch, Gibbon was a West Point graduate and an accomplished career soldier. Unlike Hatch, Gibbon worked hard to shift the primary identification of his troops from their regiments to the brigade. A strict disciplinarian, he routinely "invaded" the regiments with inspections and new regulations intended to bring them more closely into line with regular army standards. He also introduced a major innovation. The regiments of the brigade were now required to wear a distinctive uniform, highlighted by leggings and black Hardee hats highly unusual in volunteer regiments, which typically wore kepis or forage caps.

Like Sherman's proscription on tents, Gibbon's insistence on the black Hardee hats was an embedding mechanism. Gibbon wanted a unit that thought of itself as a brigade, not as an aggregation of regiments. And he indeed achieved an impressive degree of success. The brigade became known first as the Black Hat Brigade and then, thanks to a reputation for stalwart fighting in several major battles, as the Iron Brigade, easily the most famous brigade in the Army of the Potomac.

Yet even this formidable pride in the brigade never eclipsed the primacy of the Nineteenth Indiana as the locus of its soldiers' loyalty. Initially the men of the Nineteenth violently resisted Gibbon's attempt to forge a well-integrated brigade, despised him as a tyrant, and—encouraged by Colonel Meredith, their regimental "father"—actually refused to buy the leggings that Gibbon insisted that the men of his brigade wear. Meredith justified his resistance on the dubious ground that the cost of the leggings would be unfairly deducted from the soldiers' clothing allowance. Gibbon retaliated severely, even threatening to bombard the regiment with artillery if it did not comply. The tension between Meredith and Gibbon never abated. The men of the Nineteenth backed their colonel, and Meredith and several of his subordinates did not hesitate to contact powerful political patrons in a largely successful effort to neutralize Gibbon's attempt to dominate the Nineteenth. Despite the so-called Legging Mutiny, Meredith's position as colonel was never in jeopardy. Eventually, when Gibbon went on to division command and Meredith assumed command of the brigade, among his first acts—highly popular with the Nineteenth—was to revoke Gibbon's order requiring the troops to pay for the despised leggings.[47] If even within the Iron Brigade, the soldiers' first allegiance remained to their regiments, it is no surprise that soldiers in most regiments felt only a modest identification with their brigades and even less with their divisions, whose composition and commanders continually shifted.

Conclusion

Although organizational culture was hardly the sole explanation for success or failure on the battlefield, it merits greater attention than it has so far received. Of particular value would be studies of the brigade and division levels that connected the senior leadership and regimental culture. These appear to have been influenced more by the former than the latter, since officers interested in promotion would naturally look to the culture of the high command.

Gerald Prokopowicz surely is correct in postulating that the regimental culture gave Civil War armies the durability to survive battles in which losses of 30 to 70 percent were normal. (In contrast, the modern U.S. Army considers a unit that sustains 25 percent casualties to have been effectively destroyed.) This culture also inoculated soldiers against battlefield defeats, since they usually blamed them on senior commanders or other regiments and believed that their own regiments had acquitted themselves nobly.

Even so, no amount of regimental esprit de corps could supply the strategic wisdom and operational prowess needed to win the war. What, then, could have been done to improve the hierarchical senior leadership culture? Many potential solutions were simply unavailable. The extensive staff system characteristic of modern military organizations—and already well developed in the Prussian general staff—did not yet exist. Although Civil War armies did have officers who handled such matters as equipment and ration supply, they had nothing like the large staffs who assist modern commanders in the planning, monitoring, and execution of operations. Instead, most officers who assisted Civil War army and corps commanders were little more than glorified clerks.[48] As a result, these commanders were usually overburdened and overstressed, traits that led to short tempers and mutual suspicion.

The Union and Confederate War Departments also had limited ability to transmit effective senior leadership techniques from one field army to another. Officers who worked directly under Grant or Lee might learn the secrets of their success, but no institutional mechanism existed to pass these along, and the mere transfer of officers from one army to another had only a negligible impact on their well-established cultures.

Even so, one partial remedy stands out. While the strategic guidance supplied by Presidents Lincoln and Davis was entirely legitimate, their chronic interference in personnel matters and their indulgence or even encouragement of disgruntled subordinates who violated the chain of command set a poor example and often compromised the ability of army commanders to be masters of their own house.

Ultimately, in the postwar decades, the problem of toxic senior leadership cultures was partly solved by increased professionalization of the officer corps through advanced military education and a distancing from political involvement. Yet it continues to affect military operations to this day. One simply cannot thrust strong personalities together in stressful environments and expect cordial relationships to emerge naturally. Grant's and Lee's intuitive grasp of organizational culture must be intentionally studied and mastered.

NOTES

1. *War of the Rebellion: A Compilation of the Official Records of the Union and Confederate Armies*, 128 vols. (Washington, DC: U.S. Government Printing Office, 1880–1901), vol. 30, part 1, p. 635 (hereafter *OR*).

2. Quoted in Peter Cozzens, *This Terrible Sound: The Battle of Chickamauga* (Urbana: University of Illinois Press, 1992), 363.

3. Report of Colonel Emerson Opdycke, September 26, 1863, *OR* series I, vol. 30, pt. 1, p. 706.

4. Ralsa C. Rice, *Yankee Tigers: Through the Civil War with the 125th Ohio*, ed. Richard A. Baumgartner and Larry M. Strayer (Huntington, WV: Blue Acorn Press, 1992), 65.

5. Ibid., 69.

6. Charles T. Clark, *Opdycke Tigers, 125th O.V.I.: A History of the Regiment and the Campaigns and Battles of the Army of the Cumberland* (Columbus, OH: Spahr & Glenn, 1895), 105.

7. Clifford Geertz, *The Interpretation of Cultures* (New York: Basic Books, 1973), 5.

8. William Glenn Robertson, *The Staff Ride, Prepared by the U.S. Center for Military History* (Washington, DC: U.S. Government Printing Office, 1987), v.

9. The Center for Strategic Leadership at the U.S. Army War College, for example, routinely offers a three-day strategic leadership development program for senior business executives, capped by a daylong staff ride of the Gettysburg battlefield. For an overview of the program, see Center for Strategic Leadership, available at http://www.csl.army.mil/SLEP.aspx (accessed August 24, 2010).

10. Stephen J. Gerras, Leonard Wong, and Charles D. Allen, "Organizational Culture: Applying a Hybrid Model in the U.S. Army," *Strategic Culture: Selected Readings*, U.S. Army War College Academic Year 2010 (Carlisle Barracks, PA: U.S. Army War College, 2009), 114–44.

11. Edgar H. Schein, *Organizational Culture and Leadership*, 3rd ed. (San Francisco: Jossey-Bass, 2004), 25–38.

12. Gerras, Wong, and Allen, "Organizational Culture," 119.

13. The inspiration for the GLOBE study was derived from the pioneering work of Geert Hofstede, *Culture's Consequences: International Differences in Work-Related Values* (Beverly Hills, CA: Sage, 1980).

14. Gerras, Wong, and Allen, "Organizational Culture," 120–21; Robert J. House, Paul J. Hanges, Mansour Javidan, Peter W. Dorfman, and Vipin Gupta, *Culture, Leadership, and Organizations* (Thousand Oaks, CA: Sage, 2004).

15. Gerras, Wong, and Allen, "Organizational Culture," 116–17. See also Kim S. Cameron and Robert E. Quinn, *Diagnosing and Changing Organizational Culture* (Reading, PA: Addison-Wesley, 1999).

16. Gerras, Wong, and Allen, "Organizational Culture," 117.

17. Alfred D. Chandler Jr., *The Visible Hand: The Managerial Revolution in American Business* (Cambridge, MA: Harvard University Press, 1977), 485.

18. Schein, *Organizational Culture and Leadership*, 291–317; W. Clay Hamner, ed., *Organizational Shock* (New York: Wiley, 1980).

19. Michael C. C. Adams, *Our Masters the Rebels: A Speculation on Union Military Failure in the East, 1861–1865* (Cambridge, MA: Harvard University Press, 1978); Grady McWhiney and Perry D. Jamieson, *Attack and Die: Civil War Military Tactics and the Southern Heritage* (Tuscaloosa: University of Alabama Press, 1982).

20. Gerald J. Prokopowicz, *All for the Regiment: The Army of the Ohio, 1861–1862* (Chapel Hill: University of North Carolina Press, 2001), 4.

21. Walter H. Herbert, *Fighting Joe Hooker* (1944; repr., Lincoln: University of Nebraska Press, 1999), 284–87.

22. Steven E. Woodworth, *Nothing but Victory: The Army of the Tennessee, 1861–1865* (New York: Knopf, 2005), ix.

23. See Joseph T. Glatthaar, *Partners in Command: The Relationships between Leaders in the Civil War* (New York: Free Press, 1994), 135–90; and Steven E. Woodworth, ed., *Grant's Lieutenants*, 2 vols. (Lawrence: University Press of Kansas, 2001, 2008).

24. Stephen R. Taaffe, *Commanding the Army of the Potomac* (Lawrence: University Press of Kansas, 2006), 9–13.

25. Stephen W. Sears, *Controversies and Commanders: Dispatches from the Army of the Potomac* (Boston: Houghton Mifflin, 1999), 131–66.

26. Horace Porter, *Campaigning with Grant* (1897; repr., Bloomington: Indiana University Press, 1961), 69–70.

27. Mark Grimsley, *And Keep Moving On: The Virginia Campaign, May–June 1864* (Lincoln: University of Nebraska Press, 2002). For the concept of coping versus control, I am indebted to my colleague Alan D. Beyerchen.

28. Entry for May 19, 1864, in David W. Lowe, ed., *Meade's Army: The Private Notebooks of Lt. Col. Theodore Lyman* (Kent, OH: Kent State University Press, 2007), 164–65.

29. Clifford Dowdey and Louis H. Manarin, eds., *The Wartime Papers of R. E. Lee* (New York: Bramhall House, 1961), 221.

30. William Allan, "Memoranda of Conversations with General Robert E. Lee," in *Lee the Soldier*, ed. Gary W. Gallagher (Lincoln: University of Nebraska Press, 1996), 17.

31. Douglas Southall Freeman, *Lee's Lieutenants: A Study in Command*, 3 vols. (New York: Scribner, 1942–1944). Freeman details Lee's purges after the Seven Days (1:606–14); after Antietam (2:250–83); after Chancellorsville (2:683–714); and during the Overland campaign (3:496–514).

32. For Lee's relationship with Hill, see James I. Robertson Jr., *General A. P. Hill: The Story of a Confederate Warrior* (New York: Random House, 1987). On Ewell's removal, see Donald C. Pfanz, *Richard S. Ewell: A Soldier's Life* (Chapel Hill: University of North Carolina Press, 1998), 397–402.

33. Contrasting analyses of Lee's decision are Robert K. Krick, "The Army of Northern Virginia in 1862: The Circumstances, Its Opportunities, and Why It Should Not Have Been at Sharpsburg," in *Antietam: Essays on the 1862 Maryland Campaign*, ed. Gary W. Gallagher (Kent, OH: Kent State University Press, 1989), 35–55; and Joseph L. Harsh, who defends Lee in *Taken at the Flood: Robert E. Lee and Confederate Strategy in the Maryland Campaign of 1862* (Kent, OH: Kent State University Press, 1999), 354–67, 361, 369, 444–45.

34. Steven E. Woodworth, *Jefferson Davis and His Generals: The Failure of Confederate Command in the West* (Lawrence: University Press of Kansas, 1990), 160–62.

35. Steven E. Woodworth, "Davis, Bragg, and Confederate Command in the West," in *Jefferson Davis's Generals*, ed. Gabor S. Boritt (New York: Oxford University Press, 1999), 65–83.

36. Woodworth, *Jefferson Davis and His Generals*, 230–32.

37. Larry J. Daniel, *Days of Glory: The Army of the Cumberland, 1861–1865* (Baton Rouge: Louisiana State University Press, 2004), 126–35, 174.

38. This definition draws on Steven M. Jones, *Improving Accountability for Effective Command Climate: A Strategic Imperative* (Carlisle Barracks, PA: Strategic Studies Institute, 2003).

39. Daniel, *Days of Glory*, xii–xiii.

40. T. Harry Williams, *Lincoln and His Generals* (New York: Knopf, 1952), 276–85; Daniel, *Days of Glory*, 246, 281.

41. Daniel, *Days of Glory*, xi.

42. Ibid., 379–93.

43. Sherman to Grant, June 18, 1864, in *Sherman's Civil War: Selected Correspondence of William T. Sherman, 1860–1865*, ed. Brooks D. Simpson and Jean V. Berlin (Chapel Hill: University of North Carolina Press, 1999), 655.

44. Ibid.

45. Reid Mitchell perceptively analyzes this dynamic in *The Vacant Chair: The Northern Soldier Leaves Home* (New York: Oxford University Press, 1993), esp. 39–54.

46. Ezra J. Warner, ed., *Generals in Blue: Lives of the Union Commanders* (Baton Rouge: Louisiana State University Press, 1964), 319–20.

47. Alan Graff, *On Many a Bloody Field: Four Years in the Iron Brigade* (Bloomington: Indiana University Press, 1996), esp. 124–38.

48. J. Boone Bartholomees Jr., *Buff Facings and Gilt Buttons: Staff and Headquarters Operations in the Army of Northern Virginia, 1861–1865* (Columbia: University of South Carolina Press, 1998); R. Steven Jones, *The Right Hand of Command: Use & Disuse of Personal Staffs in the Civil War* (Mechanicsburg, PA: Stackpole Books, 2000).

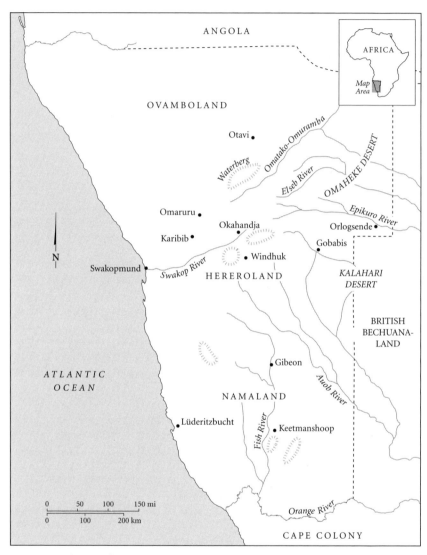

German Southwest Africa

7

German Military Culture and the Colonial War in Southwest Africa, 1904–1907

ISABEL V. HULL

From its unification in 1870/71 until World War I, imperial Germany's only military engagements were overseas. In several of the larger colonial conflicts, the military demonstrated its tendency to adopt extreme, even dysfunctional, policies of destruction, which it did so again during the world war. This chapter explores how Germany's military culture predisposed commanders to use excessive force and how the military's place in German political culture made it difficult to rein in that force once it had been unleashed. The example I use is Germany's largest prewar engagement, suppressing the revolt in Southwest Africa between 1904 and 1907, during which two African peoples suffered genocide or near genocide as a direct result of military operations.[1]

Military culture describes the lessons that military organizations have learned from their past struggles with foreign armies, with domestic competitors for resources, and with domestic critics—in short, the challenges they have surmounted in the environments in which they operate. These lessons gradually disappear from consciousness as they become embedded in habits, basic assumptions, default programs, and scripts that seem so obviously correct and natural that those inside the organizational culture have trouble thinking beyond or against them. Furthermore, because they deal in violence and death and thus have developed imperative command structures, militaries typically have "strong" organizational cultures, insulating them even further from insiders' critical insight.[2]

The Prusso-German military shared many significant features of its military culture with other late nineteenth- and early twentieth-century European armies. Some of the most important were the habits and techniques resulting from the military's basic task of being the expert wielder of violent force, the imperative command structure, the industrial-technological revolution in firepower, gender uniformity and shared ideals of masculinity, and the modern organizational-bureaucratic structure.

But the Prusso-German military also was unique in some respects. Its preeminent importance to the monarchy and, increasingly, to the national imaginary; its constitutional protection from civilian or critical scrutiny; its general staff system that dominated training, doctrine, and planning; its system of "mission tactics" stressing independence, activism, and responsibility even in the most junior officers; its assumptions about the pure, existential nature of warfare, from which it derived an expansive definition of "military necessity"; and its narrow conception of military victory—all these were peculiar traits of the German army. All of them are reflected in how the revolt in Southwest Africa was suppressed. For even though it was a colonial war, the men who fought it were not part of a colonial army. Germany had none. They and their officers, with the exception of a few members of the local armed force of the colony (the *Schutztruppe*), were sent from home to quash the rebellion. Their methods either were those of European warfare or were derived from European armies' assumptions about war. Although the colonial situation tended to confirm and strengthen the destructive tendencies of military culture, for the most part it did not create them.

The Revolt in Southwest Africa, 1904–1907

In the twenty years since Germany established a protectorate over Southwest Africa (SWA) in 1883, about two thousand, mostly male, settlers had come to the arid, sparsely populated colony. A combination of factors, not least of which was white pressure on native lands, caused the dominant tribe in the colony's center, the cattle-herding Herero, to rise in revolt in January 1904. They were followed in rebellion by the much less numerous Nama to the south, in October 1904. Crushing these uprisings took over three years, cost almost 600 million deutsche marks, and involved fourteen thousand soldiers transferred from the German army.

The Germans found the fighting extremely difficult, unused as they were to desert conditions in which no infrastructure of roads, telegraphs, or waterlines eased their movements. The military effort was Germany's largest before 1914. Some 1,500 men died, half of them from illness.[3] But the Herero and Nama lost infinitely more. A handful of modern writers have cited poor statistics to justify their denial of the vast demographic catastrophe.[4] Well-informed contemporary observers and postwar demographic data agree, however, on the immensity of the human destruction suffered by Africans.

Most historians accept a death rate of between 75 and 80 percent for the Herero (out of an original population of 60,000 to 80,000 people) and of about 45 to 50 percent for the Nama (whose prewar numbers were around 20,000).[5] Official German military statistics admitted that the internment camps, which contained not just surrendering male rebels but also women and children, had compiled a death rate of 45 percent.[6] In addition to these enormous numbers, the commander who set this military policy, Lieutenant General Lothar von Trotha (June 1904 to November 1905), announced in October 1904 his intention to achieve a final solution in SWA, in which mass death to the point of extermination was an acceptable outcome.

Neither the genocide nor, more generally, the final solution in SWA was ordered in Berlin. If Trotha had received such an order, even a verbal one, he surely would have said so when he later defended his extremism in private correspondence with his superior, Chief of Staff Alfred von Schlieffen, with Chancellor (Bernhard, prince von) Bülow, and with SWA Governor Colonel Theodor Leutwein.[7] As it was, he explained that "I received no instructions or directives from His Majesty upon my appointment to commander in Southwest Africa. His Majesty simply said that he expected me to crush the uprising by all means and explain to him later why it had begun."[8] The phrase "by all means" was a standard expression routinely used in connection with colonial revolts.[9]

Not only was no order given, Trotha's *Vernichtungspolitik* (policy of destruction) was opposed by Governor Leutwein, Chancellor Bülow, the Social Democrats and Left Liberals in the Reichstag, missionaries, even ruthless social Darwinists like Paul Rohrbach, who was in SWA when the revolt broke out, and, finally and belatedly, also by the white settlers there, who did not want their labor supply eliminated. The settlers' inflammatory rhetoric at the beginning of the revolt, however, certainly contributed to an atmosphere conducive of annihilation.[10]

In the absence of an order and in the face of much opposition, the extreme human destruction in SWA developed out of military practices. The institutional prerequisite for this extremism was therefore total military control over military policy and over the colony. This control occurred in two stages. The first was the immediate transfer of authority from the governor, himself a soldier experienced in putting down revolts, to the general staff back in Germany. Although Governor Leutwein still prosecuted the initial campaigns (from January to June 1904), he took his orders from the general staff rather than from the chancellor via the Foreign Office, which was the normal chain of command in the colonies. The "civilians" were unseated in favor of military experts because it was in the kaiser's constitutional power (his *Kommandogewalt*) to do so, and because the revolt was immediately identified as a national security issue. The deaths of 158 white settlers (98 percent of them male) at the revolt's start impressed even colonial skeptics in the Reichstag who had a duty to protect German settlers. Even more threatening was the rebels' challenge to the German state's authority and prestige. The director of the Colonial Office, Dr. Oscar W. Stübel, declared in the Reichstag to general approval that "Germany's honor demands the repression of the uprising by all means."[11] If the rebellion were not decisively crushed, Germany's ability to be a colonial power would seem doubtful, and therefore its status as a great power after the British model would be diminished. *Weltpolitik* (world policy) and great-power politics made a mere colonial revolt into a major national security threat.

The second stage in the consolidation of military power occurred because of strictly military judgments. In April 1904 Governor Leutwein won a difficult military victory at Oviumbo, driving the Herero permanently into a defensive position at Waterberg. But because Leutwein had momentarily retreated for strategic reasons, the general staff viewed Oviumbo as a defeat. This misjudgment rested on a series of basic assumptions embedded in German military culture. First were heightened expectations of easy victory by superior Europeans over inferior Africans (a type of generalized race-thinking ubiquitous in the imperial situation and common to all colonial armies).[12] Second was a peculiar German military investment in cheap, quick, symbolically decisive victories. Quick victory circumvented the civilian oversight that came with extra Reichstag military appropriations. The overvaluation of speed was especially desirable to demonstrate absolute German military superiority, since the military—thanks to its own efforts and those of the monarch, Conservatives, and ultranationalist agitators—had become synonymous with imperial stability, social discipline, and Germany's future as a prosperous great power. In short, the German military had tremendous symbolic-political weight, so its defeat, even a momentary strategic retreat, was unbearable and unthinkable.

Consequently, the chiefs of the general staff and the military cabinet convinced the kaiser to replace Leutwein with Trotha, who earlier had distinguished himself as a ruthless suppressor of native revolts in German East Africa. When Trotha arrived in SWA in June 1904, he declared martial law, and in November, when he and Leutwein clashed over *Vernichtungspolitik*, Trotha replaced Leutwein as governor. SWA thus remained under total military control until Trotha's own removal and return to Berlin in November 1905.

Putting the military in charge thus was the result of many complicated factors: Germany's constitutional setup (which gave the kaiser and his military advisers sweeping power), national foreign policy (*Weltpolitik*), national identification heightened by acceptance of the doctrine of national security (even by former opponents of colonialism in the Catholic center and left liberal parties), and central tenets of military doctrine (which themselves were formed in interaction with important characteristics of Germany's political culture).

With Trotha's arrival in SWA, there began the logical unfolding of the German military's standard operating procedures on the levels of both doctrine and practice (i.e., on both the conscious and the habitual and un-self-reflexive levels). The resulting pattern can be divided into six moments.

The Military Pattern of Development toward Extremes of Destruction

1. Vernichtung

Late nineteenth-century German military doctrine held that the destruction (*Vernichtung*) of the enemy was the goal of warfare. When Carl von Clausewitz originally enunciated this principle, he meant "destruction of the enemy's military forces." Although Wilhelminians meant the same thing, in an age when industrialism and technological growth threatened to expand military targets to include civilians and the economy,[13] it is perhaps significant that the phrase had been reduced to simply "destruction of the enemy." Nevertheless, military men believed their foe to be primarily soldiers.

By the 1890s, *Vernichtung* had developed into a specific dogma that called for swift, offensive movement, if possible culminating in a single, concentric battle of annihilation. While the "cult of the offensive" was characteristic of most European military cultures at this time, the single battle of annihilation was peculiarly German.[14] It is most evident in Schlieffen's famous plan, but it also was the basis for German naval strategy.[15] In both cases, the dogma was a response to perceived German weakness: on land, in response to "encirclement" by France and Russia; and at sea, in the face of the world's greatest naval power, Britain. Extreme offense was the simultaneous concentration of all one's forces; the hope that the country's technological and technical prowess might overcome numerical weakness; the daring, even foolhardy risking of the country's entire effort at a single stroke; the demand of extreme self-sacrifice from the country's troops and sailors; and the discounting of logistical limits and the enemy's possible responses. All these features of the dogma were required to transcend Germany's inferiority and to permit it to behave like a world power, a paramount power, instead of merely one of the five European "great powers." The dogma of the single battle of annihilation was thus the military reflection of that curious mix of ambition and desperation characteristic of Wilhelminian politics.[16]

This dogma was the default program, the "prescription for victory" in which all German officers were trained.[17] Although it was developed for European circumstances, the dogma was applied randomly in the colonies, where it was almost impossible to achieve. Lack of infrastructure made the movement of supplies and the concentration of men extremely difficult; worse, huge supply trains prevented mobility and flexibility, precisely what guerrilla wars required.

Not surprisingly, therefore, the single battle of annihilation was what Lieutenant General Trotha attempted in SWA. He spent June and July inching his forces forward until they had nearly surrounded the Waterberg, the last main water source before the Omaheke desert, where an estimated sixty thousand Herero, the entire people, were holed up. The terrain was so difficult that by the time the attack began, the German forces, new arrivals from Europe, were exhausted and had used up their fodder and water. Trotha then deployed his forces unevenly, blocking a breakthrough west back into the center of the colony while leaving the eastern route into the desert more sparsely defended. One historian even concluded that Trotha wanted the Herero to escape into the desert where they would die.[18] This is surely wrong, for Trotha not only informed Berlin just before the battle that "I will attack the enemy simultaneously with all units, in order to destroy [*vernichten*] him," as the dogma required; but he also had built a stockade for the eight thousand prisoners (the maximum official estimate of Herero warriors) he expected to take and even had ordered one thousand chains for them.[19] Everybody expected a great German victory; civilian administrators, missionaries, and businessmen were already meeting to divide the prisoners among themselves.[20] Instead, due partly to two errors by unit commanders, the Herero suffered only light casualties and escaped into the desert.

Trotha had now (August 11, 1904) achieved a victory somewhat like Governor Leutwein's at Oviumbo. He had in fact defeated the Herero. Their leaders concluded they could not win, and they sent out peace feelers. They never again posed a serious military risk or engaged in regular battle. But according to the inflated German military standards of the day, this was not enough to qualify as a victory. It was not a total victory of force in which the enemy was dead or captured or submitted unconditionally. It had not demonstrated German military invincibility and therefore had not convincingly reestablished German authority and order.

2. Rejection of Negotiations

If the object of German military intervention had been to defeat the Herero, then Trotha should now have negotiated the Hereros' surrender, as Governor Leutwein urged him to do. But negotiations were unthinkable. Trotha later (1909) explained why: Without a breakthrough,

> then the possibility of negotiation would have existed, and a regular court would have brought the murderers and ringleaders to the gallows; the weapons and cows would have gone to the government; and the rest of the tribes would have returned to the sunshine of the all-highest [i.e., His Majesty's] mercy.

In any case, there could be no question of negotiations in the immediate aftermath of the battle if Trotha did not want to testify to his own weakness and embarrassment (*Ohnmacht und Verlegenheit*). This would have been immediately clear to the enemy and would have meant a renewal of the war as soon as the band had recovered from the first shock.[21]

For Trotha and for many of his fellow officers, anything short of a total victory of military force signaled weakness and constituted a security threat. Again, we see the exceedingly high standards of victory that the German military had manufactured for itself.

Trotha's intransigence, however, was encouraged by several other factors. Both the kaiser and widespread public opinion as it was reflected in the bourgeois press at the beginning of the revolt rejected negotiations until the rebels had been "punished."[22] This trope of colonial warfare, eternalized in the phrase "punitive expedition," construed rebels as outlaws and understood punishment in the old-fashioned way as physical suffering rather than as the incarceration appropriate to (one's own) citizens. Infliction of physical suffering was what one did to one's inferiors, and the military instrument was singularly apt, since it was one of the last spheres in Europe that still permitted flogging and degradation (though it was increasingly controversial).

Thus a number of separate cultural strands combined to make negotiation questionable, especially since it carried the suggestion of some equality between the negotiating parties and recognized the political existence of indigenous groups that German colonialism, at any rate, was trying to erase.[23]

3. Pursuit (*Verfolgung*)

If the single battle of annihilation was the first default program of German military doctrine, pursuit was the second. As all commanders knew, if the first did not succeed, then they should pursue the enemy ruthlessly until they either had forced "him" (as the books always labeled the enemy) to fight, thus recreating the conditions of the battle of annihilation, or they had ground his forces into oblivion. Not surprisingly, Trotha immediately ordered such a pursuit and, until the end of September, chased the chimera of a final, decisive "battle" with the Herero.[24]

In fact, the parlous state of the German troops and their mounts dictated that most soldiers remain behind at the waterholes, forming a kind of cordon against the Hereros' reinfiltration into the colony, while the two most resilient units pursued the fleeing Herero deeper into the waterless desert. Only the very first skirmish resembled a battle. The rest, although listed as "battles" or "fights" in the official history and reported in the telegrams to Berlin as such, instead were encounters in which German troops fired on fleeing Africans. A very small number of Herero, perhaps two thousand, made it through the desert and into Bechuanaland on the other side. Some even managed to slip through the cordon back into SWA, where they tried to eke out an existence on the veld. But the great majority of the Herero people died of thirst during the "pursuit," as the surviving daughter of the chief Zacharia graphically described it to Trotha at the beginning of October, as the skeletons beside the dried river beds attested, and as the official history concluded, describing the "shocking fate [*erschütternde Schicksal*] that the mass of the people had met in the desert": "The punishment [*Strafgericht*] had come to an end. The Hereros had ceased to be an independent tribe."[25]

The mass death of the Herero people was therefore the result of a standard military procedure, described (and perhaps experienced) by most of the German participants as conventional combat. Mass death came from the practices of waging war, not (yet) from an announced policy aiming at genocide. Perhaps this is one reason why the participants, even Trotha himself, doubted the magnitude of the dying, even though they had daily proof of it. For many, it seemed the Herero had simply vanished, and German officers were seized by the fear that they would return to continue the war. This fear contributed to Trotha's decision to make the clearance of all Herero people the actual goal of military policy. Before turning to this decision, however, we must examine more closely the practices that made mass killing easy or likely by encouraging or habituating soldiers to indiscriminate slaughter. That is, a great many Herero died not of thirst but by being shot. These practices can be located in institutional habits, deep-seated expectations on the part of troops, and specific orders concerning war conduct.

4. Practices Conducive to Mass Killing

Many scholars have noted that suffering, frustrated troops are more apt to engage in retaliatory atrocities than are others.[26] Some of the reasons that Germany's troops in SWA suffered and became frustrated were circumstantial, but there also were structural-institutional reasons that made unnecessary suffering likely. One of the main reasons was inadequate provisions; field troops received two-thirds rations, and malnutrition and scurvy were widespread. In addition, medical treatment was wholly inadequate, as the official postwar report acknowledged.[27]

Provisioning (logistics) was the stepchild of the German military. No ambitious officer chose to specialize in it, for German military culture stressed fighting above any and all ancillary activities. Even the Schlieffen plan's otherwise minute choreography left critical aspects of provisioning to the chance of finding food and fodder near the battlefield.[28] Aside from the premium placed on combat, the traditional Prussian aversion to those archcivilian concerns of economics and management played a strong role in relegating logistics to the sidelines, despite the advancing "professionalization" of the officer corps before 1914.[29] The gap between Germany's military and colonial ambitions and its actual power to achieve them (evident in the vagueness of *Weltpolitik* and in all of Germany's war planning) would only have encouraged the general staff to overlook realistic planning that threatened to expose the unreality of world-power dreams.

In the colonies, haphazard provisioning was fatal. Colonies typically lacked a developed infrastructure and reserves of familiar food and potable water, yet the dogma of the battle of annihilation required huge amounts of men and matériel, the very stuff of European superiority. In short, logistical failure was virtually preprogrammed in the colonies.

This problem might have been resolved by training small units of colonial-warfare specialists, who, acclimated to overseas conditions, could have moved as lightly and swiftly as the indigenous peoples did. But Germany was a new imperial power and was dedicated to the principle of colonialism on the cheap. The suggestion to form an expensive colonial force was repeatedly rejected. The alternative, relying on African allies, worked in German East Africa, but not in SWA, where the influx of metropolitan soldiers brought with it the conviction that "natives" were unreliable and that Germans, superior by nature and by training, should do everything themselves.[30]

The failures of logistics and preparation, which were deeply institutionalized defects, were all the more shocking because of the high expectations they disappointed. The general racial hubris of Europeans in Africa (and elsewhere), combined with the specific military hubris of the Prusso-German military, meant that troops expected a quick and easy victory. They almost seemed offended when that sort of victory eluded them. And frustrated hubris is surely one of the most dangerous kinds.

But German troops had another expectation that at first glance seems incompatible with colonial combat. They had been trained for a conventional European war. They were therefore prepared to fight uniformed soldiers, clearly demarcated from civilians, equipped with standard weapons, and behaving according to European standards (e.g., attacking openly and surrendering when wounded). Instead, they met a foe who might be wearing a German *Schutztruppe* uniform (stolen from a fallen soldier) or be indistinguishable except by sex from noncombatants; who fought stealthily; who often had to resort to homemade weapons that left dirty, ragged wounds; who fought until death; who killed wounded German troops; and who engaged in the ritual mutilation of dead soldiers.

The expectations of conventional European warfare were, of course, the foundation of international law, which had been codified in a series of recent conferences. That is, conventional behavior and those who abided by it were covered by legal protection, and those who violated these conventions were subject to reprisals. At the international conferences, the German delegates, military and civilian, had distinguished themselves by their uniquely high standards of "order" and conventionality.[31] German representatives were far less willing to grant regular combatant status (and thus the protection of the Geneva Convention for prisoners of war) to irregular troops than were the representatives of France or of smaller European nations. And the Germans were far readier to sanction severe reprisals against civilians for a whole range of activities that other nations found acceptable, even patriotic.[32] In short, Germany held a much more rigid conception of order and propriety than did other European powers, and it was quick to label the unconventional a violation of international law even in Europe, much less in a colony where most legal experts determined that international law did not apply in the first place. Wherever international law did not apply, whether because of unconventional practices or colonial exclusion, German military officials and many jurists argued that there were no limits at all to sheer force. Consequently, the spiral toward the unlimited was a predictable, dynamic result of Germany's institutionalized practices, which came close to guaranteeing failure while simultaneously nourishing high expectations of the country's own military conduct and unrealistic expectations concerning that of its foes.

In SWA the status of Herero and Nama warriors was set by these European expectations. The imperial order of December 28, 1899, Criminal Procedure in the Army in Wartime, called for the summary execution of foreign civilians participating in combat against German soldiers. As rebels, indigenous warriors were in the same category as illegal combatants. They thus were subject to the "customs of war" (*Kriegsbrauch*); that is, officers could execute them summarily if they caught them red-handed. Trotha issued orders to this effect upon his arrival in June 1904. Abandoning courts-martial (the practice under Leutwein) for the summary execution of armed males was a further step in the intensification of force.[33]

There is other evidence that soldiers in SWA received official encouragement to kill beyond the normal bounds of war. This is a controversial matter, and elsewhere I have discussed at length the complicated evidentiary basis for the judgments I offer here.[34] Circumstantial evidence, but no surviving written order or direct acknowledgment by the participants, suggests that when Lieutenant General von Trotha assumed command in SWA in June 1904, he ordered the troops (as opposed to permitting officers to summarily execute armed enemies) to kill all adult Herero males when they commenced the battle of Waterberg. Such an order would have meant killing the male wounded and prisoners but sparing women and children. Whether the motivation for such an order was the assumption that in colonial warfare all adult (no age given) males were, ipso facto, warriors, that this policy would wipe out all further military and especially political resistance, or that revenge was necessary for the Herero's affront to German authority or to the conventions of European warfare is impossible to reconstruct with certainty. Even if such an order was never given, which is possible, Trotha nevertheless made public statements upon his arrival that "no war may be conducted humanely against nonhumans [*Unmenschen*]," thereby indicating his approval of "sharp" or extreme conduct by his soldiers.[35] Even without a direct order, then, German soldiers would have received the impression before the battle that excessive force was expected or certainly condoned by their commanding officer.

The massacre accompanying the battle of Waterberg was therefore antici- pated, if perhaps not entirely intentional. The indiscriminate killing of the wounded, male prisoners, women, and children also has been a subject of controversy, but eyewitness reports on both sides confirm that it occurred at Waterberg and probably continued during the "pursuit."[36] Trotha him- self tried to regain control of his troops and to focus their excessive force on adult males, in an order issued immediately after Waterberg that forbade the killing of women and children but expressly permitted the shooting of "all armed men who were captured."[37] Trotha thus attempted to widen the bounds of the usually permissible while imposing limits against wholesale slaughter. This balancing act was probably not successful. Evidence of vari- ous kinds indicates that troops released from one major prohibition found it hard to observe others.[38] The "pursuit" consisted largely of German sol- diers shooting at fleeing Africans, regardless of their status or condition. I do not wish to suggest that all units shot everyone they encountered; prisoners (male and female) were taken, and some, especially adult women, survived the war. In fact, the very lopsided postwar demographic ratio of women to men shows that there was a tendency to spare women, as Trotha had ordered. Nevertheless, the general pattern of conduct during the "pursuit" was wide- spread shooting, including that of male prisoners. Relentless shooting, in addition to the direct deaths it caused, pushed dehydrated, desperate people back into the desert, where they died en masse. There was little to choose between these two techniques of mass death. The "pursuit," which was both a standard operating procedure and a set of practices developing from the circumstances of SWA, effectively destroyed most of the Herero people by the end of September 1904.

5. Trotha's October Proclamation: Annihilation as an Explicit Goal

On October 2, 1904, Lieutenant General von Trotha issued a proclamation to the Herero people. After alluding to their crimes, he concluded,

> The Herero people must leave this land. If it does not, I will force it to do so by using the great gun [artillery]. Within the German border every male Herero, armed or unarmed, with or without cattle, will be shot to death. I will no longer receive women or children, but will drive them back to their people or have them shot at. These are my words to the Herero people.[39]

To the German troops he explained what he meant:

> I assume absolutely that this proclamation will result in taking no more male prisoners, but will not degenerate into atrocities against women and children. The latter will run away if one shoots at them a couple of times. . The troops will remain conscious of the good reputation of the German soldier.

The most puzzling aspect of Trotha's proclamation has always been its timing, coming after the actions and effects that it "orders" to be taken. The proclamation does three things: it makes explicit and uniform the already customary tactics employed by German troops ("no more male prisoners"); it attempts once again to regain control over troops tempted to commit "atrocities"; and it takes the effect of the "pursuit" (the complete disappearance of the Herero) as the explicit aim of military policy. Not surprisingly, surviving documents indicate no change in military conduct in the weeks after October 2.[40]

Trotha's proclamation was his response to the failure of the second default program of German military doctrine: pursuit. The troops had not managed to get the Herero to turn and fight so that they could be clearly defeated in battle. On September 29, exhausted, suffering German troops had arrived at the last known waterhole in the colony, but apart from finding a few Herero, the expected final battle did not occur. As he did after Waterberg, Trotha now sought to escape pressure to negotiate, the obvious alternative under the circumstances. Knowing that his proclamation would be "controversial," as he put it, he explained his decision in a letter to Chief of the General Staff von Schlieffen:

> For me, it is merely a question of how to end the war with the Herero. My opinion is completely opposite to that of the governor and some "old Africans." They have wanted to negotiate for a long time and describe the Herero nation as a necessary labor force for the future use of the colony. I am of an entirely different opinion. I believe that the nation must be destroyed as such, or since this was not possible using tactical blows, it must be expelled from the land operatively and by means of detailed actions.[41]

Farther along in the letter, when he describes what will happen to the women and children turned back by German troops, Trotha admits that he is talking about mass death, not simply disappearance: "I think it better that the nation perish rather than infect our troops and affect our water and food."[42] Nonetheless, engaging in the doublethink typical of the campaign, Trotha sums up the possibilities: "They must either die in the desert or try to cross the Bechuanaland border." We know that only about two thousand Herero made it across that border.

Over the course of the campaign, Trotha had thus moved from one sort of finality to a far larger one. The single battle of annihilation was supposed to "destroy" the nation politically, by killing and capturing all its warriors and forcing the people to submit to unconditional surrender. When that failed (even though by different standards of reckoning, Waterberg was a success), the pursuit was supposed to achieve the same thing. The "pursuit," too, was a success insofar as it destroyed the bulk of the people, but it neither unequivocally demonstrated the superiority of German arms in a conventional battle nor restored unquestioned state authority or order, since surviving Herero might stealthily return to the colony. Therefore, the next logical unconditional solution was not surrender but disappearance. This could take two forms: expulsion or death. Trotha did not care which. The point was to achieve a total and final solution of force: the permanent end of any possibility of further revolt, disorder, or challenge to German authority.

6. Death by Imprisonment

In order to give this solution-by-force the greatest chance against the solution-by-negotiation, Trotha sent notice of his proclamation by slow boat, rather than telegraph, and to the chief of staff only, rather than to the chancellor as well. When his proclamation finally arrived in Berlin in late November 1904, both Schlieffen and Bülow rejected Trotha's policy but, significantly, not for the same reasons. Bülow cited humanitarian, economic, political, and diplomatic grounds, whereas Schlieffen merely judged *Vernichtungspolitik* to be impractical.[43] The military's bias toward accepting extreme human destruction was once again demonstrated.

Nevertheless, with the (reluctant) help of the chief of the military cabinet, both Bülow and Schlieffen persuaded the kaiser to reverse Trotha's policy and offer amnesty to surrendering, unarmed, and innocent Herero. In the meanwhile, the Nama clans had revolted, and ultimately, civilians and warriors of both peoples were collected into internment camps, which defined the last phase of the war.

Internment camps, especially when they held primarily or exclusively civilians, were, at that time, called *concentration camps*. They were an imperial-military invention, designed to frustrate guerrilla warfare by removing the civilian population and thus exposing the remaining fighters to easier and clearer conditions of battle. Both Britain and Spain had established concentration camps before the Germans considered them in 1904. The death rates in such camps were high because European militaries were not trained in, nor did they attach much priority to, mastering the complex logistics required to maintain women, children, the aged, and the ill in overcrowded, hastily built but quasi-permanent locations.[44]

For a number of reasons, the German military attached an even lower priority to the needs of the imprisoned. The higher symbolic value attached to the military in Germany resulted in producing, if possible, an exaggerated valuation of actual fighting and therefore relegated all other, noncombat considerations to a zone of indifference, if not disdain. The institutionalized disregard for adequate provisioning and the concomitant expectation of German suffering already had set a low standard of care, which, of course, was even lower for the "enemy": Herero prisoners, whether warrior or civilian, could not be treated better than Germany's own troops.[45] Racism worsened their treatment still more, not just in the idiosyncratic cases of outright viciousness, but in more important structural ways, whether because of the widespread belief that "natives" required less food than Europeans or because the Germans simply did not bother to note what food Africans could digest. Administrative incompetence was widespread and made worse by the constant rotation of officers, a practice applied equally, and with equally bad effects, in the field.

The most lethal factor, however, was the desire to punish. This motive is clear in the official rations for African prisoners, set under and approved by Trotha. Prisoners received one-fifth the meat of the most punitive ration Great Britain had permitted for civilians interned during the Boer War and only one-sixth of the two-thirds ration that German field troops received, which already had caused widespread malnutrition and scurvy among the *Schutztruppe*. No provisions were taken against scurvy, and no regular milk portion was provided, even though milk in some form was the principal staple of the Hereros' diet. The official ration, like the official allotment of blankets and clothing, was designed to produce extreme suffering at the very least. Disease and death were clearly acceptable by-products of this treatment. When Trotha left SWA, his successors raised and varied the official ration, but not by much. Their internal correspondence indicates that they did not want African prisoners to die, but the factors just listed set hard limits to the amount of amelio ration they dared to introduce.[46] Internment in SWA thus was a lethal mixture of conviction and administrative indifference. The German military acknowledged a death rate of about 45 percent in its camps in SWA, compared with about 25 percent in the British camps in South Africa.[47]

The deaths in the British camps were ultimately stopped by citizens' political intervention and outraged public opinion, which led civilian political leaders to remove the camps' administration from military hands. In Germany, however, such an outcome was not possible, mainly because of several features of Germany's political culture. First, both the constitution and accepted practice relegated almost complete control over warfare to the military experts. Colonial critics of Trotha's *Vernichtungspolitik* were simply ignored, since they had no business interfering in military matters. High-level bureaucrats in SWA, chiefly Deputy Governor Hans von Tecklenburg and his successor, Deputy Governor Oskar Hintrager, accepted the military's nearly paranoid arguments about security and their punitive schema and consequently agreed with the lethal policies the military pursued. Indeed, they even added to these by demanding the deportation to other colonies of surviving rebels and their families.[48] But the deportees' death rates were even higher than the death rates in the camps in SWA. Meanwhile, the missionaries' informed criticism of both the conduct of the war and the camp conditions was disqualified from the beginning by Chancellor Bülow's misguided but well-established tactic of vilifying the missionaries as disloyal in time of war. The government and its conservative and bourgeois allies had always labeled Socialists as traitors, so Socialist criticism in the Reichstag had considerably less effect than similar attacks in the British Parliament, where loyal opposition was a time-honored tradition. Therefore, divide-and-rule, the presumption of military infallibility, and the civilian government's indiscriminate use of nationalist mobilization techniques all combined to insulate military policy from outside intervention.

Therefore, the camps could be stopped only from inside, through the intervention of a freethinking commander, Colonel Ludwig von Estorff. His horror at the conditions he found was surpassed only by his feelings of personal honor: "For such hangmen's services I can neither detail my officers, nor can I accept responsibility," he notified Berlin.[49] He closed the worst camp on his own orders and cleared it in fewer than two days.

Conclusion

I have argued here that the tendency for the German military to gravitate toward destructive extremes was built into its military culture, understood as its habitual practices and the (largely unexamined) basic assumptions embedded in its doctrines and administration.[50] The imperial situation did nothing to contravene these habits or inclinations and everything to encourage them. Already pernicious assumptions of race thinking developed into genuine racism under the shock of imperial practices. Many of these factors encouraged European troops toward a spiral of revenge: the difficulty and frustrations of colonial warfare made worse by structural deficits in planning and administration, the enemy's strange or "exotic" fighting practices, and the difficulties distinguishing civilians from warriors in guerrilla wars. Worse, the colonies had fewer brakes inhibiting unnecessary violence, since international law was widely thought inapplicable there. In settler colonies, the non-economically-minded (which is to say almost all military men) could regard indigenous peoples as expendable, and the restraints provided by identification or the intervention of observers sympathetic to the "natives" were largely missing.[51]

It is important to underscore that while German military culture differed somewhat from the cultures of other late nineteenth- / early twentieth-century European armies (chiefly by being even more purely military), European military culture in this period tended to apply progressively more force when lesser operations failed, as they often did in the colonies. Thus Germany's military culture and its imperial dilemmas were recognizably European or Western. Germany's chief difference lay in its political culture and institutions. Otto von Bismarck's effort to safeguard the conservative Prussian monarchy had yielded a national constitution that intentionally truncated parliamentary power and shielded the military from civilian oversight. The structure of government and the resulting political culture were, not surprisingly, less capable than, for example, comparative British or French institutions in subsequently curbing the military's tendencies to go to extremes. German political institutions were thus less able to slow the development toward destruction, a failure that therefore encouraged the further institutionalization of this tendency inside the military to a degree found nowhere else. This is the often-cited "autism" of the German military, which meant that the propensity to grasp at extremes of destruction was reinforced and more deeply ingrained and therefore more likely to be used in future.[52]

The genocide in SWA was part of a pattern of developmental possibilities; it was not an aberration. A very similar outcome resulted from 1905 to 1907 in German East Africa, where the tactic of slash and burn used to crush all political resistance during the Maji-Maji revolt ended in the deaths by starvation of an estimated two hundred thousand to three hundred thousand Africans, completely and permanently depopulating several large districts in the colony.[53] Although the two events are not identical, they do clearly illustrate the military's institutional preference for solving political problems with total, unlimited force.

This developmental logic, which during the Wilhelminian period was not enunciated as an a priori goal, continued to operate during World War I. The European theater of war, with its limits imposed by identification with the enemy, international law, and other factors, acted as a brake to the full-blown development of the logic, but its operations nonetheless were visible in every place. The mass deportation (and typically bad treatment) of civilians from occupied Belgium, northern France, and the eastern territories; ubiquitous forced labor; lethal ill treatment of prisoners of war; unlimited economic exploitation of occupied zones; and total destruction of areas relinquished during retreats were some of the most striking standard procedures of the German war effort in Europe from 1914 to 1918.[54] The complex story of the extermination of the Armenians by Germany's ally, Turkey, beginning in 1915 also has links to military culture. The genocide was not German policy; rather, it was the idea of a few radical members of the ruling Committee of Union and Progress. Once it was launched, many German observers on the spot, including some military men, were shocked and tried to persuade their government to intervene to stop the killings. But certain high-ranking German military advisers to the Turks had recommended the deportations, and they accepted the resulting genocide. Military-security arguments ("military necessity") identical to those adduced in SWA and German East Africa were decisive in preventing the German government from effectively resisting its ally's policy.[55]

The spiral of violence and destruction visible in the colonies before the world war thus assumed far greater dimensions after 1914. The basic assumptions and scripts of imperial German military culture continued to determine how Germany conducted the world war and, afterward, how its military, and increasing numbers of its civilian, leaders interpreted that war and applied those lessons during the next world war.

NOTES

1. An earlier version of this chapter was published as I. V. Hull, "Military Culture and the Production of 'Final Solutions' in the Colonies: The Example of Wilhelminian Germany," in *Genocide in Historical Perspective*, ed. Robert Gellately and Ben Kiernan (New York: Cambridge University Press, 2003), 141–62, and is used here with permission.

2. On military culture, see Isabel V. Hull, *Absolute Destruction: Military Culture and the Practices of War in Imperial Germany* (Ithaca, NY: Cornell University Press, 2005), part 2. Note that this usage differs slightly from the categories and definitions as presented

in chapter 1 of this volume but is retained here to accord with my longer discussion in *Absolute Destruction*.

3. Kommando der Schutztruppen im Reichs-Kolonialamt, *Sanitäts-Bericht über die Kaiserliche Schutztruppe für Südwestafrika während des Herero – und Hottentottenaufstandes für die Zeit vom 1. Januar 1904 bis 31. März 1907* (Berlin: E. S. Mittler und Sohn, 1909), 2:405.

4. Gert Sudholt, *Die deutsche Eingeborenenpolitik in Südwestafrika; von den Anfängen bis 1904* (Hildesheim: Georg Olms Verlag, 1975), 40–44; Brigitte Lau, "Uncertain Certainties: The Herero-German War of 1904," *Migabus* 2 (1989): 4–5, 8; and Günter Spraul, "Der 'Völkermord' an den Herero; Untersuchungen zu einer neuen Kontinuitätsthese," *Geschichte in Wissenschaft und Unterricht* 39, no. 12 (1988): 713–39.

5. Horst Drechsler, *"Let Us Die Fighting": The Struggle of the Herero and the Nama against German Imperialism (1884–1915)*, trans. Bernd Zollner (London: Zed Books, 1980), 214; Helmut Bley, *South-West Africa under German Rule* (Evanston, IL: Northwestern University Press, 1971), 151–52; Horst Gründer, *Geschichte der deutschen Kolonien*, 3rd ed. (Paderborn: Ferdinand Schöningh, 1995), 121.

6. Schutztruppe Kommando, "Sterblichkeit in den Kriegsgefangenenlagern in Südwest-Afrika," Nr. KA II. 1181, undated, Bundesarchiv-Berlin [BAB], R 1001, Nr. 2140, pp. 161–62.

7. This correspondence is in BAB, R 1001, Nr. 2089. August Bebel, the Social Democratic leader, surmised in the Reichstag that Trotha probably received a verbal order, *Stenographische Berichte über die Verhandlungen des Reichstags*, XI Legislaturperiode, sess. 2, 1905/1906, vol. 218, 131st Sitzung, December 1, 1906, 4060.

8. Trotha to Leutwein, Windhuk (copy), November 5, 1904, BAB, R 1001, Nr. 2089, pp. 101–3.

9. Hull, *Absolute Destruction*, 29.

10. For a detailed account of the Southwest African campaign, see Hull, *Absolute Destruction*, chaps. 1–3.

11. Sten. Ber., vol. 199, March 17, 1904, pp. 1896, rest of debate, 1889–1906.

12. On race-thinking versus racism, see Hannah Arendt, *The Origins of Totalitarianism* (New York: World, 1951), 183–86.

13. (General) Julius von Hartmann, "Militärische Nothwendigkeit und Humanität. Ein kritischer Versuch," *Deutsche Rundschau* 13 (1877): 455, 461; *Deutsche Rundschau* 14 (1878): 71–91.

14. Stephen van Evera, "The Cult of the Offensive and the Origins of the First World War," *International Security* 9, no. 1 (summer 1984): 58–107; Jack Snyder, *The Ideology of the Offensive: Military Decision Making and the Disasters of 1914* (Ithaca, NY: Cornell University Press, 1984); Jehuda L. Wallach, *The Dogma of the Battle of Annihilation: The Theories of Clausewitz and Schlieffen and Their Impact on the German Conduct of Two World Wars* (Westport, CT: Greenwood, 1986).

15. On the Schlieffen plan as reflective of Germany's military culture, see Hull, *Absolute Destruction*, chap. 7.

16. Summed up in Kurt Riezler's marvelous phrase, "the necessity of the impossible." See Kurt Riezler, *Die Erforderlichkeit des Unmöglichen* (Munich: Georg Müller, 1913); Hartmut Pogge von Strandmann and Imanuel Geiss, *Die Erforderlichkeit des Unmöglichen* (Frankfurt: Europäische Verlagsanstalt, 1965).

17. Schlieffen's phrase; see Wallach, *The Dogma of the Battle*, 124.

18. Horst Drechsler, "The Hereros of South-West Africa," in *The History and Sociology of Genocide*, ed. Frank Robert Chalk and Kurt Jonassohn (New Haven, CT: Yale University Press, 1990), 241–42.

19. Lothar von Trotha, "Directive for the Attack against the Herero," August 4, 1904, cited in General Staff, *Die Kämpfe der deutschen Truppen in Südwestafrika: Auf Grund amtlichen Materials*, 2 vols. (Berlin, 1906/1907), 1:153; Paul Rohrbach, diary entry of August 10, 1904, in Paul Rohrbach, *Aus Südwestafrikas schweren Tagen: Blätter von Arbeit und Abschied* (Berlin: Wilhelm Weicher, 1909), 167; and August Franke's diary entry of August 5, 1904, Bundesarchiv-Koblenz, Nachlass Franke, Nr. 3, p. 85. For further corroborating statements from contemporaries of Trotha's intentions, see Hull, *Absolute Destruction*, 33–37.

20. Missionaries Dannert, Lang, Hanefeld, Elger, Brockmann, and Wandres to Rohrbach, August 1, 1904, Vereinigte Evangelische Mission-Wuppertal, C/o, 5; Rohrbach, *Aus Südwestafrikas schweren Tagen*, 167; District Administrator Burgsdorff to Governor, Nr. 1364, Gibeon, August 18, 1904, BA-Berlin, Kaiserliches Gouvernement Deutsch-Südwest-Afrika, Zentralbureau Windhoek (R 151 F), D.IV.L.E., vol. 1, p. 1.

21. Lothar von Trotha, "Politik und Kriegführung," *Berliner Neueste Nachrichten*, February 3, 1909, p. 1.

22. The liberal *Berliner Zeitung*, for example, called for "punishment [Bestrafung]," but when alleged atrocities by German troops were reported, it hastened to add that while "a certain strictness is necessary [in handling the revolt], this must not degenerate into brutality." See von Gädke, "Die militärische Lage in Deutsch-Südwestafrika," *Berliner Zeitung*, February 4, 1904), 1; and the untitled article of Nr. 141, March 17, 1904, p. 1. Kaiser Wilhelm had forbidden negotiations without his prior consent.

23. Colonial Director Stübel had set the goal of suppressing the revolt as "end[ing] the quasi-independence the natives still enjoyed in politics," Sten. Ber., January 19, 1904, 364.

24. Trotha, tel. August 12, 1904, Hamakari, reprinted in Conrad Rust, *Krieg und Frieden im Hererolande: Aufzeichnungen aus dem Kriegsjahre 1904* (Leipzig: I. A. Kittler, 1905), 376–77; Trotha to Bülow, tel. Okahandja, September 25, 1904, BAB, R 1001, Nr. 2116, p. 25; Lothar von Trotha diary, entries August 11 to October 3, 1904, Trotha Family Archives, Nachlass Lothar von Trotha, Nr. 315.

25. Trotha to Bülow, tel. Northeast Epata, October 1, 1904, BAB, R 1001, Nr. 2116, pp. 35–36; General Staff, *Die Kämpfe der deutschen Truppen*, 1:214.

26. For example, Robert Jay Lifton, "Existential Evil," in *Sanctions for Evil; Sources of Social Destructiveness*, ed. Nevitt Sanford and Craig Comstock (San Francisco: Jossey-Bass, 1971), 37, 38; C. Fourniau, "Colonial Wars before 1914: The Case of France in Indochina," in *Imperialism and War: Essays on Colonial Wars in Asia and Africa*, ed. J. A. de Moor and H. L. Wesseling (Leiden: Brill, 1989), 83.

27. "Überblick über die bei der Entsendung von Verstärkungen für die Schutztruppe in Südwest-Afrika gesammelten Erfahrungen und die in der Kommissionsberatungen zu erörternden Fragen, 1. Nov. 1908," Bundesarchiv-Militärarchiv Freiburg, RW 51, vol. 18, 74–81; Kommando der Schutztruppe, *Sanitäts-Bericht*, I.

28. Martin van Creveld, *Supplying War: Logistics from Wallerstein to Patton* (Cambridge: Cambridge University Press, 1977), chap. 4.

29. Michael Geyer, "The Past as Future: the German Officer Corps as Profession," in *German Professions, 1800–1950*, ed. Geoffrey Cocks and Konrad H. Jarausch (Oxford:

Oxford University Press, 1990), 183–212; Morris Janowitz, "Professionalization of Military Elites," in *On Social Organization and Social Control*, by Morris Janowitz (Chicago: University of Chicago Press, 1991), 99–112.

30. On Germany's indigenous troops in East Africa, see Michelle R. Moyd, "Becoming Askari: African Soldiers and Everyday Colonialism in German East Africa, 1850–1918" (PhD diss., Cornell University, 2008).

31. Geoffrey Best, *Humanity in Warfare* (New York: Columbia University Press, 1980), 172–79, 180–89, 195–99, 226.

32. Isabel V. Hull, "'Military Necessity' and the Laws of War in Imperial Germany," in *Order, Conflict, Violence*, ed. Stathis Kalyvas, Ian Shapiro, and Tarek Masoud (Cambridge: Cambridge University Press, 2008), 352–77.

33. Compare Zimmerer's interpretation of von Trotha's order in Jürgen Zimmerer, "Kriegsgefangene im Kolonialkrieg: Der Krieg gegen die Herero und Nama in Deutsch Südwestafrika (1904–1907)," in *In der Hand des Feindes; Kriegsgefangenschaft von der Antike bis zum Zweiten Weltkrieg*, ed. Rüdiger Overmans (Cologne: Böhlau Verlag, 1999), 282. On Kriegsbrauch, see Gerd Hankel, *Die Leipziger Prozesse: Deutsche Kriegsverbrechen und ihre strafrechtliche Verfolgung nach dem Ersten Weltkrieg* (Hamburg: Hamburg Edition, 2003), 215, 229–40.

34. Hull, *Absolute Destruction*, 44–55.

35. Otto Dannhauer (military correspondent), "Brief aus Deutsch-Südwestafrika," *Berliner Lokalanzeiger*, August 2, 1904, pp. 1–2, written June 26, 1904.

36. Hull, *Absolute Destruction*, 44–55.

37. Schlieffen to Bülow, Nr. 13297, Berlin, December 16, 1904, BAB, R 1001, Nr. 2089, p. 107; letter of Trotha's chief of staff, Lieutenant Colonel von Beaulieu, cited in General Staff, *Die Kämpfe der deutschen Truppen*, 1:186.

38. Wayne E. Lee, *Barbarians and Brothers: Anglo-American Warfare, 1500–1865* (New York: Oxford University Press, 2011), chap. 8.

39. Trotha, Proclamation of October 2, 1904, copy, J. Nr. 3737, BAB, R 1001, Nr. 2089, p. 7; another copy in "Kaiserliche Schutztruppen und sonstige deutsche Landstreitkräfte in Übersee" [RW 51], "Militärgeschichtliches Forschungsamt: Dokumentenzentrale, Schutztruppe Südwestafrika" [vol. 2], BA-MA Freiburg. Reprinted in Conrad Rust, *Krieg und Frieden im Hererolande*, 385; *Vorwärts*, no. 294 (December 16, 1905); Drechsler, *"Let Us Die Fighting,"* 243; Jon M. Bridgman, *The Revolt of the Herero* (Berkeley: University of California Press, 1981), 128.

40. Hull, *Absolute Destruction*, 58–61.

41. Trotha to Schlieffen, Okatarobaka, October 4, 1904, BA-Berlin, R 1001, Nr. 2089, pp. 5–6. Partly reprinted in Drechsler, *"Let Us Die Fighting,"* 160–61; Horst Drechsler, *Aufstände in Südwestafrika: Der Kampf der Herero und Nama 1904 bis 1907 gegen die deutsche Kolonialherrschaft* (Berlin: Dietz, 1984), 86–87; Drechsler, "The Hereros of South-West Africa," 244–45; and Bley, *South-West Africa under German Rule*, 164.

42. While the food and water situation was indeed serious, this excuse did not motivate the proclamation; it merely justified causing the certain death of harmless civilians. On justification, as opposed to motivation, see Martha Finnemore, "Constructing Norms of Humanitarian Intervention," in *The Culture of National Security: Norms and Identity in World Politics*, ed. Peter J. Katzenstein (New York: Columbia University Press, 1996), 159; Neil J. Smelser, "Some Determinants of Destructive Behavior," and Edward M. Opton Jr.,

"It Never Happened and Besides They Deserved It," both in *Sanctions for Evil: Sources of Social Destructiveness*, ed. Nevitt Sanford and Craig Comstock (San Francisco: Jossey-Bass, 1971), 23 and 63–67.

43. Bley, *Southwest-Africa under German Rule*, 166–67; Schlieffen to Colonial Department, Nr. 12383, Berlin, November 23, 1904, BA-Berlin, R 1001, Nr. 2089, pp. 3–4.

44. See the scathing criticisms leveled by the Fawcett Commission at the British military administration in South Africa during the Boer War: Great Britain, Parliament, *Report on the Concentration Camps in South Africa by the Committee of Ladies Appointed by the Secretary of State for War Containing Reports on the Camps in Natal, the Orange River Colony and the Transvaal*, Cd. 893 (London, 1902), 6–7, 16–18.

45. This was a standard principle: General Staff, *Die Kriegsbrauch im Landkriege*, 15; C. Lueder, "Das Landkriegsrecht im Besonderen," in *Handbuch des Völkerrechts*, vol. 4, ed. Franz von Holtzendorff (Hamburg, 1889), 435; Christian Meurer, *Die Haager Friedenskonferenz*, vol. 2, *Das Kriegsrecht der Haager Konferenz* (Munich: J. Schweitzer, 1907), 122.

46. For data and discussion of provisioning the camps, see Hull, *Absolute Destruction*, chap. 3 and 153–57.

47. S. Burridge Spies, *Methods of Barbarism? Roberts and Kitchener and Civilians in the Boer Republics January 1900–May 1902* (Cape Town: Human and Rousseau, 1977), 268; Thomas Pakenham, *The Boer War* (London: Weidenfeld & Nicholson, 1979), 518; Hull, *Absolute Destruction*, 88–90.

48. Hull, *Absolute Destruction*, 79–90.

49. Estorff to Command of Schutztruppe in Berlin, tel. Nr. 461, Windhuk, April 10, 1907, BAB, R 1001, Nr. 2140, p. 88.

50. The conception of military culture that I use comes from a combination of cultural anthropology and organizational culture theory. Space limitations, however, prevent a discussion of this concept here. See Hull, *Absolute Destruction*, chap. 4.

51. Militaries are thoroughly uneconomical institutions. See Hans Paul Bahrdt, *Die Gesellschaft und ihre Soldaten: zur Soziologie des Militärs* (Munich: C. H. Beck, 1987).

52. On autism in organizations, wee Dieter Senghaas, *Rüstung und Militarismus* (Frankfurt: Suhrkamp, 1972), 46–54; Bernd Schulte, "Die Armee des Kaiserreichs im Spannungsfeld zwischen struktureller Begrenzung und Kriegsrealität, 1871–1914," in *Europäische Krise und Erster Weltkrieg: Beiträge zur Militärpolitik des Kaiserreichs, 1871⊠1914*, by Bernd Schulte (Frankfurt: Peter Lang, 1983), 72; Martin Kutz, *Realitätsflucht und Aggression im deutschen Militär* (Baden-Baden: Nomos Verlagsgesellschaft, 1990).

53. The best account is by Detlev Bald, "Afrikanischer Kampf gegen koloniale Herrschaft: Der Maji-Maji-Aufstand in Ostafrika," *Militärgeschichtliche Mitteilungen* 19 (1976): 23–50. On casualties, see John Iliffe, *A Modern History of Tanganyika* (Cambridge: Cambridge University Press, 1979), 165, 199–200.

54. Hull, *Absolute Destruction*, chaps. 9–10, 12.

55. See Vakahn N. Dadrian, *German Responsibility in the Armenian Genocide: A Review of the Historical Evidence of German Complicity* (Watertown, MA: Blue Crane Books, 1996); Christoph Dinkel, "German Officers and the Armenian Genocide," *Armenian Review* 44, no. 1 (spring 1991): 77–133.

8

Connecting Culture and the Battlefield

Britain and the Empire Fight the Hundred Days

DAVID SILBEY

This chapter explores the connections between culture and the battlefield, examining how each influenced the other and suggesting that the social, national, and cultural contexts will inform us more deeply about each one. I use the summer and fall campaigns of 1918, particularly those of the British Expeditionary Force, to see whether those battles and encounters reveal anything about British and Dominion culture and whether it reveals anything to us about those battles and encounters. More specifically, I look at the Canadian Corps, the New Zealand Division, and the Australian Imperial Force and the way in which nationalism affected their operational decisions and, in turn, how their operational decisions played a role in the development of nationalisms. Whereas most operational histories extend back only as far as the rear echelons, or perhaps to the political masters back home, this chapter explores how domestic ideas and visions extended all the way to the battlefield. Conversely, whereas most cultural histories extend forward only to the training depot and then leap forward to postconflict memorialization, this chapter looks at how the operational decisions and the battles themselves drove, as they happened, cultural development.

We are far beyond the "new military history," I think.[1] So far, in fact, that it may be a cliché to say so. This label was created as an attempt to integrate social history with military history and produce "history from the bottom up," as opposed to "history from the top down." The paradigmatic example of this is John Keegan's *The Face of Battle*.[2] Keegan's book marked the start of redefining military history, focusing on the experience of the ordinary combatants. But labeling this approach the "new" military history may actually have harmed more than it helped. By implicitly contrasting itself with the "old" military history, the new military history created a division where none should have existed. Sides were chosen and lines were drawn between operational history ("drums and trumpets" was its label) and social military history (we need a similarly evocative and slightly dismissive phrase for social military history). A war started where none should have, with people declaring sides: "Operational history, once synonymous with military history, has become something of a historiographical stepchild of late. The 'new military history' of the 1960s and 1970s . . . seemed willing to discuss everything about armies but the actual wars they fought. It has been an unfortunate state of affairs."[3] The results were often a failure to cross-pollinate between the two and a conscious reluctance to cross the line between new and old.

This avoidance was problematic. The new modes of studying history over the last half century—social history; oral history; world history; race, class, and gender studies; cultural studies; and the linguistic turn, to name just a few—all are, at their base, *tools* for the study of the history itself. They are ways of prying into the world of the past and breaking it open for analysis and understanding. Military historians were surely shortchanging themselves by not using these new tools themselves.[4] Worse, they were cutting themselves off from the rest of the historical profession by failing to incorporate the tools of the trade. The new military history aimed to incorporate social history, so military history should likewise aim to incorporate all historical tools, both modern and traditional.[5]

Military historians have started to do this. In his *Carnage and Culture*, Victor Davis Hanson tried to develop a universal theory of history to explain Western dominance by focusing on the culture of those Western powers and how it formed a particular kind of overwhelming military structure.[6] Hanson's approach had numerous failings and has been widely critiqued, but it was at least an attempt to discuss the culture.[7] John Lynn's response, in *Battle*, was another such attempt.[8] Rather than concentrate on the West, Lynn explored a range of cultures and militaries and tried to link them. Despite some problems, Lynn's approach was a valiant attempt to suggest that the larger cultural structure had a global effect on militaries and wars, without Hanson's presumption that the West was inherently and eternally superior.[9] In fact, that presumption has long corrupted the little cultural analysis that military history did have (as it did in all kinds of history) into a reimposition of racial and nationalist visions of the world, with the West being inherently aggressive and straightforward and "orientals" being sly and indirect.

We still do not have ground-level studies of the interaction between culture and war that will progress to the kinds of examinations that Lynn and Hanson attempted. Before envisioning culture and war on a large scale, military historians must construct the bricks for the foundation, through more books like *The Cheese and the Worms* and *The Return of Martin Guerre*.[10] As Jeremy Black observed in his useful survey of the state of military history,

> The detailed work that [the cultural approach] requires has simply not been tackled for most of the world. As a result, we are overly dependent on a rather narrow range of research. Not only is much of the world only imperfectly covered, but there is scant evidence for the attitudes that are important if we are to assess cultural factors. Hopefully this will be redressed, and, in a decade or two, we will be able to look back at the current work on the "cultural turn" and understand it as the tentative scholarship that is all that it can realistically claim to be.[11]

This does not mean that military historians *must* use all their tools all the time. But they should understand the tools available, even if they decide not to use them. Understanding the tools would offer insights into situations that might not be obvious when looking at them in the traditional way. An example of this, and an example of the kind of foundational cultural work for which Black calls, is Carol Reardon's *Pickett's Charge in History and Memory*, which analyzes the battle of Gettysburg and the Civil War in ways not possible without new methods of inquiry.[12]

An exception to this lack of basic cultural studies of warfare may be the studies of the memorialization of World War I. These are a common part of the new wave of historiography of World War I that has come out in the past two decades, most notably by people like Jay Winter.[13] But even here the wariness of the two sides is apparent. Parallel to the memorialization stream is one that looks more carefully at the operational level of warfare between 1914 and 1918.[14] These two parallel streams have nonetheless tended to remain segregated from each other, to the detriment of both. For example, much of the memorialization literature discusses how people chose to remember the conflict but is not sufficiently skeptical about how the war itself is portrayed in those memorials. Any suggestion that the actual war itself was more complicated than Paul Fussell's mud-and-blood description has usually been ignored. For example, in *Sites of Memory, Sites of Mourning*, Jay Winter examines the way in which "those too old to fight had created an imaginary war, filled with medieval knights, noble warriors, and sacred moments of sacrifice." War poets—those with actual combat experience—reacted with fury, Winter insisted, to this "banal" and "obscene" imaginary war, instead writing about the war's horrifying reality. But Winter's example of the "imaginary war," as he himself noted, is the account of an actual French combat soldier's experience, widely re-publicized no doubt, but with as much claim to being real as that of the war poets. Winter refused to accept that, though, and assumed that the cynical views of the war poets were the only possible correct perception of the war.[15]

Even when works did try to bring together the two strands, they sometimes were handicapped by the lack of a larger intersection between military history and the larger world. Joanna Bourke's *An Intimate History of Killing*, while laudable in its attempt to look historically at the personal experience of killing, is handicapped by her lack of interest in and sympathy for things military.[16]

Even though military historians long ago abandoned the simple battle narrative, the field is now in a similar situation with regard to culture. Militaries and wars do not simply appear, and they are neither built nor waged according to some universal principles that do not vary from nation to nation, society to society, and people to people. Instead, they are constructions of the cultures and societies that wage the wars, built according to the principles, beliefs, and myths of those cultures. Without understanding how those principles, beliefs, and myths create the militaries and the wars, military historians essentially shun their responsibility to analyze and comprehend war and its institutions. Failing that means failing their central and, indeed, only mission. As Mao Zedong pointed out, culture is the ocean in which the wars swim, invisible to the fish, but essential.

1918

This chapter tries to intersect culture and the battlefield by looking at the British Expeditionary Force (BEF) in the summer and fall of 1918, when Entente forces pushed the Germans back nearly to the border of Germany itself and essentially forced the Germans to sue for peace. Until recently, this period in 1918 has been neglected; instead, the British military history of World War I has been concerned with the initial campaigns of 1914, the Somme attack of 1916, the Passchendaele offensive of 1917, and the German offensives of spring 1918. A history that covered the peaks of British interest would leap from the high points of 1914 and 1916/1917 and finish with Field Marshal Douglas Haig's famous "backs to the wall" special order of April 11, 1918, standing stranded months away from the actual end of the war. According to this conception, victory came largely because of German exhaustion. This vision has changed at the scholarly level in the past two decades, although at a popular level the perception remains mired in the mud of exhaustion.[17]

Nonetheless, much remains to be done on a scholarly level. Figuring out how the Entente won is hardly complete, especially at the tactical and operational level, and figuring out what winning meant in 1918 to the soldiers and the nations fighting has hardly been touched.[18] From Amiens in August to the armistice in November, Entente forces were moving forward relatively steadily, though still suffering casualties that rivaled those of 1916/1917. Obviously, I cannot fill in the entirety of this historiographical gap in this chapter, so I will concentrate on how the victory in 1918 was, for elements of the BEF, a consciously nationalist one. More than that, 1918 was a victory in which nationalism influenced operational decisions and operational decisions influenced nationalism. In essence, then, nationalism was driven by and drove operational concerns and decisions.

Each country's nationalism was, to a large extent, nurtured by what I call *national moments*: events, people, or things seen by populations as being peculiarly representative of their nation. An American example is Bunker Hill, which has come to stand as a national moment, as have Pearl Harbor, V-E Day, and 9/11. For a certain segment of the Irish population, the Battle of the Boyne is a national moment. Although national moments are sometimes categorized in that way only long after the moment itself, they often become such moments even while they are happening or shortly afterward.

There were a substantial number of national moments in World War I. For example, the long, bloody, and fruitless amphibious landing at Gallipoli in Turkey in 1915, at the time and afterward, was seen as a watershed in the Australian and New Zealand national identities.[19] Indeed, from Gallipoli came ANZAC Day (the technical term for the Australia–New Zealand Army Corps within the British army), a holiday celebrating the landing as a national moment. In 1921 an Australian explained,

> A celebration of this day, on which Australia, by the valor of her sons, became entitled through an ordeal of blood, fire, and suffering to take her place among the great nations of the world, and to stand on equal terms with those peoples, both past and present, who have given of their best that humanity might benefit.[20]

No longer was Australia simply "'a joint in the tail of a great Empire.'"[21] Instead, it was its own nation, defined by war and celebrated on the "fifty-third Sunday."

A particular note about Gallipoli was that it included a conscious distinction from the British for much of its power. For the "ANZACs," the British were, and are, regarded in many ways more as villains than the supposed enemy, Turkey, was. That vision was, for example, still evident in the Mel Gibson film *Gallipoli*, but it was certainly a strong feeling in 1915.[22] Its effect was to distinguish the ANZACs from the British, a distinction that was felt unnecessary with regard to the Turks. Establishing a nationalism in this case required establishing a sense of difference between the mother country and former colony. Australia was different from England, and Australians were different from the English. This led to the stereotype of the Australian soldier's brash unruly personality, which contrasted with the obedience of the British Tommies:

> An officer, inspecting the first line of resistance:
> "What soldiers are in this trench, my man?"
> "First Sussex Regiment, sir."
> After going along a little further, he questions again:
> "What soldiers are in this trench, my man?"
> "What the —— has it go to do with you?"
> "Oh, this is the Australian trench," the officer said, quite surprised.[23]

For the Canadians, a national moment similar to Gallipoli was the 1917 battle of Vimy Ridge.[24] "Canada's war of independence," one historian wrote, "was fought between 1914 and 1918, with the Battle of Vimy Ridge marking the watershed between colony and nation."[25] Such a vision of progress has defined Canadian historiography since the war ended, to the extent that the abilities and skills of Canadian forces first on the western front are underestimated—"admirable raw material," as one historian put it—which was the better to show Canadian progression and advancement.[26] Canadian soldiers in 1914/1915 are, in this literature's telling, the rough colonials of myth standing in sharp contrast to the polished citizen-soldiers of 1917/1918.[27] The narrative needs of the national moment had overcome the demands of strict analysis.

By contrast, it would be more difficult to find such a national moment in the Great War for, say, Wales.[28] This is not to judge Welsh nationalism, but it does suggest that national moments are particularly important when a nationalism is either defining or redefining itself. For the Dominion countries, World War I was the intersection of a growing national self-awareness with the demand for a great effort by the mother country. It was, in essence, a crossroads for those nationalisms and thus particularly ripe for the development of national moments.[29]

Let us trace this sense of national and cultural uniqueness through 1918 to find the ways that the victories of that year became part of a national moment. Throughout the war, for domestic consumption, the Dominion forces actively cultivated a vision of the conflict as a national effort, especially through the famed Australian correspondent C. E. W. Bean, which influenced recruits for the Australian Imperial Force.[30] Furthermore, major Dominion forces, like the Australians and Canadians, were largely kept together rather than interspersed into "British" units, and they were given some autonomy in the planning and execution of their assaults. Field Marshal Douglas Haig used the forces this way because of their perceived martial valor, because both countries' divisions were larger than the typical British division, and because of nationalist political pressure from the colonies. Although this is not new information, it is important to note how national concerns influenced organizational decisions.

In addition, Haig himself reinforced that sense by isolating the national elements within the BEF in his dispatches, highlighting the battles as not just a British effort but the effort of a collection of nationalisms. In his account of the battle of the Somme, Haig wrote that

> troops from every part of the British Isles, and from every Dominion and quarter of the Empire, whether Regulars, Territorials, or men of the New Armies, have borne a share in the Battle of the Somme. While some have been more fortunate than others in opportunities for distinction, all have done their duty nobly.[31]

This was not merely a British effort or an imperial effort; it was the effort of "every part of the British Isles, and . . . every Dominion and quarter of the Empire." Specifically, Haig listed the troops and units by their nationality in his later dispatches. So when he described an attack during the third battle of Ypres (Passchendaele), he noted in September 1917 that "Australian, English, Scottish, and South African troops were employed."[32] A month later, in talking about an attack on October 4, 1917, Haig wrote, "The attack was carried out by Australian, New Zealand and English divisions, including among the latter a few Scottish, Irish, and Welsh battalions, and was successful at all points."[33] Again, the effort was effectively an Australian, New Zealand, English, Scottish, Irish, and Welsh effort, rather than a British effort.

This was more than an affectation on Haig's part or an attempt to placate the empire. Haig genuinely felt that the Dominion formations were superior, as he told Arthur Currie, the Canadian commander, in the summer of 1918:

> With tears showing plainly in his eyes, he said something like this: "In all the dark days this spring—and God knows they were dark enough—one comforting thought came to me, that I still had the Canadian Corps unused and fresh; and I felt that I could not be defeated until the Corps had been in action."[34]

Although this might have been a commander talking to a subordinate who had some uncomfortable political powers, Haig's motivation is somewhat besides the point. Rather, he was making a nationalist point about an operational situation, one that elevated the Canadian Corps as carrying a special martial virtue.

The segregation of countries' troops created large, homogenous forces who had time to grow familiar with one another at both the tactical and operational levels.[35] Not surprising, they proved to be effective in the offensives of 1918. In essence, then, what was at least partly a decision based on nationalism came to have specific operational effects. The Canadians and Australians were segregated (at least partly) because they represented their own particular countries, and segregation made them more effective tactically. Nationalism became a useful method of organizing large corps of forces into "shock" troops, because they were organized and trained to lead assaults and could be moved relatively easily from one battlefield to another. The successes of those shock troops in turn reinforced and built the nationalism that fueled them.

The combination of segregation and operational effectiveness encouraged the strong distinction among Canadian, Australian, and British soldiers. The Australians and Canadians felt themselves militarily superior to the rest of the British Expeditionary Force. "They had a contempt for Britishers to begin with," one British officer remembered. "I myself heard the expression 'Not bad for a Britisher' used by one about some successful feat of British arms."[36] They believed they were excellent soldiers because of their national origin. Likewise, Arthur Currie, the commander of the Canadian Corps, wrote in January 1918,

> I cannot begin to express to you the regard in which Canadians are held in the Allied Armies. They are looked upon as being the most efficient Corps

on the whole Western Front. There are many factors which contribute to that efficiency. In the first place, our men are full of resource and when a difficulty or situation confronts which has not been provided for, they are not the kind to stand around and do nothing simply because they have "no instructions." It is always well to do something, and the natural common sense, which is such a pronounced Canadian characteristic, usually tells one the best thing to do nine times out of ten.[37]

"Such a pronounced Canadian characteristic" was Currie's way of invoking Canadianness and implicitly contrasting the Canadian soldiers with the English.

To further distinguish the Dominion soldiers and, by extension, the Dominions themselves, they were described as behaving differently, as acting uniquely Canadian or Australian, particularly in discussions of discipline and obedience. The English were portrayed as adherents of mindless "spit and polish," unlike the more flexible colonials. "Our men are well-disciplined," Currie might say of the Canadians, but then he would explicitly redefine discipline to separate the Canadians from the English:

To me, discipline is simply the self-control which makes you do the right thing at all times. We are given a conscience which tells us what is right, and what is wrong, and at our schools and in our training camps we are taught the right way of doing military things. If we have the self-control to do that right thing always, we are well disciplined, and in the Canadian Corps I am proud to say the standards of discipline set and maintained is high.[38]

Currie thus reinvented the image of the Canadians as raw frontier colonists by making that stereotype a virtue of common sense and doing the right thing.

The summer of 1918 was a particularly propitious time for victories. The exhaustion of the German army in the spring offensives and the maturation of both the British and French armies into all-arms forces capable of effective operations meant that substantial victories were likely. As a result, the Entente won the war a year earlier than many expected. In addition, the Dominion troops had been primed to be the lead units in an attack, since for example, the Canadian Corps had been largely spared by the German offensives of spring 1918. They were therefore one of the few remaining organized forces that could be used for counterattack.

The use of the Australians and Canadians as shock troops in the summer offensives meant that such battles would almost inevitably be seen as victories for particular nationalities as well as for the Entente.[39] This is nowhere more clear than the offensive at Amiens. Haig's vision had been drawn to the possibilities of an offensive there by the success of the Australian Corps in that area during the winter and spring of 1918. German fortifications were particularly weak along the line in that area, and so the British offensive, which started on August 8 and was spearheaded by the Australians and Canadians, was successful.[40] As he had done before, Haig described it in explicitly nationalist ways: "The brilliant and predominating part taken by the Canadian and Australian Corps in this battle is worthy of the highest commendation. The skill and determination of these troops proved irresistible, and at all points met with rapid and complete success."[41] Each time an assault led by Australians or Canadians led to (often unprecedented) success—Hamel, Amiens, St. Quentin, Canal du Nord—much of the credit redounded to the Dominion troops, increasing their feelings of superiority to the British and making it more likely that they would be used in such a role again. Consequently, on August 13, 1918, Arthur Currie sent a special order in the aftermath of the Amiens attack stating that "Canada has always placed the most implicit confidence in her Army. How nobly has that confidence been justified: and with what pride the story of your gallant success been read in the home land."[42] Currie further noted in his diary on September 27, 1918, that a German colonel, a POW, had told him that "in the German Army everyone agreed that the Canadian Corps were most to be feared in all the Allied Armies."[43]

Even the form of the war came to be identified through a nationalist lens more suited to the Australians or Canadians. As an Australian lieutenant explained in 1918: "This style of war suits us better and the men are keen. . . . We fight in open fields, among hedges and farm houses and dig trenches all over the country. We have got right away from fixed trench warfare."[44] The tension was obvious between the "open" warfare, which the lieutenant felt particularly suited to Australians, and the "fixed trench warfare," which, he implied, was more English.

This feeling of nationalist self-confidence could even explain setbacks. That is, they were not the result of a lack of effort or quality on the part of the attacking soldiers, but the reaction of the Germans who, knowing that they faced Australians or Canadians, poured a much larger number of reinforcements into the defense than they otherwise would have. Currie said this in October 1918:

The Germans fought us exceedingly hard all the way, for whenever the Canadian Corps goes into battle he seems to throw a far higher proportion of men and ammunition at us than he does at any other part of the front. He assumes that if he stops the Canadian Corps, everything else stops.[45]

This may have been true, and given Haig's continuing use of both the Australians and the Canadians as shock troops, Currie may have been correct that the Germans focused on halting those formations. But at the same time, this conclusion also was convenient. Victory was due to the superior soldiers of a particular nation; failure, or even lack of overwhelming success, was the result of the Germans' focusing on stopping the superior soldiers of a particular nation.

Finally, the creation of such large national forces and their use as shock troops created issues of security. The movement of the Canadian Corps before Amiens, for example, was a nightmare for those concerned with keeping such information from the Germans. General Sir Henry Rawlinson wrote in his diary that "wherever the Canadians go they always create suspicion. I must publish several lying orders to deceive my own people who do chatter so."[46] It was much more difficult for Rawlinson to conceal the movements of a large cohesive national group of soldiers than it would have been to assemble a similar-size group that did not have the same cohesion. In this case, then, the military and nationalist advantages created their own security disadvantages.

As the campaign wrapped up, the nationalist narrative become one of a redemption that followed failure. The disaster of Gallipoli and the abortive follow-on to Vimy Ridge were vindicated by the triumph of November 11, 1918. In a sense, the national moment of Gallipoli and Vimy Ridge—gallantry in the midst of slaughter—had been bookended by the national moment of Amiens and Canal du Nord—gallantry in service of victory. Even more important, nationalism, the battlefield, and operational decisions clearly interacted. The essential operational decision was to use several large bodies of troops with established bonds as mobile shock forces, moving them to where they were needed. The most readily available of those were the Canadian Corps and the Australian Imperial Force, tied together by bonds of national culture and with home governments insisting on their unity. Using them that way was almost inescapable. Their battlefield success in 1918 then redounded to the national culture, and their successes became Canadian and Australian, as well as Entente, successes.

The narrative of the war that emerged after the conflict ended continued this nationalist bent. Histories of the 1918 campaign tend to center on the feats of the American, Australian, and Canadian forces, and the Entente's overall operational achievements have been somewhat neglected. In a sense, the historiography has focused more on *who* in the Entente forces won the war, as opposed to *how* they won.[47] Thus, for example, almost immediately after the war, a popular history of the victorious campaign, entitled *Canada's Hundred Days*, appeared in Canada.[48] The value judgment—that the experience of the Hundred Days must be broken down by nationality—was obvious. Similarly, "without the Diggers, the Allies would probably have lost the war," another historian later confidently declared.[49] The *British Official Histories*, written by Sir James Edmonds, continued this discussion over the next several decades: Who deserved credit for the victory? Who deserved the blame? Were particular nationalities being treated fairly?[50]

Even when the historiography did extend to the operational level, the story was often one of competing nationalisms. This might take the form of contrasting implicitly or explicitly the Canadian General Arthur Currie, the Australian John Monash, the American John J. Pershing, and often a British general like Sir Henry Rawlinson.[51] Or it might look at how the BEF operated by focusing on particular nationalisms to discern, for example, "distinctive Canadian tactical methods."[52] It might analyze one particular nationalism in a battle, as did Glyn Harper with New Zealand and Passchendaele.[53] This tendency led historians to extract the performance of particular nationalities in 1918 rather than to evaluate the operation as a whole, and it created a back-and-forth about the relative worth and efforts of particular nationalities. Thus, such judgments as "the Canadian Corps, like the Australian divisions on the Western Front, appears to have been better led and more effective than its British counterparts" became common.[54]

In essence, operational discussions were distorted by nationalist concerns because of the nationalist ways in which the operations were organized. If a particular battle was identified with a particular nation, then criticism of the execution of that battle became criticism of that nation.[55] An example before 1918 is the battle of Poziéres in 1916. Part of the larger battle of the Somme, Poziéres resulted in heavy Australian casualties, becoming, in C. E. W. Bean's phrase, "more densely sown with Australian sacrifice than any other place on earth."[56] Poziéres symbolized for the Australians an Australian battle and the centerpiece of action on the western front during late

July to early August 1916. Not surprising, British and Australian perceptions of the importance of Poziéres differed. Sir James Edmonds, the British official historian, reviewed C. E. W. Bean's drafts of his history of the war and complained about his overemphasis on Poziéres: "Your narrative [Edmonds wrote to Bean] time after time gives the impression that nothing was going on except at Poziéres." That was not the case, Edmonds insisted: "The most important fighting at the end of July was at Delville Wood and then at Guillemont." Poziéres was one of the many "operations of a minor character . . . going on all along the British and French front."[57] In a sense, both men were right. Edmonds was correct to point out that many other, similar operations were being carried out at the same time, but Bean was correct that it was Poziéres, and Poziéres alone, that served as a foundation for a national mythology.

This distinction reinforced the nationalist mythology of young nations like Australia or New Zealand or Canada. They had overcome the blundering of the British at Gallipoli and Vimy Ridge and emerged triumphant in 1918.[58] They had saved the western front after the British collapse during the German spring offensives and then won the war in the summer and fall.[59] Such memorialization reinforced a distinctive identity and distinguished it from that of the imperial motherland. For the Dominions, the legend after the war was one of a particularly Dominion effectiveness at war, built on a foundation of their native culture.

The best example of this was the legend of the "digger," the Australian soldier, whose stereotype echoed Arthur Currie's earlier discussion of "discipline." The Australians were undisciplined and wild—completely different from the English—but not when it *really* counted. As Ambrose Cull, an Australian officer, wrote in his 1919 memoir: "The fact is that in the essentials of discipline, absolute obedience in battle, the end at which all the ridiculed formalities of peacetime aim, the Australian had no superior. He not only possessed discipline, but was proud of possessing it."[60]

Cull's obvious comparison was with the English, the avatars of the "ridiculed formalities of peacetime." The Australians may not have matched in the English in parade-ground spit and polish, but that was because the Australians understood when discipline was truly important. They did not need the parade ground because they were "brave, have natural fighting instincts and are fine specimens of manhood."[61] All these characteristics created the "myth of the digger" in which the Australian national character—so distinctive from the British—fed into the Australian soldier and had proved to be not only adequate but superior.[62]

I am not suggesting that the historiography was necessarily wrong in suggesting that Australian or Canadian units were more effective than British units. Indeed, they may well have been more effective, particularly given the way that Haig used them. Having said that, the initial historiography of the American effort in World War I was similarly triumphal, and only recently has the scholarship begun to demonstrate that American efforts were not always successful.[63]

How, then, did the victorious campaigns of 1918 play out in the postwar era? Like the earlier years, that last year of the war had to fit into a narrative of nationalist generation. The year of victory became a year of Australian and Canadian victory, too, and one that mingled overcoming the Germans with overcoming the limitations of the British. It was the story of the rural men and boys of Australia and Canada going to war, usually making long journeys to do so, being almost undone in the early going—whether by English incompetence at Gallipoli or the gas at second Ypres—but both redeemed by the valor of the nation's soldiers. The narratives end in the ultimate redemption of 1918, when victory was achieved with the particular nationality leading the way. For the Australians, 1918 was "emphatic and everlasting proof of its soldiers' high performance."[64] That victory was not merely to help the mother country but, as General Sir Archibald Macdonnell noted in 1925, was done by Canadian soldiers "to save their country."[65]

Any recounting of 1918 thus had to reemphasize the central role of a particular nationality in winning the final battles. If the men of that nation had not taken a special and specific role in the victory, it could not have been a victory for the nation. For 1918 to be a national moment, the analysis of the victory had to be in explicitly national, and often comparative, terms. Soon after the war, two Canadian generals compared what the Canadian Corps had managed with what the American Expeditionary Force had accomplished. Needless to say, the Canadians came out ahead.[66] Moreover, the Canadians had fought above their weight, making "a contribution to the military resolution of the war out of all proportion to its relatively small size."[67]

The Americans, however, were not the main comparison; instead, it was the colonial motherland of England. As an Australian wrote about Amiens, "At last it had come: a 'British triumph' on the Western Front and don't worry that Canadians and Australians did the best work while the British troops to the north struggled."[68] The quotation marks around "British triumph" are ironic, as Amiens was an Australian and Canadian triumph, one that was achieved despite the British.

The valor of the particular nationalities in 1918 had to be emphasized after the war in order for the narrative to remain solid. If Gallipoli and Vimy

Ridge were the starting points of the narrative and required emphasis, then 1918 was the end of the narrative and also required a particular emphasis. Ian McGibbon's book on New Zealand military history from the middle of the nineteenth century to the first few decades of the twentieth century ended in 1915 and was entitled *The Path to Gallipoli*, as if everything in that country's military history was leading up to those moments on the peninsula.[69] Echoing this idea, C. E. W. Bean published a shorter version of his official history of the Australian effort in World War I, which he entitled *ANZAC to Amiens*.[70] To be fair, he deliberately focused on the Australians, but the title indicates exactly what Bean thought that Australian story was.

One of the fascinating characteristics of this emphasis is the way in which a particular nationality's valor had to be recognized by outsiders. It was not enough that the Canadians themselves felt elite; they had to be recognized as elite by the rest of the world. Thus, in *Canada's Hundred Days,* John Livesay quotes a story that highlighted Ferdinand Foch's admiration for the Canadian Corps:

> [In the spring of 1918] Foch was asked to use the Canadian Corps to stem the tide of invasion. "No," came the reply—so the story goes—"I cannot afford to do that. By their valor the Canadian troops won back at Vimy the most valuable of our remaining coal fields. These are the nerve center of France. We cannot afford to entrust their defense out of the hands of my Canadians."[71]

Canada's valor was a *public* valor, and its nationalism was a *public* nationalism.

But what makes this story even more telling is that Livesay admitted that it may not have been true: "This story may be apocryphal," he wrote before telling it. "It does not matter, for in essence it is true." On one hand, Livesay felt compelled to show that Canadian courage was a watchword for Foch, but on the other hand, he asserted that whether Foch actually ever spoke of "my Canadians," the valor would nonetheless be real.

In a similar echo of mingled public admiration of an eternal truth, a historian of the Canadian Corps quoted Arthur Conan Doyle as saying that "'there are no better soldiers in the world than those of the Dominions.'" The historian, however, did not say that Conan Doyle was "arguing" or "asserting" it but that Conan Doyle was "conceding" it. That is, he was not making a judgment open to dispute but admitting a truth that could not be qualified or denied.[72]

The effects of such judgments on the operational analysis of the battles of 1918 were profound. One of these effects was not specific to nationalism but was a general failing. The perception of the Hundred Days in 1918 as the final victory (and in the British historiography often positioned as a victory achieved by German collapse rather than Entente success) tended to obscure the immensely high casualties between August and November 1918, which, in many cases, were substantially higher than those of the previous years. Indeed, the Canadian Corps suffered the highest casualty rates of the war not during Ypres or Vimy Ridge but during the Hundred Days, a fact "often lost sight of in the historical literature."[73] Because such heavy casualties did not fit well with the narrative of victory, they have tended to be ignored.

The second failing of the operational historiography of 1918 is the tendency to extract the national levies from all the great and supporting structures that surrounded them. It is not uncommon to ignore such things as logistics in recounting wars, but it is notable that both World Wars I and II actually produced a number of legendary logistics stories, such as the La voie sacrée at Verdun in 1915 or the Red Ball Express in Normandy in 1944. There are no similar legends for logistics feats in 1918. It is suggestive that the logistics apparatuses for the Dominion forces were predominantly English rather than ANZAC or Canadian. The heroism on La voie sacrée was French and, in the Red Ball Express, American. Telling their stories in a nationalist account reinforced *la gloire* or the red, white, and blue. Telling the stories of the British logistics services' achievements in 1918 did nothing to reinforce Canadian or ANZAC patriotism, so seemingly they have disappeared from the record.

Conclusion

The very act of raising and sending a Canadian Army abroad fundamentally altered Canada's dominion status and required substantial constitutional adjustments by the Canadian government.[74] From the beginning, the participation of Britain's colonies altered their status and self-conception, an alteration that only deepened as the war progressed. That evolution was influenced by and influenced the operational level of the war. Using the Canadian Corps and the Australian Imperial Force as distinct bodies within the British Expeditionary Force made them implicitly representative of their nations. It was an effective strategy as a way to build elite bodies of troops within the BEF by using their nascent sense of nationalism and cultural similarity as bonding devices. But it had consequences. The victories of 1918 were not only victories for the Entente; they also were victories for Canada and Australia. Moreover, they confirmed the sense, begun in early moments like Gallipoli or Vimy Ridge, that these nationalisms were distinct and were, in fundamental ways, superior to that of the British imperial motherland. Australian soldiers might have been speaking for all Australians when they complained to British troops returning from an assault that the Australians had "done more than their share of the dirty work when things were hard" and that now the British troops were "getting all the fun when the going was good."[75] In 1914, at the start of the war, an Australian minister stated that Australians were "British first, and Australian second."[76] But by 1918, that sentiment no longer held; the Australians and Canadians were British second, if at all. This distance was reinforced by the postwar historiography, one that reshaped the operational events on the ground in a way that fed into each national mythos but obscured the reality of the fighting. As I have pointed out, operations on the battlefield shaped national culture, and national culture shaped operations on the battlefield, both in 1918 and afterward.

If that is my specific argument, then my larger argument goes back to the usefulness of modern tools of historiography to military history. They surely are not the only or even the necessarily dominant mode of interpretation for matters military. Nonetheless, I do not think that we should limit our understanding of warfare to only the most traditional paradigms.

This raises the final question of what to offer back.[77] What does "military history" or the "history of war" offer to the larger historical project? Are we defined simply by our topic of study, or is there some methodology reserved for military historians? I would, in fact, argue that there is. It is perhaps not the only methodology, but military historians seem to me to be uniquely skilled at deciphering and analyzing the role in history of organizations and groups, both formal and informal. We are, after all, focused on institutions and groups as one of the foundations of our history. In a world of "history from the top down" and "history from the bottom up," such organizations and groups have been, and are, neglected. "History from the middle"—as Paul Kennedy called it—does not have quite the same ring, but it is critically useful all the same.[78]

NOTES

1. Edward M. Coffman, "The New American Military History," *Military Affairs*, 48, no. 1 (1984): 1–5.

2. John Keegan, *The Face of Battle* (London: Cape, 1976).

3. Robert Michael Citino, *The German Way of War: From the Thirty Years' War to the Third Reich* (Lawrence: University Press of Kansas, 2005), xvii.

4. Not to pick on Robert Citino, but to write a book entitled *The German Way of War* and argue that there has been a centuries-long consistency in the way that Prussian and

then German officers approach warfare without looking at the Prussian society from which they came seems an odd choice.

5. David C. Evans and Mark R. Peattie, *Kaigun: Strategy, Tactics, and Technology in the Imperial Japanese Navy, 1887–1941* (Annapolis, MD: Naval Institute Press, 1997), 511–12. See also Richard J. Smethurst, *A Social Basis for Prewar Japanese Militarism: The Army and the Rural Community* (Berkeley: University of California Press, 1974); Wayne E. Lee, "Mind and Matter—Cultural Analysis in American Military History: A Look At the State of the Field," *Journal of American History* 93, no. 4 (2007): 1116–42.

6. Victor Davis Hanson, *Carnage and Culture: Landmark Battles in the Rise of Western Power* (New York: Doubleday, 2001).

7. See Steven Willett, "History from the Clouds," *Arion* 10, no. 1 (spring/summer 2002): 157–78. Ignore the uncritical Hal Elliott Wert, "Carnage and Culture: Landmark Battles in the Rise of Western Power (review)," *Journal of Military History* 67, no. 2 (2003): 545–47.

8. John A. Lynn, *Battle: A History of Combat and Culture*, rev. and updated ed. (Cambridge, MA: Westview Press, 2004).

9. Gunther E. Rothenberg, "Review of *Battle: A History of Combat and Culture* by John A. Lynn," *Journal of Military History* 68, no. 3 (2004): 943–45.

10. Carlo Ginzburg, *The Cheese and the Worms: The Cosmos of a Sixteenth-Century Miller* (Baltimore: Johns Hopkins University Press, 1992); Natalie Zemon Davis, *The Return of Martin Guerre* (Cambridge, MA: Harvard University Press, 1984).

11. Jeremy Black, "Determinisms and Other Issues," *Journal of Military History* 68, no. 4 (2004): 1227.

12. Carol Reardon, *Pickett's Charge in History and Memory* (Chapel Hill: University of North Carolina Press, 2003).

13. For a discussion of the historiographical development of memorialization, see Jay Winter and Antoine Prost, *The Great War in History: Debates and Controversies, 1914 to the Present* (Cambridge: Cambridge University Press, 2005).

14. For example, Robin Prior and Trevor Wilson, *Passchendaele: The Untold Story* (New Haven, CT: Yale University Press, 1996); Robin Prior and Trevor Wilson, *The Somme* (New Haven, CT: Yale University Press, 2005); Peter Hart, *The Somme* (London: Cassell Military Paperbacks, 2006); Nigel Steel and Peter Hart, *Defeat at Gallipoli* (London: Papermac, 1995); Nigel Steel and Peter Hart, *Passchendaele: The Sacrificial Ground* (London: Cassell, 2001); Robert H. Ferrell, *America's Deadliest Battle: Meuse-Argonne, 1918* (Lawrence: University Press of Kansas, 2007); Michael S. Neiberg, *The Second Battle of the Marne* (Bloomington: Indiana University Press, 2008).

15. J. M. Winter, *Sites of Memory, Sites of Mourning: The Great War in European Cultural History* (Cambridge: Cambridge University Press, 1995), 204–10.

16. Joanna Bourke, *An Intimate History of Killing: Face-to-Face Killing in Twentieth-Century Warfare* (New York: Basic Books, 1999); for a useful review illustrating this point, see Graham Fuschak, Review of Joanna Bourke, *An Intimate History of Killing: Face to Face Killing in 20th Century Warfare, Journal of Military History* 64, no. 3 (2000), 915–16.

17. Daniel Todman, *The Great War: Myth and Memory* (London: Hambledon, 2005), is particularly good on the disconnect between scholarly and popular perceptions of World War I.

18. See John Keegan, *The First World War*, 1st U.S. ed. (New York: Knopf, 1999), for example, the great bulk of which is on 1914 to 1916.

19. Graham Seal, *Inventing Anzac: The Digger and National Mythology* (St. Lucia: University of Queensland Press, with API Network and Curtin University of Technology, 2004); Craig Wilcox and Janice Aldridge, *The Great War, Gains and Losses: Anzac and Empire* (Canberra: Australian War Memorial, Australian National University, 1995).

20. Quoted in Seal, *Inventing Anzac*, 113.

21. Quoted in Jeff Kildea, *Anzacs and Ireland* (Sydney: University of New South Wales Press, 2007), 213.

22. For *Gallipoli*, see Stuart Ward, "'A War Memorial in Celluloid': The Gallipoli Legend in Australian Cinema, 1940s–1980s," in *Gallipoli: Making History*, ed. Jenny Macleod (London: F. Cass Routledge, 2004), 59–72; Rose Lucas, "The Gendered Battlefield: Sex and Death in *Gallipoli*," in *Gender and War: Australians at War in the Twentieth Century*, ed. Joy Damousi and Marilyn Lake (Cambridge: Cambridge University Press, 1995), 148–61.

23. Quoted in Seal, *Inventing Anzac*, 44.

24. Larry Worthington, *Amid the Guns Below: The Story of the Canadian Corps, 1914–1919* (Toronto: McClelland and Stewart, 1965); John Alexander Swettenham, *To Seize the Victory: The Canadian Corps in World War I* (Toronto: Ryerson Press, 1965); Shane B. Schreiber, *Shock Army of the British Empire: The Canadian Corps in the Last 100 Days of the Great War* (St. Catharines, ON: Vanwell, 2004); Donald James Goodspeed, *The Road Past Vimy: The Canadian Corps 1914–1918* (Toronto: Macmillan, 1969); Tim Cook, *No Place to Run: The Canadian Corps and Gas Warfare in the First World War* (Vancouver: University of British Columbia Press, 1999); René Chartrand and G. A. Embleton, *The Canadian Corps in World War I* (Oxford: Osprey, 2007); Angus Brown et al., *In the Footsteps of the Canadian Corps: Canada's First World War 1914–1918* (Ottawa: Magic Light, 2006).

25. Jeffrey Williams, "Review of *Canada and the Battle of Vimy Ridge, 9–12 April 1917* by Brereton Greenhouse and Stephen J. Harris," *Journal of Military History* 57, no. 1 (1993): 157–58.

26. Andrew Iarocci, *Shoestring Soldiers: The 1st Canadian Division At War, 1914–1915* (Toronto: University of Toronto Press, 2008), 8.

27. Ibid., 6.

28. Angela Gaffney, *Aftermath: Remembering the Great War in Wales* (Cardiff: University of Wales Press, 1998), is useful on this.

29. Mark David Sheftall, *Altered Memories of the Great War: Divergent Narratives of Britain, Australia, New Zealand and Canada* (London: I. B. Tauris, 2010), does a wonderful job analyzing the different ways in which World War I fed into a variety of colonial nationalisms.

30. John Frank Williams, *ANZACS, the Media and the Great War* (Sydney: University of New South Wales, 1999) is better on Bean than Ross is but still is useful.

31. Douglas Haig and J. H. Boraston, *Sir Douglas Haig's Despatches (December 1915–April 1919)* (London: J. M. Dent & Sons, 1919), 54.

32. Haig and Boraston, *Sir Douglas Haig's Despatches*, 121.

33. Ibid., 125.

34. Shane B. Schreiber, *Shock Army of the British Empire: The Canadian Corps in the Last 100 Days of the Great War* (St. Catharines, ON: Vanwell, 2004), 18.

35. For an analysis of the effect of this on the Canadian Corps, see Ian M. Brown, "Not Glamorous, but Effective: The Canadian Corps and the Set-Piece Attack, 1917–1918," *Journal of Military History* 58 (1994): 421–44.

36. Peter Hart, *1918: A Very British Victory* (New York: Weidenfeld & Nicolson, 2008), 257.

37. Mark Osborne Humphries, ed., *The Selected Papers of Sir Arthur Currie* (Waterloo, ON: LCMSDS Press of Wilfred Laurier University, 2008), 72.

38. Ibid., 73.

39. G. D. Sheffield, *Forgotten Victory: The First World War: Myths and Realities* (London: Headline, 2001), 239.

40. J. P. Harris, *Douglas Haig and the First World War* (Cambridge: Cambridge University Press, 2008), 486.

41. Haig and Boraston, *Sir Douglas Haig's Despatches*, 261.

42. Humphries, *The Selected Papers of Sir Arthur Currie*, 104.

43. Ibid., 119.

44. Jeffrey Grey, *A Military History of Australia*, 3rd ed. (Port Melbourne: Cambridge University Press, 2008), 108–9.

45. Ibid., 127.

46. Quoted in Sydney Wise, "Amiens, August 1918: A Glimpse of the Future?" in *Canada and the Great War: Western Front Association Papers*, ed. Briton Cooper Busch (Montreal: McGill–Queen's University Press, 2003), 177.

47. For a measured discussion of competing claims, with particular focus on the French, see Robert A Doughty, *Pyrrhic Victory: French Strategy and Operations in the Great War* (Cambridge, MA: Belknap Press of Harvard University Press, 2005), 504–6.

48. John Frederick Bligh Livesay, *Canada's Hundred Days: With the Canadian Corps from Amiens to Mons, Aug. 8–Nov. 11, 1918* (Toronto: T. Allen, 1919).

49. John Laffin, quoted in Dale Blair, *Dinkum Diggers: An Australian Battalion at War* (Melbourne: University of Melbourne Press, 2001), 135.

50. Andrew Green, *Writing the Great War: Sir James Edmonds and the Official Histories, 1915–1948* (Portland, OR: F. Cass, 2003), 113.

51. Tim Travers, "The Allied Victories, 1918," in *The Oxford Illustrated History of the First World War*, ed. Hew Strachan (Oxford: Oxford Paperbacks, 2000), 278–91, esp. 284–87.

52. W. A. B. Douglas, "Marching to Different Drums: Canadian Military History," *Journal of Military History* 56 (1992): 257.

53. Glyn Harper, *Massacre at Passchendaele: The New Zealand Story* (Auckland: Harper-Collins, 2000).

54. Douglas, "Marching to Different Drums."

55. For an example of the way this can happen (albeit in an earlier battle), see Timothy H. E. Travers, "Allies in Conflict: The British and Canadian Official Historians and the Real Story of Second Ypres (1915)," *Journal of Contemporary History* 24 (1989): 301–25.

56. Quoted in Grey, *A Military History of Australia*, 102.

57. Williams, *Anzacs, the Media and the Great War*, 145.

58. Tim Cook, *Clio's Warriors: Canadian Historians and the Writing of the World Wars* (Vancouver: University of British Columbia Press, 2006) discusses this effectively. See also Tim Cook, *Shock Troops: Canadians Fighting the Great War, 1917–1918* (Toronto: Penguin, 2009).

59. Blair, *Dinkum Diggers*, 135.

60. Seal, *Inventing Anzac*, 81.

61. This is actually a quotation from James Edmonds, critiquing C. E. W. Bean's account of the war in the 1920s. See Williams, *ANZACS*, 6.

62. Jane Ross, *The Myth of the Digger: The Australian Soldier in Two World Wars* (Sydney: Hale & Iremonger, 1985).

63. Mark E. Grotelueschen, *The AEF Way of War: The American Army and Combat in World War I* (New York: Cambridge University Press, 2007); David F. Trask, *The AEF and Coalition Warmaking, 1917–1918* (Lawrence: University Press of Kansas, 1993).

64. Blair, *Dinkum Diggers*, 134.

65. Quoted in Jonathan F. Vance, "Remembering Armageddon," in *Canada and the First World War: Essays in Honour of Robert Craig Brown*, ed. Robert Craig Brown and David Clark MacKenzie (Toronto: University of Toronto Press, 2005), 428.

66. Schreiber, *Shock Army*, 133.

67. Ibid., 142.

68. Les Carlyon, "Dark Victories," in *Best Australian Essays 2008*, ed. David Marr (Sydney: Black, 2008), 122.

69. I. C. McGibbon, *The Path to Gallipoli: Defending New Zealand, 1840–1915* (Wellington: GP Books, 1991).

70. C. E. W. Bean, *Anzac to Amiens: A Shorter History of the Australian Fighting Services in the First World War*, 3rd. ed. (Canberra: Australian War Memorial, 1952).

71. Livesay, *Canada's Hundred Days*, 7.

72. Schreiber, *Shock Army*, 2.

73. Ibid., 131.

74. Donald Vince, "Development in the Legal Status of the Canadian Military Forces, 1914–19, as Related to Dominion Status," *Canadian Journal of Economics and Political Science / Revue canadienne d'économique et de science politique* 20, no. 3 (1954): 357–70.

75. Hart, *1918*, 342.

76. John McQuilton, *Rural Australia and the Great War: From Tarrawingee to Tangambalanga* (Melbourne: University of Melbourne Press, 2001), 19.

77. A question that Roberto Rabel tried to answer, in Roberto Rabel, "War History as Public History: Past and Future," in *Going Public: The Changing Face of New Zealand History*, ed. Bronwyn Dalley and Jock Phillips (Auckland: University of Auckland Press, 2001), 55–73.

78. Paul Kennedy, "History from the Middle? The Case for the Second World War," George C. Marshall Lecture, American Historical Association meeting, January 4, 2009.

9

The American Culture of War in the Age of Artificial Limited War

—— ADRIAN R. LEWIS ——

In the aftermath of World War II, Americans accepted a new theory of war, a theory based on airpower and advanced technologies.[1] Although this theory has never proved decisive and has in fact proved indecisive again and again, it has had incredible staying power and, to this day, dominates American thinking about the conduct of war. The latest version of this theory of war is called "network centric warfare (NCW)," which is merely another evolution in airwar theories and not a "revolution in military affairs," as is too often claimed.[2] The basic problem with airwar theories is their exclusivity. From their very inception in the 1920s, proponents have emphatically claimed and believed that airpower made all other forms of war obsolete, that airpower alone was the panacea, the answer to all wars. Humanity, however, has never accepted this verdict. Humanity has consistently acted in ways demonstrating that airpower was not the decisive instrument for the conduct of war. In World War II, Korea, and Vietnam, airpower, while contributing to the outcome of the war, failed to produce decisive results; ground and naval forces were needed as well. The most recent examples are Operations Enduring Freedom and Iraqi Freedom. In these wars, we Americans again prepared to fight a high-tech war against a low-tech enemy. We again employed the most advanced airpower against an enemy who could not produce the handheld weapons he employed. We again tried to destroy our enemies from thirty thousand feet, and we again failed. The North Koreans, the Chinese Communist forces, the North Vietnamese, and now, Al Qaeda, the Taliban, and Iraqi insurgent forces all have demonstrated again and again the ability to fight and survive against overwhelming American airpower. Today we are relearning the lessons of the Vietnam War. We are relearning counterinsurgency warfare, small-unit operations, engagement with people, and the human factors, the human costs of war.

Since World War II, we Americans have consistently failed to learn from the experience of war, primarily because the way we fight is in large part a function of our culture. It is not ignorance, neglect, evil intentions, or purposeful misdirection that causes us to continuously prepare to fight the wrong war. It is culturally imbued learning, the unbounded American faith in technology, the unmitigated desire to eliminate the human costs and ugliness of ground warfare, and the unhampered pursuit of happiness that decisively influence the American conduct of war. Culturally consistent ways of thinking and acting are quite literally killing Americans in foreign lands, diminishing the United States in numerous ways, and damaging our ability to achieve political objectives in all parts of the world.

A theory of war is not enough to motivate the behavior of a people. It is not enough to cause the expenditure of billions of dollars annually and trillions of dollars over decades. The Cold War, the Soviet threat, the decline of the traditional European powers, the advent of small wars of national liberation, the invention of nuclear weapons, and a new American militarism have combined to created the environment and the conditions for putting into practice this new American vision of war. This chapter examines the evolution of the American culture of war since World War II.

The Traditional American Culture of War

The strongest roots of the American culture of war come from the American Revolution, the Civil War, and World War II.[3] Traditionally, Americans have drawn a sharp distinction between war and peace. Peace is the norm, and war is an aberration that upsets the norm. Policing actions in Central and South America, the Philippines, China, and other parts of the world were not *wars* in the American understanding of the word. Even though the U.S. Army and Marine Corps have fought all types of "small wars" in all parts of the world, in the minds of Americans these were not *real wars*. When you say "war" to Americans, two of the three most significant events in the nation's life immediately come to mind, the Civil War and World War II. Both wars are deeply rooted in American culture, and both are rich sources of myths, legends, history, and symbolism. Americans believe they know what these wars were like, what they were about, and why they ended the way they did. Hence, Americans know what *real war* ought to look like.

The Civil War and World War II formed ideas and constructs in the minds of Americans, which in turn informed our understanding of war and hence influenced our decision making. These wars created systems of beliefs, values, and ethics that help determine emotions, attitudes, and dispositions in the present that affect the decisions we make. When you say "Civil War," places such as Gettysburg and Antietam come to mind, and names like Abraham Lincoln, Robert E. Lee, and Ulysses S. Grant come to mind. Images of deeds of valor, sacrifice, and honor come to mind. The nation at war comes to mind. Although in one sense, these are only words and images, they are in fact strands of culture that combine in a complex web of meaning called *war*. In his study *The Interpretation of Culture*, Clifford Geertz wrote, "Believing, with Max Weber, that man is an animal suspended in webs of significance he himself has spun, I take culture to be those webs, and the analysis of it to be therefore not an experimental science in search of *law* but an interpretive one in search of *meaning*."4 The two most significant events in the life of the American people still hold *meaning* and continue to influence the way we think about war.

Part of that thinking has been believing that war is a national endeavor, a serious business, not a balance-of-power game played by monarchs and politicians. Real wars require the total resources of the United States, its industrial power, its military power, its intellectual power, and its manpower. Real wars require everyone to sacrifice. Americans believe that war is an aberration that upsets the American norm that humans are *not* a means to achieve some end, not a tool of the state, but *the* end. War interrupts the American "pursuit of happiness": the process of producing, accumulating, and consuming wealth. Accordingly, wars must be fought expeditiously and relentlessly in order to bring them to a swift end and a return to normalcy.

American wars must be strategically offensive, and offensive operations must commence at the earliest opportunity. The strategic defense is assumed only temporarily to mobilize the nation for war. The preference for the overwhelming use of force and an offensive strategy are basic tenets of the American culture of war. Indeed, Americans believe that this is the surest and most direct path to decisive victory. Strategically defensive wars of attrition are un-American. For the strategic defense, all that is possible is to not lose the war. Americans prefer strategies of annihilation, and although it has rarely been achieved, it has frequently been sought. Exhaustion is the strategy employed in total wars.

Ideally, American wars are operationally and tactically offensive, for the attacking forces hold the initiative. Operations focus on destroying the enemy's main army. Direct engagement of the enemy's army at the earliest opportunity is expected. Thus Americans traditionally believed that the destruction of the enemy's main army would inevitably lead to the destruction of its government and the occupation of its country. Defensive operations, therefore, were only temporary expedients. Because sustained defensive operations prolonged the war, they were un-American. Likewise, protracted wars of attrition also were operationally un-American. Americans believed that soldiers should be supplied with the best weapons, the best equipment, the best food, the best transportation, and the most advanced technologies. They believed this because they understood that the soldiers on the battlefield who were killing, being wounded, and dying were making the greatest contributions and the greatest sacrifices; therefore, no resource should be spared to give them everything they needed to fight and win.

Americans expected and anticipated complete victory, unconditional surrender. Compromise solutions and negotiated settlements could not justify the expenditure of American lives and were, at best, only partial solutions. With the occupation of the country, the corrupt ideology and leadership that had caused the war could be rooted out, and a new, democratic, capitalist, American- / Western-oriented government could be put in place. In American eyes, there was a sharp distinction between right and wrong, good and evil. When the war was won, the citizen-soldiers were to be released and returned expeditiously to their homes and their individual pursuit of happiness. Americans did not believe they were responsible for rebuilding the defeated countries or for maintaining significant forces in the regions to preserve the peace. But they would accept these conditions as long as there was no significant fighting and dying. Americans expected states and nations, like people, to stand on their own and to be responsible for their actions. This was the way that real wars, total wars, were to be conducted. Americans did not distinguish between total wars and limited wars. War was war.

In the wake of World War II, however, the traditional American culture of war no longer was sustainable. During World War II and in the early years of the "Cold War," the American culture of war underwent a fundamental transformation, caused primarily by

1. The invention of the atomic bomb, which created *artificial limited war*.
2. The invention of "revolutionary technologies"—jets, rockets, guided missiles, satellites, nuclear energy, radar, and other advanced technologies—that caused many people to believe that the nature of warfare had fundamentally changed, that a revolution in warfare had taken place, and that the new *Star Trek* vision of war was the future.
3. The assumption by the United States of new roles and new responsibilities in world affairs. These new responsibilities created the perceived necessity of spending billions, ultimately trillions, of dollars on defense. These responsi-

bilities made the preparation for war a big business, which created new, powerful industries.

4. Expanded expectations from life. The unparalleled growth of wealth and consumption; the new freedoms created by the automobile / interstate highway system and the airplane / national airport system; and the new means of marketing to Americans through television and now the Internet created expectations from life that no other people in history could have conceived. In the late 1950s and early 1960s, Americans became the planet's biggest consumers, and the repercussions are evident today.

5. The advent of a new, American militarism. One form of militarism is the expenditure of resources to acquire military equipment and maintain forces beyond those needed for defense. The existence of military capabilities, unbalanced by a similarly capable threat, positively influences the decisions for war and the use of military force. The dynamic nexus of Congress, the armed services, the defense industry, and the American people led to the development of this new form of American militarism that has influenced the decision for war, as well as the conduct of war.

All these factors came together to transform the American culture of war and, in fact, American culture. But there remains an enormous chasm between the realities of war and war as Americans conceive and understand it. The consequences of this gap in understanding were evident in Operations Enduring Freedom and Iraqi Freedom.

Nuclear Weapons and the Development of Artificial Limited War

In November 1950 a miracle took place that ever since has shaped human history. But this miracle was almost unnoticed and has not been well studied. In November 1950, the U.S. Army, having all but destroyed the (North) Korean People's Army and defeated Communist North Korea, was violently attacked by the People's Liberation Army (PLA) of Communist China. The overwhelming force of the attack, with more than 150,000 soldiers, threatened the very survival of the U.S. Eighth Army and caused the longest retreat in U.S. history. Substantial numbers of U.S., ROK (Republic of Korea), and UN forces were cut off and killed. Although many were forced to surrender, others were able to fight their way out. This outcome was one of the most critical ever faced by U.S. forces. The miracle was what did not happen. The president of the United States, Harry S. Truman, had in his power the means to annihilate the PLA using an atomic bomb. But he did not. The moment he made that decision, Truman created *artificial limited war*, a way of war that had no precedent in the American military experience, a way of war that in fact did not conform to human nature.[5]

The atomic bomb's unparalleled destructive power motivated the creation of artificial limited war. But it did not have to be this way; Truman could have used the weapon, and he would have had the full support of the American people and military leaders. Instead, he went against the American culture of war and against human nature and established the precedent that has informed the behavior of governments to this day. The atomic bomb is the most significant invention for the conduct of war ever invented. Even though it did not change human nature, it caused people to seek to change the nature of war, which had tended toward total war. Carl Clausewitz observed that

> the maximum use of force is in no way incompatible with the simultaneous use of the intellect. If one side uses force without compunction, undeterred by the bloodshed it involves, while the other side refrains, that first will gain the upper hand. That side will force the other to follow suit; each will drive its opponent toward extremes, and the only limiting factors are the counterpoises inherent in war.[6]

In other words, absolute war, while the least common, is the most natural. War is a struggle for survival. There is nothing limited about dying or killing.

In war, human nature leans toward the extremes. But the "counterpoises," inherent in all human activities, place limits on war, limits that confine its destructiveness. In the past, social and political organization, geography and terrain, the availability of resources, the necessity to eat and to grow food, transportation and communication networks, the size and speed of means conveyances, the rotation of the planet, the inability to engage at night, weather and climate conditions, freezing cold and snow, and all other forms of essential human behaviors in a given environment placed very real limitations on people's ability to kill one another. This changed, however, in the late twentieth century with the invention of airpower and nuclear weapons. The vastness of the sky, the flexibility of airpower, and the small size of nuclear weapons and their great destructive power eliminated the effects of the physical or material "counterpoises" that, in Clausewitz's day and in all previous generations, placed very real limitations on the conduct of war. By the late 1950s, those limitations no longer existed, and humanity had created the ability to destroy itself. The one remaining counterpoise, and the one to which Clausewitz gave overriding importance, was the "political" counter-poise, the calculation of gain versus cost. In a moment of tremendous sig-nificance, President Truman weighed the costs, found them too high, and set a precedent that every American president, and the political leadership of every nation possessing nuclear weapons, has followed to this day. Nonethe-less, the danger that the true nature of war will reemerge is still with us. Arti-ficial limited war is not in accord with human nature.[7] It also is not in accord with the American culture of war. In 1950, a huge chasm was created between the realities of war and the American understanding of war.

In 1953, Robert Oppenheimer, the man most responsible for producing the atomic bomb, concluded,

> We may anticipate a state of affairs in which the two Great Powers will each be in a position to put an end to the civilization and life of the other, though not without risking its own. We may be likened to two scorpions in a bottle, each capable of killing the other, but only at the risk of his own life.

By eliminating military engagements between the two superpowers, the "scorpions," and by restraining engagements of surrogate forces and engage-ments in peripheral areas, the superpowers worked to preclude decisive, annihilatory blows with nuclear weapons. These restraints however, were self-imposed. Artificial limited war required nations to limit the objectives sought, the weapons and manpower employed, the geographic area of hostil-ities, and the emotions, passions, energy, attention, and intellectual commit-ments of their people. War, in essence, became a game between the super-powers. In his 1957 study *Limited War: The Challenge to American Strategy*, Robert Osgood defined limited war as follows:

> A limited war is one in which the belligerents restrict the purpose for which they fight to concrete, well-defined objectives that do not demand the utmost military effort of which the belligerents are capable and that can be accommodated in a *negotiated settlement*. Generally speaking, a limited war actively involves only two (or very few) major belligerents in the fighting. The battle is confined to a local geographical area and directed against selected targets—primarily those of direct military importance. It demands of the belligerents only a fractional commitment of their human and physical resources. It permits their economic, social, and political pat-terns of existence to continue without serious disruption. . . . Furthermore,

a war may be limited from the perspective of one belligerent, yet virtually unlimited in the eyes of another.[8]

For the major powers, limited wars are limited only at the strategic and operational levels. At the tactical level of war, where the battles are fought and the killing, wounding, suffering, and dying take place, there is nothing limited about limited war. Weapons produce the same effect in "limited war" as they do in "total war." They destroy life. Furthermore, there is nothing limited about war when it takes place in your homeland. Therefore, there was nothing limited about the Korean War for Koreans and nothing limited about the Vietnam War for the Vietnamese, just as there was nothing limited about the American Revolution for Americans. Limited war is not logical and cannot be sufficiently explained to the American people to gain and maintain their support, nor can it be explained to any other people who have had to commit their most precious gift to it: life. To ask people to commit their most valued possession to an endeavor and then to hold back the resources that would hasten an end to the conflict and possibly save lives was (is) inexplicable. The restraints in limited war are artificially imposed, and because everyone understands this, war has an internal illogic. Although political and military leaders have accepted and fought limited wars, the American people have never accepted the doctrine or strategy of limited war. To them, defensive wars of attrition—a function of the limitation imposed on war—are un-American.

During the "Cold War," Americans lived with many illusions of strategic importance that damaged the United States' ability to achieve its political objectives through the use of military force. While Americans accepted the "policy of containment," they did not accept the limited war strategy, which is an inextricable part of it. The illusion of unlimited war, of fighting war in the traditional American way, remained in place, contrary to the policy of containment. There was no way to reconcile the American understanding of war with the theory and strategy of artificial limited war. Even though Americans accepted, at least initially, the political decisions to go to war, they never accepted the strategy for the wars in Korea and Vietnam. Consequently, their expectations were never met. As a result, the gap between expectation and reality caused some political leaders to seek to fight wars on the margins of American consciousness. President Lyndon B. Johnson, for example, sought to fight the Vietnam War in "cold blood," that is, without the full involvement of the American people, without their passion, and without their emotional participation in what has traditionally been a national endeavor.[9] Limited war put the president in opposition to the people he led, and as the war continued and expectations were not met, support for both him and the war dropped. A conscripted army, particularly in a democracy, can exist and fight only with the support of the people. A limited, protracted war of attrition is unsustainable because it violates too many cultural, long-held tenets of the conduct of war.

In 1973, after fighting a prolonged defensive war of attrition, this contradiction was resolved. Through the legislative process the American people created an all-volunteer army, thereby removing themselves legally from the conduct of the nation's wars. This citizen-soldier army was incapable of supporting limited war as conceived by Robert Osgood and Henry Kissinger and, later, as practiced by Lyndon Johnson and Robert McNamara. The American citizen-soldier army could fight a limited *offensive war*, war in which the end of hostilities was based on American forces' positive actions, but such a war also could threaten to become a total war. The ever present danger in limited war, especially if fought with an offensive strategy, is that the "true nature" of war will reemerge, with all the death and destruction made possible by nuclear weapons.

The Revolution in Military Technology

Besides this disconnect between the American vision of total war and the artificial limitation imposed by nuclear weapons, other forms of modern technology have influenced the transformation in the American culture of war. Indeed, the new, post–World War II American vision of war is evident today on evening television. It is the vision of war portrayed in the many *Star Trek* and *Battlestar Galactica* series, and it is wrong to conclude that Gene Roddenberry or any other science fiction writer created this vision alone. Rather, they tapped into the vision of the future of warfare developed in the wake of World War II. Atomic energy, jet aircraft, guided missiles, satellites, and other advanced technologies coalesced with the American drive for progress, sense of modernity, value of human life, and love of technologies to create a new American vision of war, a vision in which wars are fought from the sky and space and in great ships resembling modern aircraft carriers but with warp engines. It is a vision in which war is clean and neat, like the bridge of the *Starship Enterprise*, which was modeled on the bridge of warships like the USS *Enterprise*. It is a vision in which enemies are killed from great distances, weapons have great precision, and their destructive power is exactly measured to produce the desired results.

It is a vision in which highly educated, highly skilled technicians, with traditional military codes of ethics, honor, and valor, conduct battles primarily by giving orders to other highly trained, highly skilled technicians who actually employ these precision weapons from advanced air/space crafts. It is a vision of war in which sensor technologies enable perfect information: constantly updated accurate intelligence on the enemy situation and complete situational awareness. It is a vision in which technologies make it possible to actually see the battlefield in real time on great, theaterlike screens. It is a vision of war in which communications are instantaneous and everyone has immediate access to all the information generated by the many sensors. These sensors supposedly eliminate the "fog of war" that has plagued military leaders throughout history. They make it possible for leaders to make decisions thousands of miles from the battlefields where the fighting is taking place. It is not difficult, therefore, to see the many parallels between the American *Star Trek* vision of war and the American military's vision of "network centric warfare," the vision of war that dominated the thinking of American military and civilian leaders as they prepared for and initiated war in Afghanistan and Iraq.[10]

One of the fathers of this new vision of war was the Italian military theorist Giulio Douhet, who in 1921 wrote a book entitled *The Command of the Air*, in which he prophesized that airpower would fundamentally change the nature of war. He believed that airpower was the decisive instrument for the conduct of war and that armies and navies would be relegated to the position of auxiliary forces. He wrote,

> The brutal but inescapable conclusion we must draw is this: in face of the technical development of aviation today, in case of war the strongest army we can deploy in the Alps and the strongest navy we can dispose on our seas will prove no effective defense against determined efforts of the enemy to bomb our cities.[11]

This widely popularized vision of future warfare took firm hold in American and British circles, and in World War II, only they invested vast sums and vast human resources in this unproven theory, something they came to call "strategic bombing." According to Richard Overy,

> Public opinion in both states [the United Kingdom and the United States] was unusually susceptible to the science-fiction view of air power, first popularized by writers such as H. G. Wells, whose *War in the Air*, pub-

lished in London as long ago as 1908, painted a lurid picture of "German air fleets" destroying "the whole fabric of civilization." Wells was father to a whole generation of scaremongers, who traded on popular anxiety that bombing was somehow a uniquely unendurable experience.[12]

Long before Gene Roddenberry created Captain Kirk and the *Starship Enterprise*, the idea of a decisive war taking place in the air was prevalent. The specter of another Great War, of trench warfare, weighed heavily on the British. Their experience of the carnage at the battles of the Somme and Passchendaele and witnessed at Verdun were enough to motivate extreme efforts to avoid this type of warfare. The vision of war created by writers like H. G. Wells and the predictions of airpower enthusiasts such as Douhet and Billy Mitchell not only planted the seeds of the ideas for a better, smarter way of war, but they also added to the fears, anxieties, and concerns created during the Great War. Technological competition was (and remains) a tenet of the Western way of war. All sides tried to gain advantage through advances in technologies. The airplane was a versatile technology for reaching deep into enemy countries. Proponents of airpower believed it had the capability to destroy the enemy's cities, the will of his people, and/or his means of production and to do so quickly, thereby shortening the war and avoiding the catastrophic stalemate of 1914 to 1918.

In 1940, after the fall of France, when Britain stood alone, airpower dominated the war effort. Before the German Wehrmacht could invade Britain, it had to control the air above the invasion beaches. Britain's survival thus depended on the capabilities of the Royal Air Force's Fighter Command. At the same time that the British were fighting for their survival, the only means they had to strike back at Germany was through airpower. Hence, in the early days of World War II, airpower played a decisive role, and Prime Minister Winston Churchill and President Franklin Roosevelt never lost sight of this fact. Airpower saved Britain. In the years following the victory by the Royal Air Force, the American and British built great fleets of heavy bombers and initiated a strategic bombing campaign, the first such campaign in history. The objective of the American campaign was to destroy the enemy's means of production, his ability to make war; and the objective of the British campaign was to destroy the will of the enemy's people. Neither campaign proved decisive. More decisive were the vast land campaigns fought in the Soviet Union and, finally, the American and British landings at Normandy, France, on June 6, 1944. The proponents of airpower nevertheless claimed that airpower had won the war and that had it been employed more effectively, the ground campaign would have been unnecessary. In 1943, U.S. General Henry Arnold concluded that

> war has become vertical. We are demonstrating daily that it is possible to descend from the skies into any part of the interior of an enemy nation and destroy its power to continue the conflict. War industries, communications, power installations and supply lines are being blasted by attacks from the air. Fighting forces have been isolated, their defenses shattered and sufficient pressure brought by air power alone to force their surrender. Constant pounding from the air is breaking the will of the Axis to carry on. . . . *Strategic air power is a war-winning weapon in its own right, and is capable of striking decisive blows far behind the battle line, thereby destroying the enemy's capacity to wage war.*[13]

In August 1945, the United States demonstrated to the world the most significant innovation in the conduct of war in history. Two small atomic bombs were dropped on the Japanese cities of Hiroshima and Nagasaki, bringing World War II to an abrupt end. This technology caused many to believe that armies and navies were obsolete. Indeed, Dwight Eisenhower, the second Cold War president, asserted that

> all the developments in method, equipment, and destructive power that we were studying seemed minor innovations compared to *the revolutionary impact of the atom bomb*. . . . [E]ven without the actual experience of its employment, the reports that reached us after the first one was used at Hiroshima on August 6 left no doubt in our minds that a new era of warfare had begun.[14]

By the end of World War II, the American people had firmly embraced the air war theory.

In June 1950, when North Korea invaded South Korea, General Douglas MacArthur ordered United Nations air and naval forces to stop the advance of the (North) Korean People's Army, but the Soviet-trained and equipped army continued to advance. To save South Korea, MacArthur ordered the deployment of the four understrength and poorly equipped divisions of the U.S. Eighth Army stationed in Japan. South Korea exists today only because U.S. ground forces were available in theater. The war was not the high-tech war envisioned; in many ways it was more primitive than World War II. To be sure, airpower working with ground forces generated greater combat power than would have been possible by ground forces alone. Still, it was a joint effort that saved South Korea. In the aftermath of the war, however, this lesson was forgotten, and Korea was seen as an aberration and a mistake. Korea, however, was the future of warfare because it was the first artificial limited war.

Throughout the 1950s, Eisenhower relied on an airpower doctrine called "massive retaliation" to deter war and to secure the United States and its allies. To do this, he committed enormous resources to build the Strategic Air Command. Technological competition between the Soviet Union and the United States was the defining characteristic of the 1950s, as it touched every aspect of American life, from the workplace to the schoolhouse to the backyard bomb shelter. Then in 1957 the Soviet Union launched *Sputnik* initiating the "space race." The Soviets' capabilities shocked Americans, creating a perception of American technological inferiority and putting Eisenhower on the defensive. The Soviet satellite then motivated the creation of the National Aeronautics and Space Administration (NASA) and the Advanced Research Projects Agency (ARPA) in 1958, and it help pushed Senator John F. Kennedy into the White House. Kennedy believed there were technological gaps: a "missile gap," a "bomber gap," and a space gap. *Sputnik* reinforced his argument against the Eisenhower-Nixon administration, helping Kennedy win the White House, from which he announced the race to the moon. *Sputnik* greatly intensified the drive for technological superiority and the push into space. Science fiction books and films and real-world capabilities combined to create visions of war from space, the *Star Trek* vision of war.

The army was never convinced, however, that airpower was the decisive weapon for the conduct of war, and throughout the 1950s it waged a campaign against the policy of massive retaliation and the belief that ground forces were obsolete. In 1954 General Mark Clark wrote:

There is much talk these days about push-button warfare and the fact that the technical experts have developed such weapons of mass destruction that the role of the infantryman is now secondary. . . . However, in my opinion . . . the infantryman remains an indispensable element in any future war. Certainly he must be supported by the Air and Navy and every kind of technical weapons, but he never will be relegated to an unimportant role. He is the fellow with the stout heart and the belly full of guts, who, with his rifle and bayonet, is willing to advance another foot, fire another shot and die if need be in defense of his country.[15]

Army Generals Omar Bradley, Lawton Collins, Matthew Ridgway, Maxwell Taylor, and numerous others made similar statements, but in the prevailing environment, they seemed out of place, a throwback to earlier times. The army, and ground warfare in general, were seen as not modern, not sophisticated, not high-tech, and not in the hearts and minds of the American people and their political leaders.

The U.S. Army fought the Vietnam War entirely on the strategic defensive, the first such war in U.S. history. Airpower was the only strategic offensive arm and indeed was supposed to win the war. With a few highly controversial exceptions, the army fought the ground war entirely within the borders of South Vietnam, and consequently, the enemy always had the initiative. He could control his rate of losses and decide when and when not to fight. Although the reasons for the eventual American failure in Vietnam are complex and are still being debated, it is clear that airpower did not prove to be the hoped-for panacea.

Stalemate in Korea and failure in Vietnam, however, did not change the minds of Americans in regard to the effectiveness of airpower. American hopes for its efficacy lingered on during the waning years of the Cold War and then received sharp and much-televised reinforcement during the first Persian Gulf War in 1991. Richard Hallion explained the outcome of that war:

> The Persian Gulf War will be studied by generations of military students, for it confirmed a major transformation in the nature of warfare: the dominance of airpower. . . . Simply (if boldly) stated, air power won the Gulf war. It was not a victory of any one service, but rather the victory of coalition air power projection by armies, navies, and air forces. At one end were sophisticated stealth fighters striking out of the dark deep in Iraqi territory. At the other were the less glamorous but no less important troop and supply helicopters wending their way across the battlefield. In between was every conceivable form of air power application, short of nuclear war, including aircraft carriers, strategic bombers, tactical and strategic airlift, and cruise missiles.[16]

In Kosovo in 1999, in Afghanistan in 2001, and finally again in Iraq during Operation Iraqi Freedom in 2003, the decisive nature of airpower was trumpeted, on the last occasion under the operational doctrine of "shock and awe." But like the strategic bombing theory in World War II and the "graduated escalation" doctrine used in Vietnam, it did not work. The war evolved into an insurgency war, and ground forces were deployed to take up the fight.

While billions of dollars of the most advanced aircraft ever produced sat silently on runways, the United States was incapable of providing sufficient numbers of soldiers to implement its counterinsurgency doctrine, and soldiers were again poorly equipped for the type of war they were required to fight.

The New Role of the United States in World Affairs

The transformation of the American culture of war was in part a function of the United States' assuming new roles and responsibilities in Europe, Asia, the Middle East, and other parts of the world. In the wake of World War II, the American people slowly accepted the status of "superpower" and the role of "leader of the free world." They also accepted the strategic airpower doctrine of massive retaliation and the deployment of U.S. forces around the globe. And they accepted enormous defensive budgets. What they did not accept was the human cost of the Cold War, a cost that many had believed would be negligible because of the great advances in technology.

After President Roosevelt's death in April 1945, President Truman undertook the task of changing the American perspective on war and the world. He emphasized the special place of the United States among nations, the dominance of American power, the need to look outward, and the burden of leadership it created. He told the American people:

> Whether we like it or not, we must all recognize that the victory which we have won [World War II] has placed upon the American people the continuing burden of responsibility for world leadership. The future peace of the world will depend in large part upon whether or not the United States shows that it is really determined to continue in its role as a leader among nations. It will depend upon whether or not the United States is willing to maintain the physical strength necessary to act as a safeguard against any future aggressor. Together with the other United Nations, we must be willing to make the sacrifices necessary to protect the world from future aggressive warfare. In short, *we must be prepared to maintain in constant and immediate readiness sufficient military strength to convince any future potential aggressor that this nation, in its determination for a lasting peace, means business.*[17]

In the aftermath of World War II, the United States became a European land power with the occupation of what became West Germany, as well as what became an Asian Pacific land and sea power with the occupation of

Japan and South Korea. These new responsibilities were not simply to secure the regions against vanquished enemies; they were also to contain Communism, to stop the spread of an ideology and a social, political, and economic system that were unacceptable to Americans and the Western world.

While accepting this new role in world affairs, Truman and the American people were slow to understand exactly what this meant: the duties and requirements that went along with world leadership, and the resources required to defend such vast regions. This new level of commitment of national resources to the defense of foreign shores and to stop the spread of Communism marked a major change in U.S. foreign policy, national military strategy, and the decision-making processes in Washington. The rapid collapse of the British and French empires, the descent of the "Iron Curtain" in Eastern Europe, the Chinese Communist revolution, the Soviets' acquisition of the atomic bomb, and the outbreak of small wars of liberation in various parts of the world placed extraordinary demands on the United States. This "Cold War" resulted in creating the environment and the conditions for the transformation in American thinking about the use of military force and the conduct of war.

The Cold War (1945–1990) was a remarkable period in history, a time when the two most powerful nation-states on the planet, the United States and the Soviet Union, continuously prepared to go to war with each other, and indirectly fought wars through surrogate, peripheral, and even non-aligned states. It was a period during which the extinction of humanity became a real possibility, because each superpower had acquired the means to destroy the other, and ultimately civilization, several times over. It was a period when the superpowers employed armies of scientists and engineers in a race to develop the most destructive weapons and invincible delivery systems. It was a period when they formed strategic mutual defense alliances, NATO and the Warsaw Pact, to strengthen their ability to defend themselves and destroy their opponents. But perhaps most important, it was a period of global turmoil, when the exertions of World War II caused the collapse of European imperialism, and nationalism spread to India, China, Indochina, Africa, the Middle East, and other parts of the world. The resulting postwar process of "rearrangement" generated great suffering and carnage in developing states racked by wars as they tried to achieve statehood, establish legitimate political systems, reconcile borders that were based on the concerns of European imperialist powers, redress racial and ethnic discrimination, and recover and reorganize after decades and centuries of European rule. Critical among those new states were North Korea, South Korea, the

People's Republic of China, Pakistan, and Israel, each of which in some way challenged the balance of power between the superpowers. It was a period when states in all parts of the world expended vast resources on armies, navies, and air forces, and militarism invaded the social and political fabric of nations. It was a period when the superpowers maintained armies, navies, and air forces forward-deployed in nations around the world, influencing their economies, internal politics, and culture. It was a period of ideological entrenchment when paranoia invaded governmental institutions and the "police state" threatened democracy and individual freedoms. It was a period of great distrust, uncertainty, and anxiety, punctuated by days and weeks of fear and terror. But it also was a period of great prosperity in the United States, during which Americanism spread around the globe and American culture adjusted to the norms of being in a perpetual state of preparing for or fighting a war. The Cold War was ultimately a fight over the political, economic, social, and cultural systems that would dominate the earth. During this long, costly, and difficult fight, all parties were transformed, politically, geographically, socially, culturally, economically, and militarily.

The Cold War and the policy of containment meant intellectually that the armed forces of the United States had to remain in a permanent state of military readiness to provide the force required to maintain the peace and/or fight wars until the Soviet Union collapsed from its internal "deficiencies," as George Kennan predicted.[18] The Truman administration and the Congress, however, opposed spending the money required to maintain American forces at the state of readiness that the Joint Chiefs of Staff believed was necessary, given the Soviet threat. Memories of the Great Depression ran deep, and in the aftermath of World War II, given the totality of that war, it was difficult to imagine a ground war that would *not* escalate into nuclear war. Strategic airpower had become the decisive doctrine for the conduct of war, as it appeared to offer the United States the means of maintaining a high state of readiness without wrecking the economy or placing an enormous burden of debt on the American people. Airpower and the atomic bomb gave the nation a deterrent to war and, in the event of total war, a means of devastating the enemy's homeland. Truman also believed that American security was enhanced by diplomatic offensives and economic support to allies. Collective defense agreements, such as the North Atlantic Treaty Organization (NATO) and the Military Assistance Program were means of enhancing the security of the United States without maintaining a large standing army.

Not everyone accepted Truman's military policy, however. In 1949, Secretary of State Dean Acheson recognized that new worldwide responsibilities required a new worldwide military establishment. The United States could not go back to the pre–World War II paradigm for national defense, nor could it rely solely on airpower. In the early months of 1950, NSC-68, a classified National Security Council policy document advanced by Acheson and Paul H. Nitze, was discussed at the highest level of government. In summary, the policy paper stated:

> The issues that face us are momentous, involving the fulfillment or destruction not only of this Republic but of civilization itself. . . . In the concept of "containment," the maintenance of a strong military posture is deemed to be essential for two reasons: (1) as an ultimate guarantee of our national security and (2) as an indispensable backdrop to the conduct of the policy of "containment." Without superior aggregate military strength, in being and readily mobilizable, a policy of "containment"—which is in effect a policy of calculated and gradual coercion—is no more than a policy bluff. . . . We have failed to implement adequately these two fundamental aspects of "containment." In the face of obviously mounting Soviet military strength ours has declined. . . . [W]e must, by means of a rapid and sustained build-up of the political, economic, and military strength of the free world, and by means of an affirmative program intended to wrest the initiative from the Soviet Union, confront it with convincing evidence of the determination and ability of the free world to frustrate the Kremlin design of a world dominated by its will. . . . [T]he cold war is in fact a real war in which the survival of the free world is at stake.[19]

NSC-68 was designed to be a blunt instrument to move Truman to increase defense spending. The events of 1949, especially the collapse of the Nationalist government in China, convinced Acheson and Nitze that the Soviet Union had the initiative around the world. Their response, embodied in NSC-68, divided the world into good and evil, creating a simplistic formulation designed to be easily understood. Nevertheless, concerned about the budget and the economy, Truman wavered and ordered a follow-up study of NSC-68's implications. Then in June 1950, North Korea attacked South Korea. A shaken Truman now fully comprehended and accepted the new duties of the United States in the management of world affairs. The Cold War provided the reasons to expend enormous national resources on airpower, and NSC-68 provided the necessary documentation to advance the argument.

NCS-68 was referenced by every subsequent administration during the Cold War. It provided the justification for continued military expenditures.

Still, while Americans were willing to spend their tax dollars on bombers, they were not willing to send their sons and daughters to defend Koreans and Vietnamese. In 1965, the first year of the Americanization of the Vietnam War, President Johnson also sought to explain to the American people the new role of the United States in international affairs:

> There are those who wonder why we have a responsibility there. Well, we have it there for the same reason that we have a responsibility for the defense of Europe. World War II was fought in both Europe and Asia and when it ended we found ourselves with continued responsibility for the defense of freedom.[20]

Even though American foreign and military policies and strategies had changed substantially after World War II, the American people had changed little in their vision and expectation of war. One reason was that the partial mobilization for war caused confusion. The American people were unhappy with the partial success in Korea, with the stalemate that left North Korea in existence, and with the way the war was fought—a defensive war of attrition. The biggest problem, however, were the human costs, the sacrifices required.

The American people were not asked whether they wanted to fight the Cold War. They were not asked whether they wanted to station hundreds of thousands of soldiers around the world. Americans did accept the policy of containment and the status of superpower. They also accepted the enormous dollar costs of the Cold War, but they never agreed to pay the human costs it involved. They never agreed to make the sacrifice that containment might require. In fact, they were told again and again that technology had replaced people in the conduct of war. But it did not work that way in Korea, and it failed spectacularly during the Vietnam War. Nothing about that war seemed to match what the American people had been led to expect, and after a decade of bleeding in Vietnam, in 1973 the American people removed themselves from the conduct of the nation's wars.

The Culture of Wealth and Consumption: The Pursuit of Happiness

Writing during the last days of the Roman Empire, Flavius Vegetius Renatus observed that "the chief strength of our armies, then, should be recruited from the country. For it is certain that the less a man is acquainted with the sweets of life, the less reason he has to be afraid of death." A more accurate assessment of human nature is that the less a man has, the greater will be the apparent benefits of military service. Furthermore, the martial spirit is easier to implant in poorly educated individuals, because they have a limited vision of the world and fewer options in life. Men who toil in fields or labor in industry are physically and psychologically more adaptable to the toils of the battlefield. As a student of the U.S. Army in the Korean War pointed out,

> [N]o army can change entirely—either for better or for worse—the civilians to whom it issues uniforms, supplies, and rifles. As a man has lived as a civilian so can he be expected to fight as a soldier. Americans in Korea displayed prodigious reliance on the use of firepower; they became unduly concerned with putting in their time and getting out; they grew accustomed to fighting on a level of physical luxury probably unparalleled in world history to that time. In stark contrast to the American reverence for the programs of "R&R" (rest and recuperation) and the "Big R" (rotation back to the US), Chinese Communist soldiers fought—much as they had lived—with little hope of leaving the frontline until the war ended or until they became casualties. *Whether the US can maintain the requisite balance between a liberal society which is the master of its armed force and a professional soldiery which is free to preserve the military ethic is the vital question to which the American way of war in Korea offers limited but significant testimony.*[21]

The affluence of much of modern America is diametrically opposed to the destitute conditions of the battlefield. Two of the things that make life most precious are the expectations from life and the finality of death. War at the edge of the battlefield where the killing takes place is ultimately a selfless endeavor. The culture of wealth, which emphasizes selfishness, is diametrically opposed to the culture of soldiers, which requires selflessness. Success in modern America's competitive, capitalist society is ultimately a selfish endeavor. Self-interest is the bedrock of capitalism. Many argue that greed is good for the economy and hence is good for America. But without individuals willing to act selflessly, nations cannot provide for their defense. Thus American cultural tenets conflict, and the one that receives the most reinforcement and dominates cultural production will come out on top. In recent decades, wealth and the pursuit of wealth have been the dominant forces in American life, directly influencing everything that Americans think and believe. Again, consider the words of Robert Osgood:

> Quite aside from the moral odium of war, the fear of violence and the revulsion from warfare are bound to be strong among a people who have

grown as fond of social order and material well-being as Americans. War upsets the whole scale of social priorities of an individualistic and materialistic scheme of life, so that the daily round of getting and spending is subordinate to the collective welfare of the nation in a hundred grievous ways—from taxation to death. This accounts for an emotional aversion to war, springing from essentially self-interest motives.[22]

In 2008, another student of American life, Andrew Bacevich, wrote:

For the United States the pursuit of freedom, as defined in an age of consumerism, has induced a condition of dependence—on imported goods, on imported oil, and on credit. The chief desire of the American people, whether they admit it or not, is that nothing should disrupt their access to those goods, that oil, and that credit. The chief aim of the U.S. government is to satisfy that desire, which it does in part through the distribution of largesse at home (with Congress taking the leading role) and in part through the pursuit of imperial ambitions abroad (largely the business of the executive branch).[23]

In 2008, *U.S. News & World Report* reported that

America is incredibly indebted. The debt in the financial world went from 21 percent of a $3 trillion gross domestic product in 1980 to 120 percent of a $13 trillion GDP in 2007, reflecting an astonishing accumulation of as much as $30 of debt for every $1 of equity in many firms.[24]

Consumption is necessary for human existence, for food, clothing, and shelter. But consumption is a self-centered activity, and America's wealth has produced levels of consumption known to only a very few throughout human history. Such levels of consumption necessarily influenced American culture and the way that American people live and think. The American economy and marketing practices in the latter half of the twentieth century produced a society in which from birth to death, people are told to consume. Americans thus devote much of their time and energy to the self-centered endeavor of consumption, which informs people that life is about them. No people in the history of the world have been marketed to as Americans have. In the 1950s, television entered American homes, and by the end of 1952, nineteen million TV sets were marketing to Americans. Two years later, television was the largest advertising medium in the country, and as David Halberstam noted, "Ten years later television had begun to alter the political and social fabric of the country, with stunning consequences."[25] Television influences consumption, and consumption influences every aspect of American life, including the nation's ability to produce combat soldiers and fight wars.

American affluence grew considerably during the 1950s, making possible even greater levels of consumption. The value of each American life in terms of dollars rose to exceed that of all other people on earth. Home, automobile, and television ownership increased. The interstate highway system and the commercial airline system made Americans more mobile than any other society in history. Individual freedoms, freedom from needs, and the freedom of time gave Americans a standard of living new to humankind. American expectations from life grew as the state prospered, and the definition of the "good life" changed. President Eisenhower noted,

> In 1953 we had seen the end of the Korean War. In 1954 we had won out over the economic hazard of a recession. With these problems behind us, we in the United States entered a new era of unprecedented peace and unprecedented prosperity. . . . Compared with any years of the two preceding decades, these surely must have seemed miraculous to most Americans. Not in the lifetime of millions of our citizens . . . had we previously had peace, progress, and prosperity all at one time.[26]

Wealth created new cultural tenets to produce this miraculous peace, progress, and prosperity, but they conflicted with the cultural tenets required to produce soldiers for war, thereby facilitating the transformation in American thinking about the conduct of war. Wealth in America created importance and privilege, which in many affluent groups diminished the sense of duty to the state and the willingness and ability to perform the labors of soldiers. Those people with less wealth aspired to and aggressively sought the importance and privileges of those with wealth. Families changed. The number of children per family declined, as more children meant less wealth and less personal time. In the latter half of the twentieth century, more and more Americans arguably became too "important" to fight in a war, particularly a limited war. When measured against the lifetime earning potential of a North Korean, Chinese, Vietnamese, or Iraqi citizen, American lives were worth many times more. Even though certain affluent groups continued to observe their traditional roles, others scrupulously avoided military service. Eisenhower explained the transformation in American life:

One dramatic feature of the expanding middle class was the increase in the number of white-collar workers and professional people. Widespread schooling, increasing domestic and international travel . . . and reasonable prosperity had helped turn people away from becoming laborers, while technology was making many unskilled and semiskilled jobs obsolete. More and more people were working in "services," because more and more people could afford to pay others to do work for them—from shining shoes to surgery.[27]

The physical aspects of work: getting dirty, using muscles, tolerating physical discomfort, summoning the stamina and endurance required for manual labor, and assuming the psychological disposition of laborers all were practices that better prepared people to become soldiers than did the paper-pushing jobs performed by sedentary white-collar workers.

With each subsequent decade in the latter half of the twentieth-century, the American people became physically and psychologically less capable of fighting wars. As the service industry expanded, the manufacturing industry contracted. In the 1990s, ROTC departments around the country complained that new recruits could not run a half mile, so new physical training programs were initiated to get potential cadets up to the minimal physical condition required for service, a standard that was far below that required in U.S. Army infantry units. Recruiters had the same problem, as too many Americans were too overweight to qualify for service. In 2002, 64 percent of Americans were overweight or obese,[28] so the percentage of the American population capable of becoming combat soldiers was considerably lower in 2005 than in 1945. In February 2009, *U.S. News & World Report* asserted that

our expanding girth is America's most visible health problem [and national security problem]. Not only are most adults too heavy, but obesity rates for children have more than doubled in the past 30 years. Excessive weight is a significant factor in four of the six leading causes of death; heart disease, cancer, stroke, and diabetes.[29]

This is an issue of national security. People who are overweight or obese lack the motivation, energy, confidence, and physical capabilities to serve in war or stability operations. They also lack the will and confidence to volunteer for military service. The *U.S. News & World Report* article concluded that "every year, in fact, an estimated 900,000 people die from avoidable causes: because they failed to maintain a healthy weight, eat nutritiously, and exercise, or because they smoked or drank excessively, for example. That's roughly 40 percent of all U.S. deaths." This is more Americans than were killed in all theaters of war in World War II. It is hard to imagine how the United States can remain a superpower when a significant portion of its population suffers from the debilitating effects of obesity. The absence of a national discussion about conscription, given the two long wars in Iraq and Afghanistan and the known shortages in manpower, is an indication that war and national security are subordinate to the major American endeavor, the pursuit of wealth and consumption.

To compensate for the shortage in manpower, in Iraq and Afghanistan the Pentagon started "outsourcing" war as never before. It employed private military firms, that is, civilian contractors such as Blackwater, Global Risks, DynCorp International, and Halliburton, to provide security, logistical support, maintenance, and training.[30] By July 2004, more than twenty thousand private contractors were in Iraq, and thousands more were in Afghanistan. Many of these men were carrying out "mission-critical" tasks, which the services had traditionally insisted were exclusively military functions. These private soldiers suffered more casualties than any of the armed forces of President George W. Bush's "coalition of the willing," and to some degree, they made up for the shortage of soldiers and marines. The Pentagon then expanded the practice of outsourcing war, increasing the number of privately employed individuals. But outsourcing war only further removes the American people from the obligation to serve their nation in the armed forces. As the American people become less capable and prove less willing to provide for the national defense, the number of private military firms will grow in importance and numbers. Why disturb an American citizen who makes $30,000 a year when you can employ three Egyptian subcontractors for less? Private military firms displace and conceal the cost and trauma of war, and their casualties are frequently not Americans. Moreover, these firms are not required to report killed or wounded to the Pentagon or the press. They also diminish the need for the president to explain the reasons for the war and to seek the support of the American people. Private military firms reduce the political cost of war for the decision makers in Washington. They are, in fact, a new form of mercenaries because they work for the highest bidder and have no loyalties to any particular government. Patriotism does not matter. Private military firms may be the future of warfare.

Throughout the world, Americans are believed to have an abnormally strong aversion to casualties, and if they are bloodied sufficiently, they will abandon their objectives and go home. In Lebanon, Somalia, and Kosovo, the world watched American ground forces retreat after sustaining casualties. The Vietnam War marked the origin of this perception, which has informed our enemies' strategic thinking. But there is a paradox here. No people on the planet invest as many resources and as much wealth in their war machines, the deployment of military forces, and the display of military capabilities as Americans do. Yet today, Americans are among the least capable people on earth of fighting war. The average American is physically incapable of serving in the army or the marine corps. One of the reasons that the army is too small and that political leaders rely so heavily on technology and private military firms is that too many Americans are incapable of serving in defense of the nation. Consumption is quite literally killing Americans.

War requires human engagement at the most basic level. By trying to take humanity out of war, Americans diminish their ability to influence events and people. In recent years the Bush and Obama administrations have taken war with technology to new extremes. They have employed unmanned aerial vehicles mounted with missiles to kill suspected terrorist leaders. In the process, they have killed possibly thousands of innocent people who happened to be in close proximity to the suspected terrorist. There is something very wrong with this behavior. It cannot legitimately be called war.

Militarism

Militarism distorts American culture and the American conduct of war. Militarism "covers every system of thinking and valuing and every complex of feeling which rank military institutions and ways above the ways of civilian life, carrying military and modes of acting and decision into the civilian sphere."[31] Militarism is the acceptance of and preference for military ways of thinking and acting. It is a people's acceptance of military values, ethics, and beliefs. Alfred Vagts observed that "militarism . . . has meant also the imposition of heavy burdens on a people for military purposes, to the neglect of welfare and culture, and the waste of the nation's best man power in unproductive army service."[32] Militarism does not necessarily mean the love of war. Rather, it can mean the love of the instruments of war, the bombers, fighters, aircraft carriers, and so on, plus the sense of power they produce. Militarism is a predisposition, an attitude, a way of looking at and thinking about the world that emphasizes military perspectives and means, military behaviors and solutions to problems.

Militarism is evident in the expenditure and use of resources. The expenditure of resources beyond that legitimately required for defense is militarism. For example, if a nation needs ten aircraft carriers for national defense and maintains fifteen, it is militaristic. If a nation has a submarine fleet designed to fight a specific enemy, and it continues to maintain that fleet even after that enemy has passed into history, it is militaristic. If a state has the world's most advanced air superiority fighter and replaces it with another, slightly more advanced air superiority fighter—in other words, if it is competing with itself in terms of military capabilities, it is militaristic. If a nation's political leadership elects to use military force when other options are available or to fight unnecessary wars, it is militaristic. If the political and military leadership maintains military installations that are no longer needed for national security, it is militaristic. And if a nation's people covet military technologies for the sake of possessing military technology, it is militaristic. Americans are in many ways militaristic.

During the Cold War, Americans became addicted to defense spending. Arguably, the United States needs enemies to maintain its economy and to keep its people employed and happy. Americans also became enamored with military hardware, jet aircraft, huge aircraft carriers, submarines, and the like. But this love affair with the military was one-sided, as it did not include the army or ground forces. There was nothing high-tech or sophisticated about an infantry division, small-unit warfare, or counterinsurgency operations. There were no high-tech, high-paying jobs for maintaining an army division, and few members of Congress supported the retention of significant ground forces. Consequently, the United States has maintained insufficient military capacity in ground forces and considerably more capacity than necessary in air forces. Consider the words of Army Chief of Staff General George W. Casey, testifying before the Senate Armed Service Committee in 2007:

> While we remain a resilient and committed professional force, our Army is out of balance for several reasons. The current demand for our forces exceeds the sustainable supply. We are consumed with meeting the demands of the current fight and are unable to provide ready forces as rapidly as necessary for other potential contingencies. Our Reserve Components are performing an operational role for which they were neither originally designed nor resourced. Current operational requirements for forces and limited periods between deployments necessitate a focus on counterinsurgency to the detriment of preparedness for the full range of military missions. Soldiers, families, and equipment are stretched and stressed by the demands of lengthy and repeated deployments with insuffi-

cient recovery time. . . . Army support systems including health care, education, and family support systems that were designed for the pre-9/11 era are straining under the pressure from six years at war. Overall, our readiness is being consumed as fast as we can build it.[33]

Casey's job and loyalty to the president required that he understate the magnitude of the problem; however, journalists and historians are not bound by the same rules. Consider what *Time* magazine wrote in April 2007 in an article entitled "Why Our Army Is at the Breaking Point: Exhausted Troops, Worn-out Equipment, Reduced Training, the Lessons of Iraq and Afghanistan":

> The Army's problems were long in the making, and the extended deployments in Iraq and Afghanistan have exposed them for all to see: more than a decade of under-funding for boots on the ground while cold war administrations from Richard Nixon's to Bill Clinton's spent lavishly on the Pentagon's high-tech wizardry. . . . Even now, more than four years after invading Iraq, the Pentagon seems to be investing much of its current $606 billion budget in an effort to fight the wrong war. . . . The Air Force continues to buy $330 million fighters, and the Navy $2 billion submarines. . . . The Army has been starved for cash since the cold war's end. (Its leaders gripe that from 1990 to 2005, their service pocketed just 16% of the Pentagon's hardware budget, while the Air Force got 36%, and the Navy 33%). . . . Amazingly, the Army had only 32,000 sets of body armor when the Iraq war began. . . . The military [again] badly miscalculated what the war would look like.[34]

For more than half a century, Americans have been trying to erase the human factor from war. But we have consistently failed to do so, and today's army and marine corps are again too small, underfunded, and underequipped for the missions they are given. After nearly a decade at war in the Middle East, almost everyone recognizes this fact. But the U.S. Army has been too small since World War II, and the reasons for this situation in the opening days of the Korean War remain applicable today. Out of a nation of 300 million Americans, not enough volunteers could be found to significantly expand the size of the army. At the same time, the nation continued to spend billions on weapons systems it does not need. This is militarism.

The existence of military capabilities influences the decision for war. The existence of military capabilities also influences the objectives sought through war. The Bush administration's decision for war in Iraq was based partly on the fact that the war looked easy. In fact, it looked so easy the Bush administration, unlike President George H. W. Bush's administration, sought total objectives and few allies. It sought the total destruction of the Iraqi government. Given the U.S. experience in Operation Desert Storm, given the expansion in airpower capabilities, and given the so-called revolution in military affairs, "network centric war," and "shock and awe," the Bush-Rumsfeld-Cheney team thought the war would be easy and the return home swift. They deployed too few ground forces and prematurely declared mission accomplished aboard the USS *Abraham Lincoln*. The irony is that another supposedly high-tech war, another war that was supposed to won by airpower, evolved into a primitive ground war in which soldiers had to kill the enemy in close proximity and learn to work with the local populations.

During the Cold War, Americans became militaristic. Militarism became part of the American culture, not simply the American culture of war. The production of military equipment, the development of new technology, and the sustainment of military facilities are not simply functions of military necessity; they are functions of the needs of representatives and senators to get reelected, the needs of regional economies, the needs of specific communities, the needs of various industries, and the needs of the American people. During the Cold War, the military became Big Business. Today the United States is the world's largest arms producer and dealer, and as a result, American soldiers frequently are killed or wounded by American-made weapons. Many of the best minds and best scientific institutions in America are committed to producing weapons systems and military-related technologies. Many universities depend on defense, or defense-related, contracts and grants to maintain their institutions. Many states depend on defense dollars to maintain their economies. The standard of living in certain areas of the country is directly influenced by the production or cancellation of a particular weapons system or the movement of a specific unit. In fact, the most powerful person in the United States after the president is the secretary of defense, who in 2010 managed a budget of more than $600 billion, considerably more than the gross domestic product of most nations in the world. The United States' military forces are employed in almost half the countries on the globe, directly influencing the actions of their governments, and American forces indirectly influence the actions of all the states in the world. A July 2000 study on army readiness reported that

the United States employs its Army around the world to promote stability, prevent conflict, and deter aggression. There are routinely more than

140,000 Army personnel forward stationed or deployed around the world. They are conducting an average of 300 separate missions in 70 different countries. . . . The Army is in more places doing more missions than ever before. Since 1989, the average frequency of Army contingency deployments has increased from one every four years to one every 14 weeks. Some of these (Bosnia for example) have evolved into ongoing commitments. The Army today is more than one-third smaller than it was in 1989. In practical terms, that means the number of active division has been reduced from 18 to 10. The increasing number and scope of these operations . . . lead to repetitive deployments for individual servicemembers . . . and significantly greater wear and tear on equipment.[35]

Since the terrorist attacks on September 11, 2001, the deployment of U.S. forces has increased dramatically. The U.S. Navy sails the oceans and seas of all regions of the planet. One aircraft carrier can generate more combat power than most nations on earth. The American people have grown to accept, expect, enjoy, and appreciate the status and pride that comes with the term *superpower*, a status that was and is primarily a function of military power.

The military in the United States is no longer valued for its ability to secure the United States and it allies; it is valued for itself. There is an intrinsic value, a satisfaction that many Americans receive from maintaining supercarriers, stealth bombers, and other military hardware that is the most advanced ever produced. Every year, the American film industry releases movies that highlight the capabilities of American war machines and forces. Military force is the American answer to hostile aliens, monsters, rogue asteroids, natural disasters, man-made disasters, and just about every other calamity that can afflict a people. Entire films are built around weapons systems.

The U.S. defense industry/system is *not* organized and designed to maximize the achievement of national political objectives through the conduct of war and the threat of war. Consider Eisenhower's thinking:

Eisenhower felt that much of the pressure for increased defense spending came from special interests, especially arms manufacturers and military figures, who had lobbied for pet projects, which had been underfunded or had been refused funding. He told Republican legislative leaders that, when he saw advertisements for Boeing and Douglas, he was "getting sick of the lobbies of the munitions makers. . . . You begin to see this thing isn't wholly the defense of the country, but only more money for some who are already fat cats." He commented that "the munitions makers are making tremendous efforts toward getting more contracts and in fact seem to be exerting undue influence over the senators."[36]

Boeing and other defense manufactures now lobby the American people directly. They advertise weapons systems on television and the Internet as if Americans were buying them directly. Militarism has become an established and significant cultural and economic norm for Americans.

The American Culture of War

Insufficient ground forces are but one manifestation of a larger problem. The situations in Korea and in Iraq were a function of a new American culture of war that evolved during and immediately following World War II. In brief, we Americans try to minimize the human element in war and overemphasize the role of material and technology. We recklessly invest billions of dollars in weapons technologies and have become the world's largest arms producer and dealer. We have formed a military that no longer reflects the demographics of the nation. But because of overconsumption, Americans are physically less able to fight war than at any previous time in history. We have formed professional military firms that have made war a business for financial gain, a business that can be lobbied for. We have used the people of other countries as surrogates to maintain our war effort and to fight. We have created a political system in which militarism is a major consideration, in which Congress supports the expenditure of resources on military means, not for reasons of national security, but for the welfare of their members' districts and states. We have created a system in which America's best companies and universities fight to win defense dollars for the research and development of instruments that facilitate the conduct of war. We have been too willing to employ military forces. We have sought to control and manage by military means world affairs and resources like oil to maintain the Western economy and high levels of consumption. But we have little interest in foreign peoples, particularly those in poorly developed countries. In some parts of the world, we use weapons systems with the full knowledge that innocent people will be killed or wounded. Our political leaders have embraced this new way of war because it frees them of direct responsibility and accountability to the American people. The less the American people know, the less involved they will be, and the more freedom the White House and Pentagon will have in foreign affairs, military strategy, and war. The end of conscription gave political leaders greater freedom to go to war and to wage war as they saw fit. In 1973, the American people successfully removed themselves from the conduct of the nation's wars. Since then and since the collapse of the Soviet Union, the deployment of U.S. forces has increased rapidly, and Americans have grown accustomed to being the dominant power on earth with no obligations to themselves. This is not sustainable.

NOTES

1. This chapter continues and expands the argument first advanced in my book *The American Culture of War* (New York: Routledge, 2007).

2. According to former Secretary of Defense William Cohen, "The information revolution is creating a Revolution in Military Affairs that will fundamentally change the way U.S. forces fight. We must exploit these and other technologies to dominate in battle." See William S. Cohen, *Report of the Quadrennial Defense Review* (Washington, DC: U.S. Department of Defense, 1997), iv.

3. See John Shy, "The American Military Experience," in *A People Numerous and Armed*, rev. ed., by John Shy (Ann Arbor: University of Michigan Press, 1993), 265–94; Russell Weigley, *The American Way of War* (Bloomington: Indiana University Press, 1993); and Russell Weigley, *Eisenhower's Lieutenants* (Bloomington: Indiana University Press, 1990). See also Brian McAllister Linn, *The Echo of Battle: The Army's Way of War* (Cambridge, MA: Harvard University Press, 2007).

4. Clifford Geertz, *The Interpretation of Cultures* (New York: Simon & Schuster, 1990), 5 (italics added).

5. In 1949, the Soviet Union tested its first nuclear weapon, ending the American monopoly. Even though the Soviet Union did not have the means to deliver the atomic bomb to the shores of the United States, it did have the means to deliver nuclear weapons to South Korea. Arguably the Soviet weapon acted as a deterrent.

6. Carl Clausewitz, *On War* (Princeton, NJ: Princeton University Press, 1984), 75, 76.

7. Ibid., 313. Clausewitz noted: "The bounds of military operations have been extended so far that a return to the old narrow limitations can only occur briefly, sporadically, and under special conditions. The true nature of war will break through again and again with overwhelming force, and must, therefore, be the basis of any permanent military arrangement."

8. Robert E. Osgood, *Limited War* (Chicago: University of Chicago Press, 1957), 1, 2 (italics added).

9. Harry Summers Jr., *On Strategy* (Carlisle Barracks, PA: Strategic Studies Institute, March 1982), 23, 17.

10. Joint Chiefs of Staff, *Joint Vision 2010* (Washington, DC: U.S. Department of Defense, 1996).

11. Giulio Douhet, *The Command of the Air*, in *Roots of Strategy*, book 4, ed. David Jablonsky (Mechanicsburg, PA: Stackpole Books, 1999), 284.

12. Richard Overy, *Why the Allies Won* (New York: Norton, 1995), 104, 105.

13. General Henry H. Arnold, "Air Strategy for Victory," *Flying* 33, no. 4 (October 1943): 50 (italics added).

14. Dwight D. Eisenhower, *Crusade in Europe* (Garden City, NY: Doubleday, 1948), 455, 456 (italics added).

15. Mark Clark, *From the Danube to the Yalu* (New York: Harper, 1954), 196.

16. Richard Hallion, *Storm over Iraq* (Washington, DC: Smithsonian Institution Press, 1992), 1.

17. Quoted in Lewis, *The American Culture of War*, 65 (italics added).

18. George Kennan, "The Sources of Soviet Conduct," *Foreign Affairs* 24, no. 4 (1947): 566–82.

19. NSC 68, "Report to the President Pursuant to the President's Directive of 31 January 1950," April 7, 1950, FRUS 1950, 1:235–92; reprinted in *U.S. National Security Policy and Strategy*, ed. Sam Sarkesian with Robert Vitas (New York: Greenwood Press, 1988), 38–43.

20. Lyndon B. Johnson, "Why Americans Fight in Vietnam," in *Major Problems in the History of the Vietnam War*, by Robert McMahon, 3rd ed. (Boston: Houghton Mifflin, 2003), 166.

21. James Toner, "American Society and the American Way of War: Korea and Beyond," *Parameters* 11, no. 1 (1981): 78–89 (italics added).

22. Osgood, *Limited War*, 33 (italics added).

23. Andrew Bacevich, *The Limits of Power* (New York: Henry Holt, 2008), 173.

24. Mortimer Zuckerman, editor in chief, *U.S. News & World Report*, October 27, 2008, 92.

25. David Halberstam, *The Fifties* (New York: Villard Books, 1993), x.

26. Dwight D. Eisenhower, *Mandate for Change* (Garden City, NY: Doubleday, 1963), 484, 485.

27. Ibid., 485.

28. Results of the National Health and Nutrition Examination Survey (NHANES) 1999–2000; available at www.cdc.gov/nccdphp/dnpa/obesity/trend/maps/index.htm (accessed April 19, 2011).

29. Michelle Andrews, "The State of America's Health," *U.S. New & World Report*, February 2009, 9–12.

30. See Peter Warren Singer, *Corporate Warriors* (Ithaca, NY: Cornell University Press, 2003), 230–42; and Dina Rasor and Robert Bauman, *Betraying Our Troops* (New York: Palgrave Macmillan, 2007).

31. Alfred Vagts, *A History of Militarism*, rev. ed. (New York: Free Press, 1959), 16, 17. More recently, Andrew Bacevich added to our knowledge of militarism in America with his book *The New American Militarism* (New York: Oxford University Press, 2005).

32. Vagts, *A History of Militarism*, 14.

33. General George Casey, "Chief of Staff of the Army Statement on the Army's Strategic Imperatives," testimony before the U.S. Senate Armed Services Committee, November 15, 2007; available at http://www.army.mil/-speeches/2007/11/15/6144-chief-of-staff-of-the-army-statement-on-the-armys-strategic-imperatives/ (accessed April 19, 2011).

34. Mark Thompson, "Broken Down," *Time*, April 28, p. 35.

35. Institute of Land Warfare, *The Way Ahead* (Arlington, VA: Association of the United States Army, July 2000), 5.

36. Peter Boyle, *Eisenhower: Profiles in Power* (New York: Longman, 2005), 122.

About the Contributors

LEE L. BRICE is an associate professor of ancient history at Western Illinois University. He is the author of several articles on ancient militaries and the coeditor of *Recent Directions in the Military History of the Ancient World*.

MARK GRIMSLEY is an associate professor of history at Ohio State University and the author of several books, including *And Keep Moving On: The Virginia Campaign, May–June 1864*, and *The Hard Hand of War: Union Military Policy Toward Southern Civilians, 1861–1865*.

ISABEL V. HULL is the John Stambaugh Professor of History at Cornell University. Her most recent book is *Absolute Destruction: Military Culture and the Practices of War in Imperial Germany*.

WAYNE E. LEE is a professor of history at the University of North Carolina, Chapel Hill, and the chair of the Curriculum in Peace, War, and Defense. He is the author of several books, including *Barbarians and Brothers: Anglo-American Warfare, 1500–1865*, and the editor of *Empires and Indigenes: Intercultural Alliance, Imperial Expansion, and Warfare in the Early Modern World* (NYU Press, 2010).

ADRIAN R. LEWIS is a professor of history and the director of the University of Kansas's Office of Professional Military Graduate Education. He is the author of *Omaha Beach: A Flawed Victory*, and *The American Culture of War: A History of American Military Force from World War II to Operation Iraqi Freedom*.

JOHN A. LYNN II retired from the University of Illinois at Urbana-Champaign and now holds the position of Distinguished Professor of Military History at Northwestern University. He has written several books, including *Battle: A History of Combat and Culture*, and *Women, Armies, and Warfare in Early Modern Europe*.

SARAH C. MELVILLE is an associate professor of history at Clarkson University. She is the author of *The Role of Naqia/Zakutu in Sargonid Politics* and the coeditor of *Opening the Tablet Box: Near Eastern Studies in Honor of Benjamin R. Foster*.

DAVID SILBEY is the associate director and senior lecturer of the Cornell in Washington Program. He is the author of *The British Working Class and Enthusiasm for War, 1914–1916*, and *A War of Empire and Frontier: The Philippine-American War, 1899–1902*.

KENNETH M. SWOPE is an associate professor of history and the director of the history MA program at Ball State University. He is the author of *A Dragon's Head and a Serpent's Tail: Ming China and the First Great East Asian War, 1592–1598*.

Index

Acheson, Dean, 203–4
Adams, Michael C. C., 120–21
Airpower: in American societal culture, 196–201; atomic bomb from, 191–93, 198; for Britain, 197; for Cold War, 203; counterinsurgency and, 200–201; massive retaliation and, 199; in Persian Gulf War, 200; strategic bombing from, 197–98; unmanned aerial vehicles for, 211; in Vietnam War, 200; in World War II, 197–98
Airwar theories: failure of, 187; military technologies and, 195–201; NCW as, 187, 217n2
American culture, militarism in, 214–16
American societal culture: airpower in, 196–201; America's new role in, 190–91, 201–5; artificial limited war in, 189–95, 198–99, 217n5, 217n7; failures and, 187–88; militarism in, 191, 211–16; military technology revolution in, 190, 195–201; nuclear weapons and, 191–93, 217n5, 217n7; political counterpoises in, 192–93; strategic culture related to, 5
American soldiers: casualty rate of, 210–11; Chinese Communist soldiers compared to, 206; health of, 209–11; in Korean War, 206; outsourcing for, 210; private military firms for, 210; qualifications for, 205–6, 209–10; resources for, 190
American war culture: limited wars in, 194–95; NCW in, 187, 217n2; pursuit of happiness compared to, 191, 205–11; tradition in, 188–91; transformation in, 190–91

American wars: as aberration, 189; expectations about, 189–90, 205; offensive and defensive, 189–90; peace compared to, 188; pursuit of happiness compared to, 189, 205–11; real, 188–89; total compared to limited, 189–90, 193–94. *See also specific wars*
Amiens offensive, 174
Anderson, Robert, 131
Antony, Mark (Marcus Antonius): against mutiny, 43, 57n37; Octavian against, 42–45, 50–53; subversion from, 52
ANZAC Day, 169
ANZACs. *See* Australia-New Zealand Army Corps
ANZAC to Amiens (Bean), 179
Aristocrats: honor for, 99–101; knights as, 99–100; as officers, 99–101; privileges of, 99
Armenians, genocide of, 160
Army of Northern Virginia, 127–29. *See also* Lee, Robert E.
Army of Tennessee, 129, 131, 133–34; power distance in, 130
Army of the Cumberland, 131–32; Army of the Tennessee compared to, 133–34
Army of the Potomac: control style in, 126–27; Nineteenth Indiana Volunteer Infantry Regiment in, 136–37; organization of, 125; power distance of, 125. *See also* McClellan, George B.
Army of the Tennessee, 123–24; Army of the Cumberland compared to, 133–34. *See also* Grant, Ulysses S.
Arnold, Henry, 198

Bonuses, 8; from Octavian, 43–44, 47–50, 52–53
Bouchotte, Jean-Baptiste, 108
Bourdieu, Pierre, 9
Bourke, Joanna, 168
Boyd, Robert, 9
Bragg, Braxton, 129; Polk against, 130–31
Brannan, John M., 115
Britain: for airpower, 197; Australia compared to, 170; conscription in, 104, 113n63; soldiers of, 104–5, 112n57, 113n63
British culture, 4–5
British Expeditionary Force (BEF): ANZACs compared to, 170; Australian Corps compared to, 177; Canadian Corps compared to, 178, 181; Dominion forces compared to, 173; nationalisms and, 165
British Official Histories (Edmonds), 176
Buell, Don Carlos, 131–32
Bülow, Bernhard, prince von, 145, 156, 158
Bülow, Dietrich Heinrich Freiherr von, 95
Burnside, Ambrose E., 125, 126
Bush, George W., 210, 214
Business, 214; leadership in, 117–18, 139n9; organizational culture in, 119–20

Cameron, Kim S., 119
Campaign narratives, 24
Canada's Hundred Days, 176, 179
Canadian Corps, 165; American Expeditionary Force compared to, 178; for Amiens offensive, 174; BEF compared to, 178, 181; casualty rate of, 180; discipline of, 173; distinction of, 172–73, 179; Haig for, 172; national moment for, 170; security issues for, 175; setbacks of, 174–75
Cannon, 91–92
Carnage and Culture (Hanson), 166
Casey, George W., 212–13
Casualty rate: of American soldiers, 210–11; of Canadian Corps, 180; modern compared to Civil War, 137; World War I victory related to, 179–80. *See also* Death rates
Catinat, Nicolas, 93

Center for Strategic Leadership, 118, 139n9
Chagniot, Jean, 106
Chamillart, Michel, 97
Chandler, Alfred D., 119
Chase, Salmon P., 123
China's military culture, 85n40; case study on, 64–65; Chinese culture compared to, 4; civil oversight in, 4, 62–64, 82, 84n13; Confucian-Mencian paradigm in, 62; factionalism against, 4, 63–64; *parabellum* paradigm in, 62; peasant rebels and, 84n17, 85n30; study of, 61–62, 83n1; troop salaries in, 66; virtues related to, 62, 63, 83n10. *See also* Chongzhen; Peasant rebellions; Yang He
Chinese culture, 4
Chongzhen (emperor), 65, 82–83; for pacification, 67; for taxes, 72–73; trust of, 69; vacillation of, 80–81; Wanli compared to, 81; Yang Sichang and, 71, 74, 76
Citino, Robert, 166, 181n4
Civil War, 188–89. *See also specific battles; specific officers*
Civil War field armies: commanders' impact on, 121; nature of, 121; personalities of, 120; societal cultures and, 120–21. *See also* Army of Northern Virginia; Army of Tennessee; Army of the Cumberland; Army of the Potomac; Army of the Tennessee
Civil War organizational culture: administrative coordination and, 119–20; business organizational culture compared to, 119–20; clan culture in, 119, 121–22; hierarchy culture in, 119–20, 121; societal culture related to, 6–7; without techniques transmission, 138; uncertainty avoidance for, 119. *See also* Senior leadership culture
Clan culture, 119, 121–22. *See also* Regimental culture
Clark, Charles T., 117
Clark, Mark, 199
Clausewitz, Carl von, 147, 192–93, 217n7
Cleopatra, 51
Coercion, of soldiers, 98

Cold War, 194; airpower for, 203; alliances in, 202; collective defense agreements for, 203; global rearrangement in, 202–3; NSC-68 for, 204; policy of containment for, 203–5; transformation from, 202–3

Command climate, 132

The Command of the Air (Douhet), 196

Communism, 201–5

Communist China, 191–92, 217n5

Concentration camps: criticism of, 158; death rate in, 157–58; genocide in, 156–58; provisioning in, 157; for punishment, 157–58; racism in, 157

Confucian-Mencian paradigm, 62

Confucian statecraft, 66–67

Conscription: in Britain, 104, 113n63; in France, 103–4; limited war and, 195, 216–17; of Prussians, 104; wealth related to, 210

Consumerism, 206–8

Corvisier, André, 97–98, 103, 105–6, 112n57

Cross, Edward, 103, 104, 112n57

Cull, Ambrose, 177

Culture: agency and, 9; behaviors and, 3; change and, 8–10; choices in, 3; clan, 119, 121–22; community formations and, 3; contingency and, 9; definitions of, 2–3, 117; hidden assumptions within, 3; hierarchy, 119–21; intergenerational transmission of, 3, 9; meaning of, 189; norms, 9; rational within, 1; regimental, 134–37; types of, 3–4, 8; war and, 35; world history related to, 2. *See also* Battle Culture of forebearance; Military culture; Organizational culture; Societal culture; Soldiers' culture; and specific nations (e.g. Assyria)

Currie, Arthur, 172–75

Daniel, Larry J., 132

Davis, Jefferson, 122, 129, 130

Death rates: in concentration camps, 157–58; deportation and, 158; of Herero, 145, 157–58; of Nama, 145. *See also* Genocide

De l'esprit (Helvétius), 97

Deportation: death rates and, 158; during World War I, 160

Descartes, René, 100–101

Desmoulins, Camille, 107

Destruction (*Vernichtung*), 145; of enemy, 147, 149; as extreme offensive, 147–48; for genocide, 147–49; single battle for, 148

Di Cosmo, Nicola, 61–62

Disciplina militaris, 8, 55n5; case study on, 35, 54n4; culture and, 36–37; definition of, 36; mutiny and, 38; physical components of, 38–39; punishment and rewards in, 39–41; *sacramentum* and, 37–39; tasks for, 39. *See also* Octavian

Discipline: of Australian Corps, 177, 185n61; at Battle of Mollwitz, 89; of Canadian Corps, 173; collective synchronized, 101–2; drill as, 101–2; from Octavian, 45, 49–51, 53–54

Discipline of Augustus. *See* Octavian

Dominion culture: British culture compared to, 4–5; nationalism in, 4–5, 171. *See also* Australian Corps; Canadian Corps

Dominion forces: BEF compared to, 173; as nation's representations, 180; New Zealand Division, 165, 169–71; segregation within, 172

Douhet, Guilio, 196

Doyle, Arthur Conan, 179

Drill: as discipline, 101–2; for esprit de corps, 105

Dubois-Crancé, Edmond Louis Alexis, 107

Dumouriez, Charles, 107–8

Early, Jubal A., 128

Economics: bonuses, 8, 43–44, 47–50, 52–53; within militaries, 164n51; wealth, 191, 205–11

Edmonds, James, 176, 177, 185n61

Eisenhower, Dwight, 198, 199, 208–9; on special interests, 215–16

Estorff, Ludwig von, 158

Ewell, Richard S., 128

The Face of Battle (Keegan), 165–66

Fall of Nineveh Chronicle (FNC), 14

Flintlock muskets, 91

FNC. *See* Fall of Nineveh Chronicle

Foch, Ferdinand, 179

Foote, Andrew, 124

France, 106. *See also* French Revolution
Frederick II (the Great), 92–95; battle of
  Mollwitz for, 89, 109; on esprit de corps,
  105; on soldiers, 96–98
Frederick William I, 100, 109
French Revolution: infantry in, 108;
  National Guard in, 107; officers in, 107–8;
  soldiers and, 107–8; tactics and, 108–9
Frey, Sylvia, 103, 104, 112n57

Gaius Marius, 39
Gallipoli, 169–70
Garfield, James, 132
Geertz, Clifford, 117, 189
Geneva Convention, 152
Genocide: of Armenians, 160; in concentration camps, 156–58; deportation and,
  158; exile compared to, 155–56; German
  military culture and, 158–60, 164nn50–51;
  from German organizational culture, 6,
  146–47; German political culture and,
  145, 158; as illegal combatants, 153; in
  imprisonment, 156–58; of Maji-Maji,
  159–60; from military practices, 145–47;
  negotiations related to, 149–50, 155,
  162n22; from politics, 146–47, 150, 162n23;
  practices conducive to, 151–54; of prisoners, 153, 154, 156–58; proclamation related
  to, 154–56; provisioning related to, 151–52,
  155–58, 163n42; pursuit related to, 150–51,
  155; Thotha for, 145, 153–56; from transfer
  of control, 145–46; troops' suffering
  related to, 151, 155–56; by Turkey, 160; *Vernichtung* for, 147–49; women and, 154–55
Gerbey, Joseph Marie Servan de, 97
Germany, 168–69. *See also* World War I
German military culture, 10n9; genocide
  and, 158–60, 164nn50–51; German
  organizational culture for, 6; in World
  War I, 160. *See also* Genocide; Herero;
  Prusso-German military
German organizational culture: genocide
  from, 6, 146–47; for German military
  culture, 6
German political culture, 144; genocide
  and, 145, 158

German strategic culture: dysfunction of,
  6; logistics related to, 151–52; provision-
  ing in, 151–52, 157–58; racism and, 159,
  164n51; troops' suffering related to, 151,
  155–56
The German Way of War (Citino), 181n4
Gheyn, Jacob de, 102
Gibbon, Edward, 97
Gibbon, John, 136–37
Gillet, Pierre, 108
GLOBE study, 118–19, 139n13
Grant, Ulysses S., 123; coping style of, 126;
  on Lee, Robert E., 126, 127; Meade and,
  126–27; partnerships for, 124; persever-
  ance of, 124; power distance for, 124;
  Thomas compared to, 133–34; uncer-
  tainty avoidance from, 124–25
Guibert, Jacques Antoine Hippolyte, 96

Haig, Douglas, 168; for Canadian Corps,
  172; for nationalism, 171–72
Halberstam, David, 207–8
Hallion, Richard, 200
Hanson, Victor David, 166
Harari, Yuval, 100–101
Hatch, John P., 136
Helvétius, Claude Adrien, 97
Herero, 6; death rate of, 145; escape of, 148;
  revolt of, 144–47, 156. *See also* Genocide
Hill, Ambrose P., 128
Hintrager, Oskar, 158
History, 2; nationalism and, 166–67; study
  tools for, 166–67, 181; universal theory
  of, 166. *See also* Military history
Hofstede, Geert, 139n13
Honor: for aristocrats, 99–101; of soldiers
  compared to officers, 105–6
Hooker, Joseph, 123, 125

Imprisonment, genocide in, 156–58
Infantry, 136–37; advance pace for, 93,
  110n9; in French Revolution, 108; the
  line for, 92–93, 97; tactics of, 89–90
Information revolution, 217n2
In-group collectivism, 119, 130; of regimental culture, 135

Institutional collectivism, 119, 130

The Interpretation of Culture (Geertz), 189

An Intimate History of Killing (Bourke), 168

Jackson, Thomas J. "Stonewall," 128

Jamieson, Perry D., 121

Jaucourt, Louis de, 96

Johnson, Lyndon B., 194–95, 205

Johnston, Albert Sidney, 129–30

Johnston, Iain, 62–63

Johnston, Joseph E., 127

Keegan, John, 165–66

Kennan, George, 203

Kennedy, John F., 199

Korean War, 191–92, 217n5; as artificial limited war, 198–99; soldiers in, 206

Lafayette, marquis de, 107–8

Leadership, 117–18, 139n9; strategy compared to tactics and, 122. *See also* Presidents; Senior leadership culture

Lee, Robert E., 126, 140n31; for aggression, 127–29; for Army of Northern Virginia, 127–29; Maryland campaign for, 128–29; against McClellan, 127

Lee, Wayne, 101

Lendon, J. E., 36

Lepidus, Marcus, 45–46

Le Roy, Claude, 103–4

Leutwein, Theodor, 145; Trotha over, 146–47, 149

Limited war, 217n7; in American war culture, 194–95; conscription and, 195, 216–17; containment compared to, 194; homelands and, 194; logic of, 194; tactics in, 194; total compared to, 189–90, 193–94. *See also* Artificial limited war

Limited War: The Challenge to American Strategy (Osgood), 193–94

Lincoln, Abraham, 122, 125–26

Livesay, John, 179

Li Zicheng, 80, 84n17, 87n111

Logistics: German strategic culture related to, 151–52; in World Wars I and II, 180

Loriga, Sabina, 103, 112n57

Louis XIV, 94, 95, 101–2

Lynn, John A., 10n6, 166

MacArthur, Douglas, 198

Macdonnell, Archibald, 178

Maji-Maji, genocide of, 159–60

Manchus, 69–70, 75, 81

Mao Zedong, 168

Marius, 37

Matchlock muskets, 90–91

McClellan, George B.: Lee, Robert E., against, 127; Lincoln and, 125; power distance from, 125

McClernand, John, 124

McCook, Alexander, 131

McGibbon, Ian, 179

McNeill, William H., 105

McPherson, James B., 124

McWhiney, Grady, 121

Meade, George G., 125; control style of, 126–27; Grant and, 126–27

Medes, 23

Medes, army of the: Assyrian armies compared to, 16; Assyrian empire's destruction by, 20–21, 23; Assyrians and, 16, 29n15; Assyrian war attack by, 18–19; Babylonia's alliance with, 19–20; Cyaxares for, 19–20

Meredith, Solomon, 136–37

Militarism: in American culture, 214–16; in American societal culture, 191, 211–16; business and, 214; definition of, 211; readiness compared to, 212–13; resources for, 211–12

Military culture: from aristocratic culture, 100; consumerism compared to, 206–8; culture of philosophy on, 100–101; definition of, 7; development of, 143, 160n2; levels of, 3, 10n6; organizational culture conflated with, 7, 10n9; social change related to, 107–10; social class and, 109–10; soldiers' culture from, 7; strategic culture related to, 7; values within, 7. *See also* China's military culture; German military culture; Roman military culture

Military history: context and, 166–68, 181n4; globalization for, 1–2; new compared to old, 165–66; operational history in, 166; paradigm shift in, 1; Western, 1–2

Military leadership, 117–18, 139n9. *See also* Senior leadership culture

Military reform: in battle culture of forbearance, 106; in France, 106; from Octavian, 53–54, 59n70; for officers, 106

Military Testament (Frederick II), 96

Mingshi, 84n16

Missionaries, 158

Montaigne, Michel de, 100

Montmorency, François-Henri de, 95

Mutiny, 38, 43, 57n37

Nabopolassar, 30n18; Babylonia's rule by, 16–20; campaigns of, 17–20; Cyaxares with, 19; defenses of, 17; diplomacy of, 19–20, 31n33; Syria's invasion by, 17, 30n21; victories of, 17–18

Nabopolassar Chronicle (NC), 14; on Assyrian war, 17, 30n19

Nama: death rate of, 145; revolt of, 144–47, 156

Napoleon, 108

Nationalisms: ANZAC Day and, 169; of Australian Imperial Force, 172; BEF and, 165; competition among, 176; in Dominion culture, 4–5, 171; Haig's for, 171–72; history and, 166–67; logistics successes related to, 180; national moments for, 169–70; operational effects from, 172, 176–77; redemption related to, 175; security issues and, 175; setbacks related to, 174–75; for Wales, 170; war style related to, 174; in World War I victory, 169, 176–80. *See also* Australian Corps; Canadian Corps; New Zealand Division

National moments: for Canadian Corps, 170; Gallipoli as, 169–70; for nationalisms, 169–70; for U.S., 169

NC. *See* Nabopolassar Chronicle

NCW. *See* Network centric warfare

Negotiations: genocide related to, 149–50, 155, 162n22; Manchu for, 69–70; politics and, 150, 162n23

Network centric warfare (NCW), 187, 217n2; science fiction of war compared to, 196–97

New Zealand Division, 165, 169–71 1918, 168–75

Nineteenth Indiana Volunteer Infantry Regiment, 136–37

Nineveh, 26, 32n55; fall of, 19–20, 31n43; FNC on, 14; size of, 25, 32n55

Nitze, Paul, 204

Normative compliance, 98–99

Octavian (Augustus), 8, 56n30; Actium campaign for, 51–54; against Antony, 42–45, 50–53; bonuses from, 43–44, 47–50, 52–53; against Cleopatra, 51; discharges from, 49–50, 52; discipline from, 45, 49–51, 53–54; first command of, 42–44; Illyricum wars for, 50–51; length of service under, 48; against Lepidus, 45–46; military reforms from, 53–54, 59n70; against Pompey, 45–46; rebellions and, 44, 46–48, 58n51; recruitment by, 43, 46; Sicily campaign of, 45–50; status rewards from, 49; subversion by, 42–43, 46–48; traditional discipline from, 45, 49–51, 53–54

Officers: aristocrats as, 99–101; in French Revolution, 107–8; honor of, 105–6; military reforms for, 106. *See also* Senior leadership culture; *specific officers*

Opdycke, Emerson, 116

Operational history, 166

Operation Iraqi Freedom, 200–201

Oppenheimer, Robert, 193

Organizational culture: artifacts in, 118; assumptions in, 6, 118–19, 139n13; in business, 119–20; definitions of, 117–20; military culture conflated with, 7, 10n9; orders and, 115–17; origins of, 120; staff rides and, 117–18, 139n9; strong, 143, 160n2; U.S. Army War College on, 118–19, 139n9; values in, 118. *See also* Civil War organizational culture; German organizational culture; Senior leadership culture

Osgood, Robert, 193–94, 206–7
Osman, Julia, 96
Overy, Richard, 196–97

Parabellum paradigm, 62
Paret, Peter, 109
The Path to Gallipoli (McGibbon), 179
Peasant rebellions, 87n110; causes of, 65–66, 67, 85n30; defense against, 70; extermination in, 72, 86n75; famine relief against, 67; Gao Yingxiang for, 66; geography and, 71; Manchu negotiations related to, 69–70; mobility of, 82; offensives against, 70; pacification toward, 67–68; participants in, 66, 84n17; successes against, 68–69; ten-sided net strategy against, 70–74; troop increases against, 70–71; Wang Jiayin for, 66; Xiong Wencan against, 70, 73–74, 76; Zuo Liangyu against, 70, 73–74, 76–77, 86n52. *See also* Yang He
Pershing, John J., 176
Persian Gulf War (1991), 200
Pickett's Charge in History and Memory (Reardon), 167
Pikes, 91
Polk, Leonidas, 130–31
Polybius, 39, 40
Pompey, Sextus, 45–46
Porter, David Dixon, 124
Power distance, 119; in Army of Tennessee, 130; of Army of the Potomac, 125; for Grant, 124; from McClellan, 125; in regimental culture, 134–35; in senior leadership culture, 124, 125, 130
Presidents: in senior leadership culture, 122, 125–26, 129–30, 138. *See also specific presidents*
Prokopowicz, Gerald J., 121, 122, 135, 137
Provisioning: in colonies, 151–52; in concentration camps, 157; genocide related to, 151–52, 155–58, 163n42; in German strategic culture, 151–52, 157–58; punishment and, 157–58. *See also* Technology
Prussians, 89–90; canton system for, 104; conscription of, 104

Prusso-German military: colonial army compared to, 144, 152; context for, 143–44, 159, 181n4; conventional warfare expectations of, 152–53; hubris of, 152; mission tactics of, 144; uniqueness of, 144
Punishment: in Assyrian strategic culture, 21–23, 31n43; capital, 39–40, 56n23; concentration camps for, 157–58; *disciplina militaris* for, 39–41; provisioning and, 157–58; in warfare, 22, 31n45

Quinn, Robert E., 119

Rabel, Roberto, 181, 185n77
Racism, 159, 164n51
Rawlinson, Henry, 175
Reardon, Carol, 167
Regimental culture: brigade in, 135–36; division in, 135–36; embedded mechanism in, 136; high performance orientation in, 135; in-group collectivism of, 135; power distance in, 134–35; senior leadership culture compared to, 134–36; uniforms for, 136–37
Remuneration, 98
Remunerative compliance, 98
Renatus, Flavius Vegetius, 205–6
Revolt, 144–47, 156. *See also* Genocide; Peasant rebellions
Rewards, 40–41; bonuses as, 8, 43–44, 47–50, 52–53
Reynolds, Joseph, 115–16
Richerson, Peter, 9
Roberts, Michael, 101
Rohrbach, Paul, 145
Roman military culture, 35; Gaius Julius Caesar, 42, 56n30; soldiers' culture compared to, 8; *virtus* in, 36, 55n7. See also *Disciplina militaris*; Octavian
Rosecrans, William S., 115–16, 132
Rush, Benjamin, 96

Sacramentum, 37–39
Saint-Germain, Claude Louis, 96–97, 108
Saint-Rémy, Pierre Surirey de, 92

Saxe, Maurice de, 95
Scharnhorst, Gerhard Johann David von, 109
Schein, Edgar H., 118, 120
Schlieffen, Alfred von, 145, 155
Schoepf, Albin, 131
Schwerin, Kurt Christoph Graf von, 89
Senior leadership culture: Army of Northern Virginia and, 127–29; Army of Tennessee and, 129–31, 133–34; Army of the Cumberland and, 131–34; Army of the Potomac and, 125–27; Army of the Tennessee and, 123–24, 133–34; command climate in, 132; embedded mechanism in, 134; founding commander in, 123–24, 131; political patrons and, 123, 130, 131, 132; power distance in, 124, 125, 130; presidents in, 122, 125–26, 129–30, 138; professional compared to political generals in, 122–23; professionalization for, 138; regimental culture compared to, 134–36; seniority and, 123; without staff system, 137–38
Sennacherib, 31n43
Seven Days' Battles, 127, 128
The Seven Military Classics (*Wu jing qi shu*), 62–63
Sherman, William T., 124, 131, 133–34
Shuzhi, Fan, 72
Siege warfare, 95
Sin-shar-ishkum: campaigns of, 18–20, 27; diplomacy of, 19–20, 31n33; inflexibility of, 19, 27; rule of, 16–20
Sites of Memory, Sites of Mourning (Winter), 167–68
Societal culture: battle culture of forbearance and, 99–101, 107–9; Civil War field armies and, 120–21; Civil War organizational culture related to, 6–7; consumerism in, 206–8; television in, 207–8; war as science fiction in, 195–96; in warfare, 3–4; wealth in, 208–9. *See also* American societal culture; Nationalisms
Soldiers: in battle culture of forbearance, 96–99, 107–8; of Britain, 104–5, 112n57, 113n63; civilians compared to, 147, 149;

coercion of, 98–99; collective synchronized discipline for, 101–2; deployment of, 214–15; desertion of, 97–98; drill for, 101–2; duels among, 106; fears of, 96–97; Frederick II on, 96–98; French, 103–4, 105–8; French Revolution and, 107–8; honor of, 105–6; in Korean War, 206; low opinions of, 96–99, 103; primary group of, 105; Prussian, 104; stereotypes of, 103, 112n57. *See also* American soldiers; Conscription; *specific armies*
Soldiers' culture, 7; bonuses in, 8, 43–44, 47–50, 52–53; culture of wealth compared to, 205–11; rewards in, 98–99; Roman military culture compared to, 8; status rewards in, 49. See also *Disciplina militaris*; Octavian; Tactics; Technology
Southwest Africa (SWA), 144–47, 156. *See also* Genocide
Soviet Union: NSC-68 and, 204; nuclear weapons of, 217n5; *Sputnik* from, 199. *See also* Cold War
Spring, Matthew, 103, 112n57
Strategic bombing, 197–98
Strategic culture, 10n9; American societal culture related to, 5; Confucian-Mencian paradigm from, 62; definition of, 5; military culture related to, 7; *parabellum* paradigm from, 62. *See also* Assyrian strategic culture; German strategic culture
Strategy, tactics compared to, 122
Stübel, Oscar W., 146, 162n23
Sun Chuanting, 75; for extermination, 72; against inconsistencies, 72; against Yang Sichang, 71–72, 86n61
Superpowers: pride as, 215; war between, 193–95
SWA. See Southwest Africa
Syria, 17, 30n21

Tactics, 144; in battle culture of forbearance, 92–95; at Battle of Mollwitz, 89–90; French Revolution and, 108–9; of infantry, 89–90; in limited war, 194; strategy compared to, 122; technology and, 108–9

Yang He, 84n16; analyses of, 66; appointment of, 65, 66; Confucian statecraft from, 66–67; criticism against, 67–68; impeachment of, 68; leniency from, 66–67; resignation of, 85n34; troop transfers under, 67. *See also* Peasant rebellions

Yang Sichang, 85n27; appointments of, 69, 76, 80, 85n40, 87n98; background of, 68; Chongzhen and, 71, 74, 76; for commanders' authority, 73; criticism against, 71–72, 75, 77–79; death of, 80; failures of, 74–80; Hong Chengchou and, 73–74; impeachment of, 75; Manchu negotiations for, 69–70; Manchus against, 75, 81; plan from, 65; resignation of, 77–78; resource allocation against, 81–82; responsibilities of, 65; revenues for, 69, 70–71, 75, 77–78, 85n41; subordinates' defiance of, 76, 78–79; Sun Chuanting against, 71–72, 86n61; ten-sided net strategy from, 70–74, 76, 77, 81–82; troop transfers and, 76, 85n26; trust for, 69. *See also* Xiong Wencan; Zhang Xianzhong; Zuo Liangyu

Zhang Xianzhong, 73; prince's death by, 80; Yang Sichang against, 75–80

Zuo Liangyu: orders against, 73; against peasant rebellions, 70, 73–74, 76–77, 86n52; Yang Sichang and, 76–77, 86n52